Life, On the Fence

To Alex
Be Sweet!

[signature]

Life, On the Fence
An Autobiography

by

Marvin D. Holladay
AKA Marv Holladay
AKA 'Doc' Holladay
AKA Marvin 'Doc' Holladay

George Ronald
Oxford

George Ronald, *Publisher*
46 High Street, Kidlington, Oxford OX5 2DN

*A catalogue record for this book is available
from the British Library*

ISBN 0–85398–454–9

Typeset by Stonehaven Press LLP, Knoxville, Tennessee
Printed and bound in Great Britain by Biddles Ltd.
www.Biddles.co.uk

Contents

I dedicate this book

to my wife Diane for her love, patience and assistance in allowing me to become the me of today;

to my father and mother, embraced in the Abhá Kingdom;

to my children Bud and Helen;

to Joseph and Leslie, the grands, and those yet to be;

to 'Smitty', Arnold Smith, for helping me to realize who I was at the very beginning, even though it took me a while to figure it out;

to every person who has touched this life – the list is way too long to include here;

and particularly to those mentioned prominently in the telling of this tale. Yes, that does include you Dave. Some people are just so self-effacing.

Preface

As I look back over this story I find that I'm not at all sure whether this is an autobiography of a musician whose life's experience led him to the recognition of his spiritual reality – through the discovery of the Bahá'í Faith – or of a spiritual person who has found how he might express himself creatively through the medium of music. Who knows? Not moi!

I began this book with the intention of writing about my discovery of the reality of the music we call jazz. As I became more involved with that community of musicians, I found that jazz was actually the indigenous classical music of America, representing the image of American people to the rest of the world. Because of my discovery, I felt that perhaps my greatest contribution would be to use my life as an example of what so many of us musicians have gone through to get a clear idea of who and what we are.

The experiences I relate here are not unique to me, although we all have different responses to these experiences and, of course, the names and associations are different. But such experiences, in the final analysis, help form our understanding of the reality both of the music and of the social circumstances of our lives.

All these events in my life seemed to have led me to the recognition of the Revelation of Bahá'u'lláh. Bahá'u'lláh says that all Revelations and the resulting religions are from the same source. Therefore each religion can readily be recognized as the same religion presented to the world progressively. So the conflict between religions appears to be based on vain imagining, since they are all valid. Each has had a dramatic impact on the whole of humanity when it was revealed.

By the way, all those AKAs identify the various stages of my life and who the people in my life understood me to be.

Marvin D. Holladay, AKA, Marvin 'Doc' Holladay

Acknowledgements

First let me say that everyone mentioned in this book had a positive influence on my life. Even those experiences that might be identified as negative had a positive effect on me by illuminating my reality. As I have often stated, I had the greatest teachers in the world, whether they knew it or not, and I am grateful to all of them:

To my father and mother, Joseph and Gladys Holladay, who despite their fears of having failed in my upbringing, were the ones who prepared me to explore and recognize reality for myself.

To my wife, Diane, who has been a constant for the past 20 years (as long as I have known her) and who continues to be that stabilizing force in my often vacillating nature. Bahá'u'lláh, who identified marriage as a 'fortress for well-being', surely must have known that Diane was in the world for me to find. Thank God that I did.

To Joanne Dawson Holladay, who made it possible for me to follow my career and who gave me two wonderful children.

To Helen Holladay Engebretsen and Marvin (Bud) Holladay, who still rank as my greatest creative achievements. Nothing really excels the procreation of the species and the opportunity to aid in the development of your children's character, which is then realized in their eventual continuation of that same process.

To Joseph and Leslie Ann, the grands Helen has provided for us to enjoy. Bud, like his father, is a late bloomer who will in his proper time do as God willeth, whatever that may be.

To Dizzy Gillespie, who was not only a role model but provided some of the most emphatic lessons in what it means to 'prefer others to ourselves' both in my life and as a musician. His profound example of Bahá'u'lláh's teaching for the development of an ever-advancing civilization, which he manifested with such simplicity and obvious joy, was ever present and nurtured all who came into his presence.

To Mike Longo for helping me to keep in touch with Dizzy's influence. From my perspective, Mike was the closest person to being a son to Dizzy that I knew.

To Wendi Momen, who turned my flow of consciousness writing into recognizable and readable prose without ever losing 'my voice'.

And last but certainly not least to Michael Fitzgerald. Michael is not only a creative soul mate but also a very dear friend. He has made so many goals possible for me through his generosity of spirit and resources and was one, with a few others, who insisted that I should make this book available to the greater public. It began when Michael asked me to record an oral history of my life for the Bahá'í archives. I still question the value of such an undertaking but Michael felt so strongly about it that I couldn't refuse him. Now there is this book, thanks to Michael. Thanks Bro! I think?

1

Shabootie

The first I really knew that I wanted to be a jazz musician was somewhere around the fifth grade. I suppose I must have been 10 years old. I knew it because my fifth grade teacher asked me what I wanted to do with the instrument I was learning to play when I grew up – I had started learning the clarinet the summer before I went into fourth grade – and I told her, to her great disappointment, that I wanted to play in a jazz band. Actually I think I said a dance band; but that's what dance bands were then, at least the ones I listened to on the radio. I believe her response was, 'Oh! I thought you'd at least want to be in a symphony orchestra,' to which I replied, 'No! I want to play in a dance band.' The end of that conversation was the beginning of riding the fence.

My mother, God bless her, was determined that my sister, Maree, and I were going to be musicians. Maree, who was four, almost four-and-a-half, years older than I, began piano studies by the age of four or five, I have been told. When I was four my mother had me in a tap dancing class in our home town of Chanute, Kansas. Those were the heydays of the Fred Astaire–Ginger Rogers movies. I must have seen all of them, and many of them twice, as well as every Nelson Eddy–Jeannette McDonald extravaganza that was ever filmed. If we had been living in a metropolitan area or, God forbid, anywhere near Hollywood, I can assure you that through my mother's will and determination I would have been in the rash of kid movies à la Shirley Temple, etc. Or, at least, a supreme effort would have been made towards that goal. She really was a bit star struck.

As a matter of fact, Shirley Temple was probably the first

love of my life, vicariously of course, through the medium of the silver screen. We were about the same age and I saw all of her movies as well. Since we were both tap dancers and all, it seemed appropriate. Fred Astaire was great and the movies were impressive but Bill Robinson (in the Shirley Temple movies) and the occasions when I got to see the Nicholas brothers dance were what really took my breath away. My style of tap dancing, however, owing to my teacher's influence, or should I say my mother's direction, was to clone Fred Astaire. This went so far as to pair me with a dancing partner who was female, cute and whose mother was able and willing to make dresses that were copies of Ginger Rogers's gowns from one of their movies.

There is a picture of me and Wanda Willene Wilson taken at the age of five. We won every contest our parents could get us into, not because we were so great, I don't imagine, but because we were clones of two of the most celebrated movie stars of our age. At least, this was so in the minds of our mothers and a substantial percentage of our midwestern culturally biased neighbours. Actually, I had had a dancing partner the year before but I don't remember what we did or anything else but I do have a picture of us together, obviously as dancers.

Since the world didn't come knocking at our door by the time I was six and in grade school, the dancing sort of disappeared and I was made a student of piano under my sister's tutelage. I think we all know how far that went. Reluctantly and begrudgingly I suffered through a few months of this torture. As a result of my inability to play anywhere near as well as my sister, however, that came to a screeching halt. Piano is so important to one's progress as a musician, regardless of what one's primary instrument may be, that as a result of my inadequacy, all the students who have come through my educational programs have learned to play piano very well as a fundamental part of their instruction. Dizzy used to say, 'Piano, that's where it's at, right in front of you on that keyboard.' I still work at the piano and regret that I didn't, or wasn't willing to, learn from my sister, who, by the way, became an excellent pianist and teacher of piano. She was just not the right one for a six-year-old little brother who had his own idea of who he was and what he was willing to be a part of or party to. This, of course, became more pronounced in later years in a very positive way.

Radio really was our lifeline to the world around us and certainly beyond us. Our other means of understanding were the movies. We broadened our perspectives through the content of the movies, which were pretty idealized. Of even more importance were the short subjects, newsreels and travel documentaries, now things of the past and unnecessary since the advent of television. The airwaves were full of the sounds of the big bands at the different ballrooms and hotels around the country. Of course, you could pick and choose the kind of music you wanted to hear, just like we do today. That is, when I could control the dial, which was more often than you'd think, considering the days in which I grew up. This is the nicest way of saying that parents decided what was listened to and viewed in most households. Rarely did you find an exception to that rule, which is a major departure from today's norm. Fortunately, for me, my parents liked the music that my sister and I also preferred.

By the way, if you can get hold of the old Betty Boop cartoons, you can find some great Duke Ellington and other notable jazz orchestras on the sound tracks. These cartoons were occasionally shown at the movie-houses in place of Donald Duck, Goofy and Mickey Mouse, etc., which were a regular feature of movie programming. Throughout my childhood our little town of 10,000 people had three movie theatres, all doing good business while catering to slightly different clientele.

The movie theatre was the center of social life for many and I was no different from them. In fact, my first date took place when I was probably six or seven. My date was Shirley Flint, who lived across the street from us. (Many years later, when I was in college, I stopped by the Flints' residence in Paola, Kansas, to see if Shirley still remembered me. Her mother informed me that she was engaged to be married to a local boy who was in succession to inherit a very productive farm. So much for finding old loves.)

To continue, it was my birthday. My dad drove Shirley and me to the movie theatre. She did look a little like Shirley Temple, now that I think about it. I got to open the door for her, buy the tickets and the popcorn. I even had enough left over to go, after the movie, to an ice cream shop where dad was to pick us up at a pre-arranged time.

My parents, I've come to realize, were very progressive for Chanute, Kansas. Speaking of my parents, I've looked back on this every so often and wondered if they knew what they were doing or if they were blessedly naïve. I guess the times were so different that you could afford to be more lenient with your children. I know that when my son, Bud, was 16 there was no way on God's earth that I would have even considered allowing him to do what my folks allowed me to do when I was that age.

Picture this: I was 16 and my favorite bands were Duke Ellington, Jimmie Lunceford, Lionel Hampton, Count Basie, Louie Jordan and the Tympani Five, Lucky Millinder, Benny Goodman, Harry James and the early beginnings of Stan Kenton. (I would refuse to listen to Guy Lombardo or anything so sickeningly sweet, or so we thought it to be. I later came to recognize that as an attitude and became more aware of the need to appreciate differences objectively.)

To go on with the story. The Jimmie Lunceford Orchestra was coming to the Playmor Ballroom in Kansas City, Missouri, on a Saturday night. (This was about six months before Jimmie died.) I wanted so much to see this band and had some money of my own, having had some kind of job or another from the age of nine or ten. That is another major difference between then and now. Anyhow, my folks said yes, I could go to Kansas City on the train, see the Lunceford band, stay over night and come back the next day.

The Saturday of the scheduled performance of the Jimmie Lunceford Orchestra at the Playmor Ballroom came and I took the 11:00 a.m. train to Kansas City from Chanute. Train travel in those days was really something special. You usually had reserved seating that was very comfortable but the *pièce de la résistance* was the dining car with silver place settings, lace tablecloths and waiters with little napkins over their arms, just like in the movies. You ordered from a menu that offered a selection of entrées that would be prepared in the kitchen on the train and served hot at your table. Then if you got restless you could go to the club car, which was an observation car with big windows, easy chairs and lounges where you could have a Coca-Cola, hobnob with the rich folks and watch the scenery go by.

The ride to KC took about two and a half hours. After arriving at the Union Station, I caught the trolley into downtown and checked into the Dixon Hotel. This was right across the street from the Muehlbach, one of the most prestigious hotels in downtown KC in those days. The lobby of the Muehlbach had big chandeliers and carpeting so plush that you felt you were sinking into it. The bellboys were dressed like the ones you saw in the movies, with all the shiny buttons down the front of their jackets. I guess you understand that the Dixon was rather modest from my description of the Muehlbach.

I got all dressed up, which meant that I wore my best Sunday-go-to-meetin' clothes and my only good shoes and slicked back my hair in a duck tail, the only way to wear your hair if you were a budding jazz musician. I got a bite to eat and caught the trolley car out to the Playmor, got my ticket well before the band was due to come on stage and found me a spot right by the bandstand as near to the saxophone section as I could get. This put me on the opposite side of the stage from the rhythm section but right next to one of the stands of the saxophone player who would be setting on the outside of the section. I could actually reach the music stand that he would use. I waited patiently, frozen to the spot so that I would not lose my place. I must admit that I went to the bathroom on my way into the ballroom and never again moved from that spot until the night was over. Oddly enough, I don't remember being particularly uncomfortable.

As 9:00 p.m. arrived, the band came on stage to start the

first set and to my great surprise and pleasure they had decided to put Joe Thomas, the primary soloist on tenor sax, on the outside of the sax section. That allowed him to get to the front of the stage and the microphone that was placed there. All the bands presented themselves that way in those days. If you felt that you needed to get more presence on your solo, you could go down front and use the microphone there; otherwise you simply blew from your position on the bandstand and played so that your sound would carry to the audience. Musicians were confident of the quality and content of their sound projection. They believed they could be heard all over the ballroom, and for the most part, they could. Anyway, it meant that I was going to stand next to Joe Thomas all night long. Wow! What a bounty for me.

The whole night was magical because I did understand something of what was going on as a result of my few years of experience with our local dance band. Hearing the musicians live was incredible. Their sound on broadcasts was great but nothing like it was live, there in the ballroom. The subtleties and shadings were much more pronounced, and when the band opened up, there was an embracing envelope of sound, undistorted, a blanket of sound with punctuations that you could feel. By this I do not mean anything related to the physical bombardment of electronically reinforced blasts that have become the norm in today's contemporary pop music. I mean the individual and collective mastery of the material and the spontaneity of improvisational skill from the soloists and from the group, sometimes by sections and sometimes by voices from different sections, interweaving melodic and harmonic ideas that constantly aid the overall expression of the content of the orchestration. Joe Thomas was out of that big tenor sax sound associated with Coleman Hawkins and Ben Webster and acknowledged by people like Don Byas, Herschel Evans, Budd Johnson, etc. I was consequently nearly mesmerized by the sheer volume of the sound coming out the end of his horn and being close enough to touch him just emphasized its vastness.

In addition to the emotional satisfaction of the musical

experience of that evening, I found that the musicians were a very congenial bunch of men as well. Thanks to Joe, I received a piece of paper with the signatures of all the guys in the band. Some added short comments like 'keep swingin'' for the kid saxophone player who stood next to Joe all night long at the Playmor Ballroom in KC, Missouri. After spending the evening listening to the on-stage banter, watching the antics of the various musicians and seeing the camaraderie, I was even more convinced that this was the way I wanted to live my life.

One Christmas Eve many years later I told this story after a gig we were doing at Basin Street East in New York with, I think, Gerald Wilson's Orchestra. The band was primarily guys from the Quincy Jones Orchestra who had been contracted by Snooky Young. The reason I told the story that night was because two of the guys who had been in the Jimmie Lunceford Band that night long ago in Kansas City were Snooky Young and Gerald Wilson. Both had been in their late teens then but were already becoming known as stellar jazz musicians. Snooky, to this day, is still considered by the musicians in the business as the best lead trumpet player we've ever had. There was another man in that Lunceford Band who I had the privilege of working with later on in New York, the alto sax man Earl Warren. What a beautifully lyrical player he was. He was also quite a character, with an incredible sense of humor.

Chanute was a small farming community in southeastern Kansas with approximately 10,000 people. Interestingly enough, 60 years later it has grown to a whopping 12,000, which should give you a pretty good idea of what goes on there. At one time it was a major stop on the Atchison, Topeka and Santa Fe railroad and had a large freight yard and roundhouse. It still has a very productive cement plant where I spent one summer doing inventory. Thank God that finally came to an end. A more boring job I can't remember.

This town, like most towns our size in Kansas, was not segregated, at least not in the schools. I learned later that this was primarily because the town simply wasn't big enough to have a segregated system. I knew that the black population lived more or less in distinct areas, even though they were dispersed around town and for the most part were on the edges of town. The exception was the eastside, which seemed to have a predominance of black homes and businesses such as a bar, a pool hall and a grocery store and some others I can't remember. However, enough multi-racial use was made of the downtown markets, grocery stores, 'Monkey Wards', Penny's and some of the other merchants, that I was not aware of the segregation that existed. In grade school we were all in the same classrooms and participated in all activities together, though there was an inclination to gravitate towards one's own group. I still didn't get the idea, even after witnessing some fights on the playground between individuals. The causes always seemed to be a result of individualized differences of opinion rather than a group or collective view. This is obviously leading to another story, so let me begin with a little background first.

In our 'Beginning Band' program, which started for us in the summer between the third and fourth grades, all those who wanted to participate actively were interested in learning to play musical instruments. As my involvement increased during the early years, I found that a few of the 'Negro' kids and I were attracted to music and liked the same kinds of music. Needless to say, as Chanute was primarily an agrarian culture, there was a general popular interest in country western music, particularly in the bands of Bob Wills and his brother, Johnny Lee Wills. There was a comparable emphasis on the dance bands of the period, such as the Tommy Dorsey and Glenn Miller bands, by most of the rest of the population. I remember in the fifth grade we had a parents' day when all the parents were invited to come to school in the evening to meet our teachers and view our artwork, very much like what is still done today. That year, a few of us who had been a part of the elementary band program in our school wanted to put together a jazz band and play for this parents' night. I do not remember whose idea it was or who proposed it to the principal but I'm sure I was a party to it. The most amazing aspect of this whole scenario was the fact that we got the approval of the principal to do it. Our band director helped us find music simple enough for us to rehearse and play at this event. We had ourselves a bandstand in the middle of the main hallway at the front of the school where we played three or four times during the evening, probably no more than two or three tunes each time, but we played. The drummer was Armond Smith, who by the time we got to high school was called 'Smitty'. Smitty was black and extremely talented. The trumpet player was a neighbor of mine named Gene Manley. I played clarinet and I believe we had a piano player whose name I can't remember but who I do remember lived next door to Gene. The rest of the group, if there were more, I don't remember at all but it seems to me that there may have been a trombone player with us. We played our version of traditional jazz (Dixieland), which went over real big with the parents and teachers, or so we thought, with the possible exception of the country western fans in attendance. We never knew.

When I was in grade school, Chanute had the extreme good fortune to have a dynamic and very competent high school band director, Al Brown. Al had built a music program that was second to none in Kansas for a school of its size and it became known throughout the state for its excellence. Of course there were programs in major cities that had more to offer and greater reputations; for example, Joliet, Illinois, had one of the supreme programs in the country during those years.

We at the grade school were the recipients of Al Brown's commitment and energy, for in the third grade we had a year of weekly lessons on the 'flutophone'. This was a type of cheap, simple recorder, which every student in the third grade learned to play.

That was followed the next summer with the opportunity to participate in a beginners' instrumental band program, if one so desired and could afford an instrument through rental or purchase. For those who didn't have the resources for that, the school owned many instruments, particularly the larger brass instruments, some saxophones, bass and alto clarinets and, of course, drums, which only required a person to own a pair of sticks and a drum pad. This pretty well accommodated everyone who was interested in being a part of the band program in Chanute.

This summer program was followed up with school bands in each and every elementary school in town where there were enough kids involved to function as one. As far as I can remember, that meant every elementary school. We had weekly rehearsals throughout the school year and this continued in the summer with band programs at all levels. Needless to say, the junior high school got a cadre of reasonably well-prepared musicians to work with and the high school had a band that reached an extremely elevated standard of performance. In a relatively small school population of 500 to 550 students, the band regularly had 100 to 125 members. During those years there was, as you would expect, an ongoing battle between the band and the athletic programs at the high school and more often than not the band won out – quite an unusual turn of events.

I remember when my sister was in the high school band. She played string bass in the concert band and glockenspiel with the marching band. The concert band became so highly respected by the state music organization that it was eventually prevented from participating in the state contests because it had, for a number of years, consistently won all the honors. The band could then only take part as a guest high school band on the invitation of the state school band organization. One year the band was invited to participate in a midwestern regional contest in Colorado Springs, Colorado, and it again won all the honors in its division. All this is to say that we younger kids had a hell of a beginning and I'm sorry it didn't last.

Al Brown, the progenitor of this music phenomenon, finally burned out so badly that he left education altogether, opened up a small music store in a neighboring town and spent the rest of his years trying to get a life back. I'm afraid he lost more than he gained on that deal. Unfortunately for me, his burn out occurred before I got to high school. The quality of the program when we arrived there was, consequently, a disaster. Mediocre was up from where it was after the departure of Al Brown. Despite the precipitous decline in the school program, there were many really good musicians who were seriously interested in playing. Unfortunately, we were left pretty much to our own resources to instruct ourselves. This was not greatly productive for us, though our spirits sure were right.

By the time I got to junior high I was the ace clarinet player for my age in town. In fact, I was brought to the junior high school to perform at an assembly as a soloist while I was still in the sixth grade. That would have been cool except by the next year the program was on its way down, as Mr Brown had resigned from burn out and the teachers who came after him had nowhere near his ability or enthusiasm for the program, music or the kids. As an example, I came into the junior high school band and immediately became the second chair clarinet player. The year before I would have been lucky to have made the second clarinet section, let alone been in a major chair assignment. Worst of all, before the year was out the kid who was first chair decided he'd rather play basketball and I was first chair. That was good for one's ego but not worth a damn for making progress on the horn, musically. The only good thing that kept coming back to me was that my taste in music and my enthusiasm for wanting to be a jazz musician was shared.

Those I shared these with were, almost to a person, black, and the group had grown. This is the age at which I think I got my first taste of being called a 'nigger lover'. Fortunately, those words came from kids I had no interest in or did not know on a social basis, so I wasn't bothered particularly. Smitty was already in high school when I was finishing my last year in junior high. We were playing with a dance band made up mostly of high school seniors who were the remnants of those good bands I referred to above.

This is how it happened. I got a call from a member of the band, letting me know they needed a tenor player to replace one of their members who'd received his draft notice. This was during the second world war. I couldn't believe my ears. These were the big guys in high school. Wow!

I asked my dad if he thought we could get me a tenor saxophone somehow, so dad and I went down to the music store in town and looked at some instruments. Look was all I could do, as I didn't have a clue how to play it. We picked one out and my dad bought it for me. I agreed to pay him back with money I would earn playing with this band. Next I went to my junior high band director and asked him if he could help me learn to play the saxophone. He gave me a fingering chart from a method book and told me to take it home and learn it, with no explanation about the difference in embouchure or anything. I realized later that music directors did not see the value of jazz and were not all that keen on anyone playing it, let alone helping someone learn it. They didn't want to teach anything other than what they perceived to be good music. We have actually made some progress in our music education systems in this regard.

I had a week to get some control of the sax for a rehearsal with the band the following week. I really can't tell you a thing about what I did or how I did it but I was there for rehearsal the next week.

Some years before, when my sister had been in high school, she had played in an all-girl dance band. The band used to rehearse in our living room, which my dad had converted, some years earlier, from a parlor and a bedroom into a single living room area. In fact, the practice dancing platform that he made me when I was four was made from leftover pieces of hardwood flooring that he used in the renovation of the living room. When I got to junior high school and took an interest in basketball, the dance floor became a backboard for a basketball hoop in the backyard. My sister played upright bass (of course, that was the only kind of bass we had in those days) with the band. They were pretty darn good for high school girls from a little town in southeastern Kansas.

I remember the lead trumpet player, Dorothy Ditmars, who had this big full sound and was, I believe, the first chair trumpet player in the high school band to achieve great acclaim. I was impressed with both the lyrical beauty of her playing and the strength and range she had at her command, which frankly put most of the high school boys to shame. After her graduation from high school she ended up as a Catholic nun. After some educational pursuits, she spent her years teaching music at a Catholic school somewhere in Kansas, I think. I can't think of one musician who came out of that incredibly successful school band program who went on to do anything with his or her music professionally.

The all-girl band was heralded all over southeastern Kansas and, as a result, was offered a summer job to play for three months at a night club in Kansas City, Missouri, which, for us, was big time. The girls' parents were not about to let their little girls go off to the big city without proper supervision, however. The problem of getting enough money to pay for the girls and for the requisite number of chaperons to be with them in KC was just unsolvable. It had nothing to do with the value of their musicianship or the quality of the band. And we all knew about the Phil Spitalny and Ina Ray Hutton all-girl orchestras, so they weren't just a novelty, except that they were from this little town in southeastern Kansas.

Many years later I became familiar with the International Sweethearts of Rhythm, the most incredible, truly jazz, all-women band you could ever want to hear. Its reputation speaks for itself, although you have to do a lot of looking to find any reference to it in your standard jazz history books. The Sweethearts originated at a school in Mississippi called Pineywoods. I understand it was a school for wayward girls at that time and is now a private boarding school. Many years later, when I was a professor of music at Oakland University in Michigan, I worked with Maurice King, the man who had been the music director of this hallmark orchestra which had the finest women jazz musicians in the country. He was then conducting for the vocal group the Spinners. An album of the recordings of the International Sweethearts of Rhythm was reissued a few years ago. I hope it is still available somewhere because you have to hear the band to realize how truly great it was.

Getting back to the story. All this reference to our family living room is to tell you that after I had been in the high school dance band for a while, the need for rehearsal space became acute. Since our living room had been used those years before for my sister's band, I didn't see why we couldn't do the same for the band I was in. I asked and had the total agreement of my folks for the rehearsals to be held in our living room, with the stipulation that there be no smoking. We started having rehearsals at my house, to the delight of our neighbors. I do not mean that sarcastically; they were delighted and used to call our house and make requests. Can you imagine that today? Of course, we were strictly acoustic, which I'm sure made a big difference to their reaction.

I'll never forget the first rehearsal. The guys started coming into the house and my mom was there to greet them graciously and make them feel at home. Anything musical going on in our house was just fine with her and my dad was just about as agreeable a person as you could hope to know. He was a very gentle soul and committed to anything that was of benefit to others. As gracious as my mother was, however, when Smitty came walking in with his drums I thought she was going to pass out. She had never dreamed of a 'negro' coming into her house. I'll give her credit though. She got hold of herself really quickly, feigned a welcome she did not feel at all and got out of our way as soon as she could. As the rehearsals continued she became more comfortable with Smitty being there. I think she learned a lot about the whole issue of prejudgment of people of another race from Smitty, as you couldn't have a more polite and considerate person in your home than he.

While Smitty, Namon Harris (later called 'Duke'), Morris Coppage and I were in junior high we shared our love of jazz and talked often about the different musicians we were listening to. Their knowledge and familiarity with the subject was way beyond mine, so these discussions were always a source of learning for me. As I mentioned, Smitty was a year ahead of the rest of us. Consequently when he went to high school that left Namon, Morris and me. The other two were a bit reserved about this white kid who was so friendly but they never closed me out. They just weren't sure I knew what I was doing and a few years later Smitty was able to show me why.

Smitty and I worked together in this band during high school. I lived closer to him than to any of the other guys in the band. My dad would let me use our family car to go to gigs. These took place a few miles outside of town at a genuine road house or, as we more affectionately called it, a 'gin mill', which was probably inappropriate since Kansas was a dry state and only 3.2 beer was sold legally. Of course, everybody knew the back roads to Missouri and the fellows made regular runs in preparation for Saturday nights. Or if you didn't mind taking your chances locally, everyone knew who the bootleggers in town were and where you could find them. I would pick up Smitty and his drums each Saturday night and we would go to the gig. We worked from 8:00 p.m. to midnight and made a whopping $3 per man, which beat the hell out of the 25 cents an hour I could get doing anything else in town.

Every night after the job, we'd head back into town and I would ask Smitty if we could stop and get something to eat at a restaurant. All the guys in the band would be there. He always had a reason to get home, usually church the next day, which was understandable, since I had to do the same thing and sing in the choir as well. I always asked and when he said, 'No', I'd take him home and go back downtown and join the guys in the restaurant. This went on for some time until finally one night Smitty said, 'O.K., let's go eat.' This was great for me because now I wouldn't have to come back later to get something to eat.

We found a place to park near the restaurant, went in, walked over to the table where the guys in the band were sitting and joined them. The waitress came over and took our orders and then announced that Smitty could pick up his plate at the counter. I said, 'What for?' and she told me that Smitty would have to take his plate outside and eat it there. Of course, this brilliant young kid had to ask, 'What for?' and watch her stummer and stammer as she tried to figure how to identify Smitty. She was able finally to get out that he was a 'niii—gro' and that they didn't serve them in the restaurant.

It took all that for me to finally get the message. Now I realized what Smitty had been trying to tell me, without telling me, all this time. I felt like an idiot and worse for putting Smitty through such an embarrassing ordeal. I got up and said, 'Forget it,' and we walked out of the restaurant after saying goodbye to the guys we were sitting with. They didn't appear to be surprised at all, only me.

We got in the car and I began to apologize for putting Smitty through such embarrassment. He just laughed and said, 'Well, I knew you didn't know what was going on, so I thought I might as well show you.' After living in this town for 16 or 17 years, I had to learn about segregation, its injustice and evils, through this kind of exposure at the expense of a young man I realized cared about me that much. Talk about being dumb! I couldn't excuse myself for just being naïve. I was plain dumb because I then saw what had been there all the time while I was growing up in Chanute, Kansas.

Then I said, 'Well, what do we do now?' He replied, 'Let's go to the Chicken Shack – it's only a couple of blocks from your house.' Sure enough, about two blocks away from my house (we lived just a short block up the hill from the railroad tracks and three blocks north of the main street), on a street just down the hill alongside the railroad tracks was this small house, of no particular description. The owners of this house had converted the living room into a small café, with seats at a counter for maybe three people and, as I remember, maybe two or three card tables with chairs. The people who owned the place welcomed me with, 'Hey! Little Joe, what you doin' here?'

Everybody in town knew my dad because he was a player with the city's semi-pro baseball team which Chanute had had for years. My dad was, first, a player of some respect and later became a coach for the team. Also, by this time I was playing American Legion ball and everybody called me 'Little Joe' after my father, whose name, obviously, was Joe. Baseball was the source of a great deal of entertainment for the town, particularly for the black population, both because they enjoyed the sport and because some of the players were local black men.

From that moment on it was the Chicken Shack for Smitty and me and, I might add, the food was better than anything I ever got downtown. To seal the deal, the jukebox at the Chicken Shack put all the other boxes in town to shame. All the best jazz bands were featured, as well as the really good rhythm and blues artists like Louie Jordan, Ruth Brown, the Johnson Brothers and Fats Domino, way before the white record companies 'discovered' him. So finally I began to comprehend and experience racism. Ignorance ain't bliss; it's just ignorance.

In case you are wondering, Shabootie is a slang term for Chanute. It was the name of a Gene Ammons tune from back in the '40s that was adopted as a pseudonym by a very exclusive local jazz contingent who resided in Chanute. Absolutely no one in Chanute would recognize that name other than those very select few young black jazz musicians who came up with it as an identification of their residence.

Smitty graduated and went immediately into the army. That was the last time I saw him until years later. After I graduated from college, I got drafted and was doing a tour of duty in Korea when Smitty and I met up, rather by accident, and got to play together again. Each recognized the progress the other had made as a musician and we appreciated each other even more. The last I heard about him was that he had retired from military service and was living in the San Francisco area, where he continued to play. After making occasional efforts to ascertain Smitty's situation over the years, on a recent stop in Chanute while touring around Oklahoma, I finally found out that he had passed on a few years before. This was a real disappointment to me as I wanted to get his input into this book before I put it out. *C'est la vie.*

You may remember my reference to the decline of the music program in the schools and my lack of competition at the junior high level. Well, things got worse when I got to high school. I went straight to first chair in the high school band, which said nothing about my proficiency on clarinet but a lot about the decline of quality in our school music program. I practiced when I felt like it, which wasn't very often, and there was so much to distract one's attention at that age – girls, cigarettes, girls, beer, girls, bootleg whiskey, girls, athletics – baseball primarily, since my mother wouldn't sign the papers for me to play football, even though I was one of the better players in school. You may ask, how did I know that? The answer is, on the Saturday afternoon after a school football game on the Friday night a bunch of the kids who played for the high school team and I, and a few others like me, would play tackle at the school football field without our parents or the coaches knowing about it. Mom thought I might break a finger and not be able to play clarinet and so forbade me to play with the football team. If she had only known that I could have broken a whole lot more than my fingers, the way I was going those Saturday afternoon games. It was crazy. We used no pads or helmets and hit just as hard as we could anyhow. If the coach had found out, I can promise you that the games would have stopped, never to happen again. As a matter of fact, this may very well have been the reason those Saturday afternoon games ended. I'm not really sure how that came about.

I can still remember Ike Stowell bearing down on me with the kind of focus on pulverizing me that the high school league's opponents must have feared. Ike became All State and played college ball for, I think, Emporia State. He went on to coach at the high school level as a career and may have gone further, I don't know. However, that day he was the only one between me and the goal line, so, as much out of fear as athletic prowess, I jumped over his tackle, he bit the dust and I scored the touchdown. My crowning achievement as a high school football player and it didn't count for anything except confidence in my ability to play the game, had I been allowed.

That brings us back to girls and, thank God, jazz. If it had not been for the dance band and trying to play jazz, I swear my musical advancement would have been totally arrested. Oh yes, I would get ready for the regional contests each spring but would usually woodshed (practice) the piece for only about two weeks before the contest and hope for the best. My senior year the, excuse the title, 'band director' gave me a nothing piece of music to learn for the spring contest, which I did. But it was such a weak piece musically that I'm surprised I even got into the final selection.

You realize that this is all hindsight, of course, as I didn't know anything about the quality of the piece at the time it was given to me. For the first time in my high school career, I did not win the highest honor. I played this same piece for an audition for a scholarship to a university that my parents wanted me to go to and the adjudicator took me aside and expressed this very sentiment. Fortunately, he added that if it had not been for the musical sensibility I had shown in the performance of the piece, I would not have been considered at all as a candidate for a scholarship at the university. I got the scholarship but don't know that it was such a good thing in the long run.

I arrived at the campus the next fall, full of enthusiasm again for music. I would get up early (anyone who knows me will not believe that I did this voluntarily, but I did) and get to a practice room early in the morning so that I would be there ahead of the other music students. All of this to be sure that I could get a room to practice in. I was going to be a serious music student in college. After the first semester I was second chair, just like back in junior high, and when the first chair player graduated that spring I was again the first chair clarinet player.

A young person, or at least this one, needs challenges and obstacles to climb over and needs work to realize whatever potential he has, particularly if he happens to be gifted in any way. It was a struggle to continue to progress. Unfortunately, I have never been terribly self-motivated and still find it difficult to be so. Here again, it was my love for jazz and the people it put me in touch with, from both the school and the community, that kept me growing. Jazz – and my first exposure to Béla Bartók. What a revelation! To top it all off, I heard, for the first time, Charlie Parker and Dizzy Gillespie. These two events were the major motivators during my last years in college.

But back to high school. I made some efforts at conformity

and wanted to get into the 'with it' crowd at school. This meant pledging a fraternity (in high school already) and trying to fit in. The fraternity thing was an introduction to where I thought I wanted to go. To add to that possibility, I joined a country club, on my own, not because my family belonged.

My parents would no more have belonged to a country club than fly to the moon, even if they had been able to join. My mother was convinced that anybody who was wealthy got there by being dishonest, cheating other people or inheriting money from a parent or relative who got it by being that way. My dad, God bless him, was a troubleshooter for Ma Bell (Southwestern Bell Telephone Company) and was really good at what he did; in fact, he had turned down offers for advancement so that he could stay in Chanute, largely because of my mother.

My dad was acknowledged by his peers and supervisors to be a top man in his field and all that with only an eighth grade education. My mom had only a sixth grade education which, I've come to understand, wasn't all that unusual for people from their generation and social status. My dad was a farm boy raised in the Ozarks of Arkansas where his family farmed and operated a saw mill. My mom was also a farm girl whose dad had a small dairy farm near a village not too far from Chanute. What a snot-nosed kid I was, to aspire to be in country club social circles. My folks seemed to understand that somehow I needed to go through this period and find out for myself who and what I was.

It didn't take too long before I became more and more uncomfortable with the racial attitudes I found. Not that they were in any way vicious or nasty but just an uninformed prejudice against people they knew nothing about. Of course, all I knew was what I could pick up by hanging around with Smitty and the people at the Chicken Shack, which was enough for me to become uneasy with the attitudes I felt from the crowd at the country club.

Now, it wasn't all bad; I should make that clear. I was recognized, by the local social group, as a very good dancer, which I was. And that gave me an introduction into an older and more sophisticated crowd, particularly to the young ladies whose peer group men were off in the military service fighting the second world war. This was the avenue by which invitations came for me to participate in the night-life of our community at quite a different social level than I had previously experienced. Needless to say, being as naïve (dumb!) as I was, I missed a lot more than I knew, which I only realized many years later. Subtle invitations of a more intimate nature went right by me and I really thought that the dancing was the point of those evenings out at the Spotlight Café, which, by the way, was only about half a block from the Chicken Shack. Oh well.

I was still working the gin joint south of town but with different musicians, many of whom were returning veterans from the war. So the musical link became more demanding, which I ate up like a starving rat. The new owners had turned the club into a kind of supper club, with a kitchen and everything, and held private parties as well as the open nights on the weekends. One summer we were working at this club five nights a week, which for Chanute was quite exceptional. What with rehearsals to work on new music, I probably played more that summer than any time before in my whole life and I loved every minute of it. There was no doubt in my mind that this was the way I wished to spend the rest of my life. That summer, between the band and the American Legion baseball team, I was in hog heaven.

An anecdote regarding baseball would be appropriate at this point. One of my team-mates and I were set up by our coach to go to a minor league tryout with the St Louis Cardinals. But the coach had decided, in his mind, that he would wait to see if we showed enough commitment to the game before he offered this opportunity to us. From his perspective, this made sense; if we didn't show enough commitment, he would let the opportunity go, even though he had made the arrangements himself. I don't think Jack Sparks, my team-mate, ever knew about the opportunity and I only found out about it during my last year in college from my father, who was that coach.

I have to admit that this was probably the only time in my

life that I was truly angry with my dad. He had always been there for me in everything I wanted to do, even when he knew I shouldn't do something but felt I would learn better by finding out for myself. This one time he made the decision for me instead of letting me find out for myself and I really would have liked to have seen just how far I could have gone in baseball. Hindsight is always 20/20 and I'm sure that my mother's desire for me to go on to college and study music was a determining factor in the decision about whether I should pursue a career in baseball. By now you've probably figured out why I was allowed to play baseball but not football. I went out for basketball and wasn't too bad but ran into some difficulty with the coach. I also had a job during the school year at a Skelly gas station, where I was making money to pay for a new Selmer clarinet that I had just bought, and the basketball coach got on my case about leaving practices a few minutes early to get to work. He handed me an ultimatum during practice one day: either quit the job or the team. And that took care of my involvement with the basketball team.

The summer after high school and before college I spent working for my brother-in-law in Minnesota building a creamery. His business was in brick masonry and I worked as a laborer. A good job but no musical activity at all, though I did go to a ballroom in Detroit Lakes to hear a territorial band one night. It sounded pretty good to me. Territorial bands, as they were called, were bands that traveled up and down the midwest, playing in various ballrooms. Most of the members lived either in a converted bus or in a trailer outfitted with bunks and some minor conveniences. The quality of life for these men was less than comfortable but they were playing seven nights a week with an occasional night off. Of course, this was without pay. God truly smiled on me in that regard. I never did work with one of those bands, though I did know at least one person who did, as a later chapter will reveal.

My birth home, with my sister Maree on the porch.
Note the Model T Ford at the side of the house.

Mom and Dad, sister
Maree and moi

My dancing partner
Glen Fagle, *left*, and
moi, aged about four

Wanda Willene
Wilson and moi,
aged five

Moi in my junior high school band uniform, Maree in the high school band uniform

In high school

The Del Morning Orchestra at Phillips University. I am at the front, far right

In the army now – my wife thinks I was handsome

Moi in Minnesota, before leaving for Korea

'Face the music'
8th Army Special Service, Korea

After Korea, in Oklahoma, 1953

Jomar Dagron Quartet
Left to right: Jo Jo Williams, Dag Walton, moi
Standing: Ron Washington

2

P.U.

Now back to college, Enid, Oklahoma, and Phillips University. I've already told you something about the beginning of my collegiate days. There were many good and productive years associated with that experience. First of all, I met some very serious and capable musicians from all over the midwest, many who had been in the service and had had extensive experience as a result of their time with Uncle Sam. I was also exposed to a wider and much more diverse musical offering than I had been familiar with, both as a listener and as a performer. For instance, it was at college that I had my first introduction to Béla Bartók, as I have already mentioned, and I experienced a major turning point in my awareness of western European classical literature. All this plus an introduction to the music of Charlie Parker and Dizzy Gillespie, which totally revolutionized the boundaries that had previously defined jazz.

It was my good fortune to have, as a fellow student, a trombone player who had spent his military career in England and while there had been able to add to his knowledge of arranging and composition in the jazz medium. While at P.U. he started a band made up of students from the college and some local musicians who were very good players. His name was Del Morning and I have much to thank him for from those years. The charts he wrote for us were of a quality that surpassed anything I had previously come into contact with and he had an understanding of what it takes to make other arrangers' charts come to fruition. I believe this was the first time I understood what made the Glenn Miller band sound the way it did. Even though I wasn't a great fan of the Miller band, I still learned to appreciate what it took to make the band sound right when playing stylistically. Thanks Del! We traveled all over the panhandle of Oklahoma and even east to Oklahoma A & M (now Oklahoma State) at Stillwater, making it possible for me to meet a much wider circle of musicians and get to know how they felt and what they thought about music.

During the first year at Phillips I made one more attempt to get on with the social scene and pledged a social club – Greek fraternities were outlawed on this campus primarily owing to its philosophy, which stemmed from its Christian orientation. I lasted one year and through the next fall's pledge period but I just couldn't cope with the whole concept of exclusivity. I had been seriously evaluating the whole idea of social exclusivity and particularly how it dealt with anyone from an African–American background. The club was a church-sponsored institution of the same Christian church that my parents had raised both me and my sister in and I continued to find there the same attitudes about black folks that I had experienced in Chanute, only more so, since I was now in Oklahoma.

The university had students from Asia and the Near East, as well as Latinos but I don't remember any African–Americans in the student body during the years I attended. This even though there was a good deal of emphasis on missionary work in Africa by the church and its educational institutions. From an old yearbook I have discovered that there were two African students at the university during the time I was there but I have no recollection of ever seeing them on campus. I also found that Phillips had a chapter of the NAACP. It was from the picture of the NAACP in the yearbook that I discovered the two African students; all the other members of the club, as it was identified in the yearbook, were white.

In Enid, Oklahoma, as well as in my home town, it was the black musicians who welcomed me and shared their knowledge and their warmth and appreciation for my love of the music. After Del graduated from P.U. there was no one to continue the band. Del found a teaching gig some-where and, of course, the library for the band went with him. In the meantime, I found a quartet with an organ player and a trumpet player who were local professionals – the trumpet player was considered in town to be the best jazz player around. The drummer and I were from the college and we found it to be a very lucrative association for us.

There was a joint on the edge of town that brought in jazz and blues groups from around the midwest, one group quite frequently. This was the Four Tons of Rhythm, whose home base was Kansas City, Missouri – remember the Jimmie Lunceford story. The group had a tenor man they called Froggy, who played with such ease that I found an excuse to spend almost every night they were in town with them. What great encouragement I used to get from these guys and an education like nothing I could have got in the classroom – teaching without criticism and replacing it with nurturing in the sensibilities of what music is about. I have said to every student that I have ever come into contact with that I've had the very best teachers in the world. These mentors have taken my sincerity at face value and given me advice, direction and encouragement. These teachers include the men and women that I have had the pleasure of working with over the years who have, sometimes without knowing it, schooled me on every aspect of the knowledge of music and the special spiritual privilege of performing it.

Sometime during those years at dear old P.U. I was invited to come to a jam session at the recreation center of a black church in Enid. I do not have any recollection of how that came about but I will never forget the experience or the people I met there. A special memory is of a young trumpet player who became a good friend to me and I'm ashamed to say that I cannot remember his name. I've tried to bring it back for years by talking about him, hoping it would show up at some moment. He was about my age, give or take a year or two – who could tell? and I never asked. We both had a commitment to the music, so much so that our respective voices really locked into each other and during those sessions at the rec. center I swear I could play anything that my imagination could conjure up. I give the credit for that both to the extreme warmth of the environment and to the spiritual dynamic of what we were doing collectively.

I have only one serious regret from those days and that association. We were taking a breather between tunes one Saturday night and my friend asked me to come the next morning to play with him and the group at their Sunday church service. I told him I wouldn't have any idea of what to play, quite honestly explaining that I felt inadequate. His reply to me was, 'Sure you can. We play the same way there that we are playing right now.' I do regret that I didn't have the courage to accept that invitation and feel I missed a major moment for my development in that period.

The associations I enjoyed with the University were many and varied, though as I indicated earlier, less than what I would have chosen for myself had I known what the alternatives were or options that were open to me. The music program at Phillips was quite good if your objective was to become some sort of educator. I was pleased with the opportunity to spend the entire year playing quality music without the usual requirement to play in a marching band which, by the way, is probably the most damaging activity to expose yourself to if your desire is to become a career performer of either jazz or classical music. This statement will be considered by many educators to be a form of blasphemy, predicated on the reality that their job security is based on the success of their marching bands at the high school or collegiate levels. It is one of the advantages of writing down your views in your latter years: you can express yourself truthfully and candidly without having to be concerned about the results of your honesty.

As an example of what I'm saying: The University of Michigan marching band did not have a single music major in it for those same reasons. The members of the marching band were from Engineering, English, Pre-Med, etc. – kids out of marching bands at high schools who were only interested in the show band kicks of traveling with the football team, just like in high school. Actually, I have much greater respect and appreciation for the drum and bugle corps that are now prevalent around the country, where they use the skills as I feel they should. A marching band is hellatious on the embouchure of any serious-minded reed player, particularly clarinet.

Enough of my kvetching.

During the summer of 1948 the Phillips University band was invited to participate in a Lions Convention in New York City where the University's president was to be installed as the president of the Lions Club international organization. This would be the one and only time that the Phillips University concert band would actually march in a parade. The practices for this event were hilarious. The organizers found, or borrowed, uniforms for the band from somewhere, quite possibly old uniforms from one of the local high schools. On the other side of the coin, we got to play at the convention as a concert band. We also were invited to perform at the Central Park band shell as a guest band, providing the first half of an evening's concert by the Edwin Franko Goldman Band, under the direction of Mr Goldman himself – which was probably the stipulation under which we were invited to perform there, professional politics being what they are and all.

However, for me the highlight of this opportunity to be in New York City was realized when a group of us were allowed, with some form of adult supervision I'm sure, to walk downtown along Broadway. When we got down around 53rd Street – we were billeted at a church on Park Avenue and 91st Street – I began to hear music wafting up and down the street from places like the Palladium Ballroom on 53rd and Birdland on Broadway between 53rd and 52nd Streets. There were at that time some of the old famous 52nd Street clubs still functioning. That was as far as I needed to go. Everybody else was on their way to Times Square. I tried to stay put but the powers prevailing in the organization would not let a still-teenaged kid go by himself in the big city. It probably was the right thing to have done but I have never forgotten the sound of that area of the city at that time. So much music flowed up and down the street, all mixed together, almost like it was supposed to be rendered that way, and the vitality and energy of it were just mesmerizing. It could have been heard as an Elliot Carter or a Charles Ives composition or maybe Schoenberg, since a given tonality was not necessary for its satisfying impact on my musical soul. At any rate, it was gorgeous to the ears of this young, small-town country boy from Kansas.

During my last couple of years at Phillips I had the privilege of playing with the faculty woodwind quintet. We played much more demanding music, which I found to be a challenge and exciting.

The greatest growth in my performance skills during my studies at Phillips came as a result of my determination to make the 'Contrasts' for clarinet, violin and piano by Béla Bartók a part of my senior recital program. This was a piece commissioned from Bartók by Benny Goodman and Joseph Szigeti.

The story goes that Bartók was in dire financial straits at the time but was a very proud man and would not accept help, and certainly not charity, from anyone. So Goodman and Szigeti put their heads together and commissioned the piece, as much as a way to offer assistance to this creative genius with an inordinate amount of pride as for the music itself. What they got, however, was a monumental work of art that has lasted and will continue to be one of the great challenges of clarinet literature. My first exposure to this work was through the recording that had been made as a result of this commission, with Bartók himself on piano. I literally fell in love with the piece the first time I heard it. When I found that I could actually purchase the composition, that set my goal for the next year and I began to attempt to learn 'Contrasts'. It was written for both B♭ and A clarinets and, fortunately for me, a part that had the A clarinet part transposed for B♭ was included. Since B♭ was all I had access to, B♭ it was going to be, all the way.

It seemed to my instructor and others that my desire to perform this piece was foolish because we did not have a violinist in the school or the city who could begin to play it. And there was no pianist at the university or elsewhere who could begin to cut the piano part. God smiled on me again. The professor of theory and composition had retired from the university the year before and his replacement was a young PhD graduate from Illinois Southern University, Eugene Ulrich, who turned out to be an excellent pianist, conversant with modern compositional techniques and an avid fan of Bartók as well. At the same time, a violinist from Greece, Andreas Makris, came to Phillips to pursue graduate studies. He was capable of fulfilling the requirements of the piece as well. As a result of these individuals, my commitment to the performance of this incredible composition was kept and learning this piece was a giant step forward in my development.

Working on this piece was the highlight of my undergraduate years. I still love the piece and developed quite a respect for Benny Goodman's clarinet playing. Actually, I thought then, and still do, that Artie Shaw was the better jazz player of the two major white jazz band leaders and later that bias was confirmed by many jazz musicians. Of course, this doesn't take into consideration the likes of Jimmy Hamilton and Barney Bigard. Jimmy was a phenomenal clarinet player and practiced all the classical literature written for the instrument in his hotel room while touring with the Ellington Orchestra. This is an insight shared with me by Clark Terry.

During those years in Enid, Oklahoma, I began to experience the difference between the way white and black jazz musicians related to me and my playing. When I would go to a white club and ask to sit in and play, I was always put off to the end of the last set of the night, which made sense; but when that time came around, they seemed to begrudge the opportunity. There was also the expectation that I would sound like whoever they thought I should sound like. On a rare occasion I would get some encouragement from white jazzers but for the most part I felt ostracized which, of course, was painful and depressing but did not deter me from my goals. The black musicians seemed to appreciate where I was trying to get to and they were more and more a source of empowerment for me as a musician. They enjoyed the fact that I didn't, or couldn't, play like everybody else and that I had my own voice, which was, I know, not very well developed yet, but it was me in there somewhere.

3

Uncle Sam

I had a college deferment from the draft board in my home town. Consequently, as soon as I graduated from Phillips I got my draft notice, which began 'Greetings', just like the veterans I knew said it would. This was the beginning of my association with the US Army. My first contact with the army, after being inducted in Kansas City, Missouri, was at the orientation at Camp Crawford, Arkansas, where we had been transported by train from KC. This is where we got our uniforms, haircuts and the first taste of latrine and KP duties – not an auspicious beginning. There followed a period of time, during which I can only remember being constantly exhausted and sore with various rashes on different parts of my body.

The interesting thing about this was that I had been doing serious manual labor every summer of my high school years, either on the railroad building bridges, with the electric company erecting pole lines or hogging bricks and mortar constructing buildings in Minnesota for my brother-in-law's father, J.B. Nordenstrom, who had decided he was going to break me and make me quit the job to prove that a kid from Kansas couldn't keep up with good Swedish boys from Minnesota. I was forewarned by both my brother-in-law and my sister that he would treat me this way. I'll never forget that experience and the sense of satisfaction when at the end of the summer J. B. shook my hand and told me that I should stay, work for him instead of go to college, make a lot of money and buy myself a new car. J. B. was quite a character and rather infamous in the area of Mora, Minnesota, and its neighboring communities.

So working hard was not in any way new to me but the army was somehow different and more debilitating than anything I had encountered and it apparently had the same objective in mind as had J. B. Nordenstrom.

Following my stay at Camp Crawford, I was sent to Fort Leonard Wood, Missouri, for basic training. There I began what was to become a very important period of development for me, both as a musician and as a human being, something which I never expected even remotely to come out of those two years. Basic training was not any different from what you would expect it to be and I will not dwell on the details of the process of dehumanization so aptly associated with entering the world of 'cannon fodder', so gloriously referred to as *esprit de corps*. This, along with other such uplifting terms, is used to justify the preparation needed to allow oneself to be eliminated, or to eliminate another person like oneself, from life on this planet under the proposition that one is doing something honorable. Stop!! This far and no further, please. Yes sir!

I will, however, introduce you to a few people I trained with and others I came into contact with as a result of being in the armed service. After the first four weeks of basic we were allowed to bring some of our personal possessions to camp, so I brought my tenor saxophone. Then I found that during our off hours we could go to the enlisted men's service club where they would often have a band that I could play with. The band was made up of other trainees and a few fellows from the service bands on the base. The baritone player was from my training company and we became regular participants in the service club band. He was from Highland Park, Michigan, and his name was Park Adams. I soon learned that he preferred to be called 'Pepper'. Pepper, as many of you will know, went on to become possibly the most respected baritone player in the world during the '60s and until his untimely death in 1987 from lung cancer. We became very good friends and he continued to be as significant a part of my professional life after my army life as he was during my two years with Uncle Sam.

Pepper, a drummer from Port Arthur, Canada, named Mac

Saunders and I were all in the same training company. The three of us would frequently get out of duties around our barracks whenever our training company commander received a command from the officer in charge of the service club, who outranked our commander. The command would be to send us to the service club to perform duties for that officer, which meant we could cut out of our training company and spend the rest of the night playing music. You know that didn't set well with our company commander. It could have been really tough on us, except that we were all exemplary soldiers and to top that off the company commander took a liking to Pepper. This happened, apparently, after some off-duty encounters at the beer hall on base during which the captain realized the breadth of Pepper's knowledge and interests and his capacity for intellectual engagement on a variety of subjects.

You will understand this more clearly if I explain to you that Pepper Adams was one of the most truly intellectual and well-read men I've ever known. His interests had no bounds and he was just as intrigued and interested in the captain's erudition as the captain was in his.

Pepper could have had at least three PhDs had he pursued them through normal academic channels. His understanding of art, painting, sculpture and other two- and three-dimensional media, complete with their respective historical contexts and significance, was clearly phenomenal. The breadth of his familiarity and comprehension of literary fields was almost legendary. Anyone who ever knew Pepper Adams will attest to his incredibly dry sense of humor, which could be almost acerbic at times, but always on target. Not only was music his passion but his mastery of theory, composition, history and musicology was such that anyone who engaged him in discussions on these topics discovered quickly enough who was the master, though you would not see it unless he was challenged, either intellectually or, God forbid, negatively.

We used to go to St Louis on a weekend pass and attend the St Louis Symphony concerts. They would allow us in for the cost of the taxes if we were in uniform and we took advantage of this, naturally. I remember the first evening that we pursued this activity the orchestra was playing a Brahms symphony and the 'Elegy for Orchestra' by Ernst Krenek. I had only heard about Krenek because he had married into my brother-in-law's family but I knew nothing about him or his music other than that familial association.

Pepper gave a complete discourse on the music to be played that night as well as a musicological exposition of the life and milieu of the composer Krenek, a lecture far more informed than any I had ever heard during my undergraduate days at Phillips. All of this information flowed from him as naturally as if he had been talking about the weather.

Now, from the vantage point of having had a career in the performance of music and completing a PhD in the field of ethnomusicology, which I made use of for 17 years while lecturing to classes, I have come to comprehend the depth and breadth of Pepper's knowledge. The best professors I've come into contact with as colleagues over the years know their subjects so well that information literally flows from their minds to their audience of one or a thousand. That was my impression of Pepper.

Some years later, when we were both in New York, Pepper called one day and asked if I'd like to go to a private showing of an exhibition of an artist that afternoon and I, of course, said, 'Sure.' I was expecting that we would go to one of the museums, most likely MOMA, since I knew that he was a member there. So it was a bit of a surprise to me when we caught a bus cross town to Sutton Place where we entered a characteristically Sutton Place environment. (When I lived in New York a lot of the wealthiest people in the city lived on Park Avenue, Fifth Avenue on the Park or Sutton Place. It may have changed dramatically since, I don't know.) The uniformed doorman asked us who we were. Pepper gave his real name, Park Adams, and we were ushered immediately into the building, the doorman having announced our arrival to whoever we were going to meet.

The artist was being given a private showing at the residence of an art dealer of obvious reputation, since the people there represented a social strata quite different from any I had ever been a part of. Pepper seemed to know many of the people there and most certainly the host but he spent his time explaining to me who the artist was and telling about his medium of expression, bringing to light the details of that expression as we viewed his works. Incredible. He was in another comfort zone. I began to wonder just how many comfort zones this man had. A more truly brilliant person I've never known and his musical legacy has been left to us through the medium of recording, attesting to his greatness as a jazz artist on baritone saxophone.

There was yet another facet of Pepper's persona. Pepper had box seat season tickets at the Polo Grounds for all the New York Giants's baseball games; in addition, every year he would arrange an engagement with some entrepreneur so that he could be wherever the Stanley Cup was to be played that year. He was an avid baseball and hockey fan and grew up watching Gordie Howe, the Red Wings and the Detroit Tigers play. I will add that he was extremely upset when the Giants decided to move from New York to San Francisco. Now, whether that was because he lost his seat at the Polo Grounds or because he didn't think they should move from New York, I don't know.

I have not been able to rationalize in my mind how a man with such a remarkable capacity for knowledge and analytical acuity would, after finding out about the lung cancer and enduring the pain and discomfort of chemotherapy, continue to smoke as if nothing had changed. How he could continue as if everything was normal is beyond my understanding. We all have, I guess, some spot in our character that we just cannot alter. With today's growing awareness of the addictive qualities of tobacco, I shouldn't be that surprised, recognizing that it was probably more the addiction than a spot on his character. However, I still can't equate that with his capacity for understanding the reality of things.

While we were playing with the service club band some of the players, who were in the Division band, explained to us how to manipulate the system. They advised us to do just that to improve our chances of getting assigned to the Division band ourselves. We should not rely on the powers that be, they told us, to recognize our talents from our dossiers. They felt that we would more useful in the band than as cannon fodder. (Sometime later I had the opportunity to look at my training dossier and was shocked to find that I had been classified as a demolition expert first and a musician second. Lordy, I would have blown up myself and everybody around me if that had been my fate. I don't recall ever successfully disarming a mine or a booby trap during my training, so how in the world the army could call me a demolition expert is absolutely unconscionable. 'That's the army, Mr Jones!')

Following the advice of the musicians, I went on sick call one morning, which meant that I went to the dispensary instead of out to the field for training. Since the line was so long, as it usually was, it was easy to walk away and grab a base taxi cab and head for the Division band headquarters. When I arrived, the guys who knew me took me to the Warrant Officer who was the commander of the band. They identified my skills to him and he then authorized an audition for me. Somebody loaned me a clarinet and I took the audition. On the recommendation of the one who auditioned me, I was then interviewed by the band commander, who told me that he could not guarantee anything but that he would put my name on his request board for assignment to the band. He explained to me that this would improve my chances but that the band was not a high priority for the army. The rest was in God's hands – my words, not his.

After training was over we all waited each morning to hear the assignments for that day, and the more days that passed without your name being called, the more anxious you became. Or at least that was my response, as you can well imagine. Finally the morning arrived when I heard my name and the relief at hearing my assignment to the 6th Armored Division Band must have been nearly audible after hearing so many others being sent to rifle and artillery units day after day. The lucky ones got orders to Europe and then there were those who were sent to the Pacific theatre which usually meant Korea.

Pepper, Mac and I all ended up in the 6th Armored Division Band at Fort Leonard Wood and associated there with a number of musicians who had been in the professional ranks in Chicago before being drafted. A beautiful alto player from Chicago, Ronnie Kolber, who later switched to baritone as I did, was one of the guys from Chicago. Some of the other Chicago cats who had outsized attitudes about who they were will not be mentioned here. I refer to them only to emphasize their reaction to Pepper, which was to snub him and his playing as being too raucous and loud; which speaks volumes, inasmuch as Pepper was the one, out of all of us, who garnered the greatest fame and respect in the world of jazz. He was not allowed to play in the Division jazz band for the reasons I have just identified, which by the way, didn't offend Pepper since he already knew more about the music and who he was than the entire band put together. The three of us – Mac, Pepper and myself – continued to play at the service club. Pepper would often sit in with the musicians at the black service club – yes, we were still segregated at that time – who were oftentimes better players of jazz than the guys from our band. I would go with Pepper on occasion but didn't have the courage to enter into that level of competition. But I surely did enjoy going with him and listening. Leroy 'the hog' Cooper, a black baritone player who was in the black army band on the base, would occasionally play at the service club. Years later, Leroy joined the Ray Charles band during the days when that band was a stellar attraction around the globe.

Mac and I used to work together off base, particularly during the summer, which was fun and kept us in the flow of what we wanted to be doing. I got an opportunity that fall to attend the Naval School of Music on TDY from our band at Leonard Wood and, of course, jumped at the offer. Anything to get away from Leonard Wood, which was out in the boonies of the Ozarks, and the parade duties that we performed daily. We were, after all an army band and that was our primary function. To remain sane you had to go to St Louis, which was an expense most of us couldn't afford very often. Pepper would take his weekend pass and return to

Detroit or go to Chicago. Realizing that the Naval School of Music, at that time, was across the river from Washington DC in Anacostia, Virginia, I was more than willing to go.

When I arrived at the N.S.M. I discovered that they had sent me as an oboe student and I thought it was a mistake since I had been put in the band as a clarinet player. So I called our band commander, the Warrant Officer, and suggested that there had been an error, that I should be there as a clarinet player and could he straighten it out with the School. He promptly informed me that I was there as a student of oboe and if I didn't want to study oboe I could come back to the Division band and he would send somebody else in my place. I studied oboe.

God works in mysterious ways. I fell in love with the oboe and particularly with the English horn, which goes along naturally with learning oboe. My instructor, Manley Sanders, was just the kind of teacher I needed. This was an experiment by the service to create more oboe/English horn players in the service bands around the country. I'm happy to report that, in my case, it was a very successful program. Not only did it offer me an opportunity to learn an instrument I would never have chosen to learn but it improved my playing on both the clarinet and saxophone. On top of that, it made me into a doubler (a category given to musicians who can play saxophone, clarinet, flute and oboe and English horn or bassoon – and some could play them all), which would pay off when I entered the music business in New York City years later.

While at the Naval School of Music I had the opportunity to associate with other musicians from all over the country. With many of these I cherished a long and continuous friendship; some later became major players in the world of music. Julian and Nathaniel Adderley, later known as Cannon-ball and Nat, is one example. We used to call Julian 'Fats'.

Another name I want you to know and I shall always remember is Maceo Hampton, who we called 'Little Jazz'. He was an incredible trumpet player, composer and arranger and Nat used to follow him around like a shadow while we were at the School. Maceo was from a very famous family of musicians from Indianapolis, Indiana, and his younger brother Slide became, and still is, well known and respected in the music business.

Once Maceo got out of the service he devoted the rest of his life to gospel music, becoming a minister of music and composing and arranging exclusively for church choirs. I will reiterate that he was a dynamite trumpet player and would have been a major contributor to music as a performer and especially as a composer/arranger. Only God knows what he could have accomplished and, as God knows, he chose, for him, the right path for the use of his skills. A truly exceptional musician was Maceo Hampton.

During the years I was touring with various orchestras I would, when passing through or working Indianapolis, call Maceo to see what was new in his life. That was how I knew about his new calling in life. But he eventually moved on to other locations and I lost touch with him. However, my memories of him are very much intact.

Another friend from that time, Gene Sisler, went on to New York and was doing Broadway shows and other substantial musical things the last I heard of him. Bob Newman took up a career as a writer and producer of recordings and did a lot of work in the jingle industry. In fact, I did a date for him in New York but never got the chance to say hello, as he was too busy with his producers. George Syrianados (Syran) was a fine tenor man but ended up working more often as a piano player. He got started while he was at the School by playing piano with Fats Adderley at a gig in DC while we were stationed there. Jimmy Sedler was also in New York after his stint in the service and I would occasionally run across him on the floor of the Musicians' Union or at Jim and Andy's, one of the major hangouts for the New York cats.

Jim and Andy's was the place to be in New York. Actually, there were four primary hangouts in midtown, each providing a casual environment for the gathering of a segment of the music industry's population. Jim and Andy's attracted mainly studio and recording session cats, which often included major jazz people as well. Many of the black musicians who were on the scene, and many of the black bands when they were in town, would hang out at Beef Steak Charlie's. Joe Harbor's Spotlight, right across the street from Birdland, was the place to find the successful club date and commercial scene musicians during the day, most notably on Wednesday afternoons when the Union floor was open. In the evening the Birdland cats would go there because it was so convenient. Charlie's and Junior's, two very successful bars, were around the corner on 52nd. Charlie's was predominantly white and attracted a lot of successful whites and a few blacks who were in jazz, whereas Junior's was more mixed. These categorizations are generalities, not absolutes, as many of us could be found in almost all of them at one time or another. Just up Broadway from Joe Harbor's place, next door to the Ed Sullivan theatre (now David Letterman's venue), was the China Song. Another segment of the population hung out there, more often than not those who were doing the studio work. Yes, they did have staff musicians in those days at each network and on shows like Ed Sullivan and Perry Como. There was another bar where you would find jazz musicians particularly, more at night than during the day because of its close proximity to the Metropole – like directly across the street. It was called the Brass Rail. These were the places that were in the midtown area between 48th Street and 54th Street between 6th Avenue and 8th Avenue. That doesn't begin to cover the musician hangouts throughout the rest of the city, Harlem, Brooklyn, Greenwich Village, Lower East Side and of course the really famous ones like Minton's, Small's Paradise, The Red Door, etc. Jazz was alive and well.

Look what happened when I started with a reference to Jim and Andy's as the place to hang . . . There were lots of places. Most are gone or changed drastically and I'm sure replaced by joints I've never heard of. Now that I have made this extensive side trip, let me get back to DC and the Naval School of Music.

There was, during those years, the Charles Hotel on 'T', I think, off 14th NW, where a local group worked in a small club in the half basement down from the street. There were jam sessions on Sunday afternoons where many of the best cats in town would set in. Some really good music would happen there. Now, if that isn't enough, add to it that the hostess for the club was one of the most beautiful women I have ever seen in my life. She was so beautiful that I can't compare her with any woman, living or dead, white, black, oriental or Native American. If I've left anybody out, include them too.

Years later when I was working at the Howard Theatre with the Quincy Jones Orchestra as a part of the Billy Eckstine show, I went to check out the Charles Hotel, which would have been not too far away, and found that it no longer existed. Too bad, as it was a special place for all to come together and share the love of the music.

During my stay at the School I had the misfortune of having one of my classmates from Phillips contact me. He wanted to get together for old times' sake. Although I had only a vague recollection of him from Phillips, I thought it would be nice to see somebody from those days, so we agreed to hang out one night. What a night! He let me choose where to go, and since there was a good service band at his station, I thought it would be cool to hear them. Big mistake. A number of the players in the band were black so I spent the whole evening listening to this guy, who was from Arkansas, curse and belittle anybody and everybody who was black. His presumption that I shared the same attitude was more than I could take. Even though I expressed my opposition to his point of view, it didn't slow him up a bit. I didn't have enough money to afford a cab all the way from his station to mine and he had a car, so I sat through the evening trying not to dump on this bigot until I could get home.

To make a long story short, when he got me to the gate of the navy receiving station I was so angry that I was actually shaking and proceeded to unload on him regarding his gross bigotry. Short of physically kicking the **** out of him, I gave him my most vitriolic verbal abuse, complete with well-chosen expletives. Would you believe this man actually called me again to see if I wanted to get together another time? Such is the depth of the ignorance and arrogance of some people.

I have no recollection of any racially-motivated incidents at the School, or at least I wasn't aware of any. They would have had to be pretty subtle if they were there, as we were totally integrated in everything we did, from our living arrangements to our activities within the School's offerings. There was so much respect and appreciation for one another at the School, something I had begun to expect from the jazz musicians who were serious about music. Racial differences were not an issue among us. However, there may very well have been others at the School, who had nothing to do with us, who had these kind of attitudes. I really don't know and I didn't care to know.

My development on the oboe and English horn was very rewarding for me, both in terms of my accomplishment on the instruments and in my relationships with my fellow students. The former seemed to earn me the respect of my peers, as they knew I was being trained for a skill I had not explored before coming to the School. Fats gave me quite a compliment after a performance of Dvorak's *New World Symphony* (the 'Going Home' theme), which our concert band had been given to play – we were in the same concert band during that part of our schooling. After we finished our respective tours of duty, Fats went on to become the Cannonball Adderley we all know. He never forgot our time and friendship at the School and though our paths crossed only rarely, when they did, usually at a jazz festival somewhere in the world, it was like old friends meeting. He never got too big for his friends. When I was at the peak of my activity in New York, he was touring constantly with Miles and that was about as big as you could get at that time.

After completing six months of TDY at the Naval School of Music, I returned to the 6th Armored Division band at Fort Leonard Wood and continued my responsibilities there. In keeping with well-established army traditions, by the end of the summer – which meant when I had been back from DC for about two months with my new-found skills on oboe and English horn, given me, ostensibly, to improve the musical tonal palette of the Division band – I received orders to transfer to the Pacific theatre of military action, which was, at that time, Korea. The logic of the army never ceases to amaze me. My orders were to report to Fort Lewis in Washington, just outside Seattle, for orientation in preparation for an overseas assignment. I spent the required leave – we all got 30 days – with my mom and dad at my sister and brother-in-law's place in Minnesota and left for Seattle from there instead of from my home in Chanute.

While waiting for a transport ship out of Seattle, I had the opportunity to get into the city quite often – after I learned how to skip out on the indoctrination classes and make my way off the base. I would then either hitchhike, which you could do easily in those days, or catch a bus into the city. Those training films were terrible and the diatribe that accompanied them even worse. I had a problem then with brainwashing and still do. I didn't rebel against the discipline and skills training that would help me to survive but to mess with the mind was objectionable to me. Even so, I found out after I was discharged and back in civilian life what effect it had on me, even though I was not aware of it at the time.

You remember that I decided to manipulate the system to get into the Division band. There is a story I want to share with you that demonstrates the flip side of my experience and to some degree validates my decision to use the system for my benefit.

Frank Foster was, as we all know, for many years the leader of the Count Basie Orchestra after the Count's passing. Before that he had spent many years with the Basie band where he became recognized as a major artist on tenor saxophone. Frank went through basic training like the rest of us but was assigned to a rifle company in Korea. He spent his time in the trenches on the front lines. I do not want to go into what that was like during the Korean conflict, but from what I do know, you needn't hear the details. Suffice it to say it ain't Hollywood. Having survived those months on the front lines, Frank was granted Little R and R (rest and recreation). There was also R and R that allowed you to leave Korea and spend a period of time in Japan at a place of your choosing. Everybody used to save up their money for that, if they were granted it. However, we are talking about Little R and R, which meant that you were brought off the front and allowed a few days in the I corps area which was at the Divisional headquarters back of the front lines. The Division band lived and worked there and often members of the band would be required to play at one of the service clubs there.

The story goes this way. Frank went to the enlisted men's service club one night after arriving from the front. He heard the group playing jazz and asked if he could borrow a tenor from one of the musicians and set in with the band. Fortunately, for him, one musician agreed and Fos' proceeded to blow everybody off the bandstand. This was such a shock that one of the musicians at the club immediately went to wake up his band leader so that he could come and hear this rifleman play. As all good stories go, the commander of the band immediately put in a transfer for Frank to the 2nd Division band. This was granted and Frank Foster spent the rest of his army days playing as he should have been from the beginning.

Frank never shared with me his experiences on the front and I don't think I want to know anyhow. But for this trick of fate and the willingness of that army musician to let Frank borrow his horn, we could very well have lost Frank Foster and all the contributions he has made, and is making, to this music. When Frank and I got together a while back I asked him about this story, and although he was not sure of the details, he told me that it was cool with him for me to share the story with you.

It was by a similar quirk of fate that the Division band offered Pepper, Mac and me a similar refuge from what could have been a terrible loss to this music, at least as far as Pepper is concerned, since he became such a major contributor to it. I don't know what happened to Mac Saunders. And I am setting here writing this book.

The three of us, Pepper, Mac and I, went all through training together. We got the opportunity to be with the

Division band together. And we were sent to the Pacific theatre, all ending up in the same 8th Army Special Service Company in Korea. There we played shows across the front at the various I corps areas as well as at the French, Turkish and British Commonwealth encampments, which included Canadian, British, New Zealand and Australian troops.

The story of how I got to Korea was probably not much different than Mac's and Pepper's, I imagine. The one thing that may have been different – though I doubt it, since military operations tend to follow the same lines of action – was my experience on the transport carrier going from the west coast of the United States to Japan.

When I left for my assignment overseas I was allowed to take one personal item, so I took my tenor sax with me and as a result the trip over to Japan was quite an adventure. The first day out to sea was devastating for some of the troops, as it was the first time most of us had traveled by sea. Many of the troops spent the first few days in agony. Fortunately for me, I was not affected physically by the roll of the ship. Consequently, for the first few days I had my choice of foods, prepared just about to order, for there were not that many of us at chow time. During this time I got hooked up with the Special Service officer and began putting together an on-board show to entertain the troops. That kept me off the duty roster for KP and deck and latrine cleaning detail.

On board this particular transport ship were troops from a Canadian regiment on their way to Korea by way of Japan. The American troops were not yet organized into units but would be assigned to regiments on arrival. Some of the Princess Pats, as the Canadian regiment was called, had entertainment experience, so our show was made up of men from both countries. Women, at this point, were not part of the fighting forces but were auxiliary to them, serving as nurses and so on. We did have a few women on board but we hardly ever saw them as they were billeted on the officers' deck and I saw them only when the officers asked for the musicians to perform at the officers' mess. Doing the show was a lot of fun and I got acquainted with men from all over Canada as well as the US. I later heard some devastating stories about that particular regiment and their military activities in Korea. I won't share the details with you but suffice it to say they were a lot braver than I could ever imagine being.

We arrived in Yokohama, Japan, and traveled by train to Camp Drake just outside Tokyo. While I was there, I was contacted by Captain Scott Defebaugh, a man from my home town of Chanute. Apparently his folks had informed him that I was being sent to the Pacific theatre, which meant that I would be coming through Camp Drake. Since he was an officer he was able to find me and arrange a pass for me to join him and some of his friends in Tokyo. This was great. I didn't expect ever to get off the base during this time of waiting to be assigned. As it turned out, I was able to go into Tokyo a few more times as I waited for my orders to be cut; others got shipped out right away.

Each morning we would line up for roll call and await our fate. Needless to say, this was not a pleasant way to begin one's day and the anxiety grew the longer you had to wait. As I said earlier, my M.O.S. showed me to be a demolitions expert and a musician. Had I known the significance of it, my identification as a demolitions expert would have scared me to death, particularly as it was listed first.

Shortly after arriving at Camp Drake I saw a sign in the base service club requesting those with entertainment and musical talents to audition for the 8th Army Special Service Company. It didn't take me long to get to that audition with my horn in hand. Although this did not guarantee me an assignment, I was told a recommendation would be put in for me. Thank God! I got orders to go to the Special Service Company in Korea. Now that wasn't the best because it could have been the Japan Company, which would have really been great duty.

We were transported to Inchon, Korea, by boat where we then embarked on a long, arduous and freezing cold trip by unheated train to Seoul. To my surprise I found that Pepper and Mac had preceded me into the same company. What a bounty. Pepper and Mac were assigned to one show platoon and I was with another. Owing to this I didn't see them much until we came home to the US about eight months later and then it was just Pepper and me. I don't remember whether Mac went home before or after us. Each detachment or platoon or show, whatever you want to call it, was an all-military personnel show put together and transported all over the front to entertain the troops stationed there. Our head-quarters company was in Seoul and we could occasionally get back there for a day or two, most often for supplies. Now and then we had a day off. Not bad duty at all. We would be billeted with different units on the front including, sometimes, units other than American. That was how I found out about the guys in the Princess Pats. The Aussies were a ball to be around. They were in many ways more American in their attitudes and so on than they were British and we had some extremely good times together, even though we were in the Korean theatre of war.

It was during one of these stops that I ran into Armond 'Smitty' Smith, my friend from my high school days. It was a ball to play with him again after so many years. We both recognized that our respective musical abilities had improved dramatically from our days together in 'Shabootie'. The friendship and understanding between us was just as clean as it had been those many years before. I asked Smitty why he had stayed in the army all those years instead of trying his wings in the musical arena outside. His reply was so well-founded and logical that it could only increase my respect for him. He said, in words to this effect, 'No matter how good I get, it's either Duke Ellington or Count Basie. The chances for that are so slim, with all the drummers out there, that I'll take this route, since I do nothing but play. I'm a Master Sergeant at the top of the non-commissioned officer rank with a comparable pay scale. My family has guaranteed care. And when I retire, I'll still only be in my forties and I'll be able to play all I want to, wherever we decide to live. And with the retirement income to back me up, I'll be able to pick and choose with whom and what music I want to play.' Makes sense to me. He was still as handsome as he was back in high school and the picture of his (incredibly beautiful) wife and kids just reinforced his philosophical position.

I remember being able to talk to Smitty about things for which others would put me down. For example, why couldn't the countries of the world do the same thing the colonies here in America did back in the 1700s and sacrifice a little of their sovereignty for a united federation, just like the beginnings of the United States? Why do the different churches all think they are the only ones in the world going to heaven? Why won't they let Smitty and me attend the same church? There was only the one exception of that black church in Enid, Oklahoma, which welcomed me when I was too dumb to accept the invitation. One of our reflections back in high school was on how beautiful the human race was going to be when we all eventually intermarried and had children who would be a reflection of all those different shades of color. We saw that we would all be various shades of a golden bronze and we thought how beautiful that would be. Smitty shared with me his mother's response to his question, posed to her when he was in early grade school, why he was darker-skinned than some of the other kids he knew. She had said, 'Well son, God just left you in the oven a little bit longer.' We both found that to be a satisfactory answer. Unfortunately, we weren't able to maintain such purity of mind inasmuch as the world around us wouldn't cooperate. I miss our talks and often wonder how we would have shared our thoughts and dreams now and what they would reveal about us. Smitty, unknown to him, was very important to me. Now that he is gone I'll never have the opportunity to explore those ideas and feelings.

Back to show time in Korea. I would like to relate an incident that occurred during one of our shows. We were playing for some Turkish troops who had just come back from the trenches up on the parallel, as it was referred to. They were a sullen lot, as was characteristic of Turkish soldiers. Or so I was told, with accompanying stories, not for public consumption, to illustrate the fighting quality of the Turks. Anyhow, we began the show and shortly after the opening song and dance we heard, and felt, artillery rounds coming awfully close to where we were. Very shortly afterwards a second round landed at an intersection probably 200 yards away from where we were playing. The Turks didn't bat an eyelid but our eyes got very large and the speed and pace of the show increased remarkably. The comedians didn't wait much for a response between jokes and the MC was turned up to fast forward, as were the tempos of the tunes we were playing. The dancers became incredibly nimble and soon the show was over and we were out of there. The troops we had been playing for didn't seem to notice anything out of the ordinary and I guess for them nothing was, but we wanted out of that area at the earliest possible moment. We weren't even interested in whether they had enjoyed the show, which we usually found out by hanging around talking, having some libations. I swear the Turks weren't afraid of anything.

We had some very good talent in our show and some that I'm not sure how it got there. Carlos Waters was the piano player and was obviously a somewhat seasoned performer or had an incredible talent, which is quite possible since he was Ethyl Waters's nephew from Camden, New Jersey, just across the river from Philadelphia. With all his talent, I never heard anything more about him after we got out of the service, and that surprises me.

We had a quartet of singers in the tradition of the Mills Brothers and Ink Spots who were very good, though they had only been put together for this show. Apparently each went his own way after Korea and I was able to get in contact with only one of them, Norris Wethington, while touring in the Buffalo, New York, area years later. All I have left of the rest are some pictures taken during our tour of duty. One comedian from the show did have a bit of a run on television in Hollywood but it didn't last very long and I don't recall seeing him on anything again. I ran into one of the singers on the show in New York City, where he had become an active background singer on the music industry scene. He was talking about some group he was in the process of putting together to travel and perform with. I don't know whatever came of it but he was an excellent musician. I also ran into our bass player who was from Milwaukee, Wisconsin, while touring through that area with the Stan Kenton Orchestra, I think. I apologize to all those guys whose names I can't remember. There are, of course, many stories to relate but few worth the telling, or the remembering for that matter, other than those I've already shared with you.

I so regret missed opportunities. One that stands out the most was the invitation to attend a concert of the Korean court orchestra playing for the court in Seoul. I knew nothing of traditional Korean music and could not appreciate the value of the opportunity to experience such an event. Had I known that I would be doing graduate work in Ethnomusicology many years later, I would have done anything to have been granted such an honor. The man who invited me had the good sense to realize the uniqueness of this opportunity and tried to interest me in sharing it with him. Too bad for me. He accepted the invitation and consequently became very good friends with the musicians in the court orchestra and, I would imagine, retained that friendship thereafter to his benefit and edification, as he was that kind of a person.

Another situation that I regret was not responding positively to an invitation to attend a performance of Kabuki at the Kabuki Sa in the Aksaksa area of Tokyo. This invitation had been extended by a young Japanese girl I met at the laundry on the base at Camp Drake, following a conversation we had about music. She offered to take me after she got off work and I let it go by. DUMB! I even messed up the opportunity to get to know a very attractive Japanese lady in the process. Double DUMB!

Then, about one month before I was scheduled to be discharged from the army, my platoon leader was authorized by the company and 8th Army Special Services to offer me the option of being given sergeant stripes (I was then a corporal) and a seven-day R and R in Japan or a discharge from the army one month early. Wouldn't you know, I chose to get out a month early and passed up the stripes as well as a week off in Japan at a resort I had picked out months before and had been saving up for. Had I taken this offer, I would have got out at the same time that I was supposed to anyway three weeks later and could have had all those advantages. Triple DUMB! Now that I look back on it, I can't believe that I could actually have been that stupid but I was.

My return to the US was again by troop ship and this time Pepper and I traveled together. We both were part of the entertainment on the trip back and spent a good bit of time playing together. I therefore had the opportunity to learn even more from him. I felt, at the time, that I might be able to become a reasonably successful R and B musician as a result of what I had accomplished in the show band. I had no thought of getting in on the jazz scene, as I knew Pepper would. My main claim to fame from my association with the show was a poor imitation of Illinois Jacquet à la his Lionel Hampton days. I would walk the crowd at the climax of our show, honking and screaming on my horn and doing outrageous physical antics. The finale was me climbing to the top of our equipment truck, honking and screaming all the way, and jumping off the top of the truck onto the stage, which was usually set up on a rice paddy, still screaming all the way down. The troops loved it and for some reason or another I never got hurt. I knew it had nothing to do with being a good musician and decided that I could at least make out being that kind of an R and B player. However, Pepper encouraged me on the way home, saying that I didn't know what I might be able to achieve and that only the future would tell. He was right, as it turned out.

4

Reluctant Teacher

My return to the States was undramatic and largely uneventful except for the disappointment of realizing that the girl I thought I was coming home to wasn't waiting for me at all. Even though I had been able to avoid the most severe associations with killing and seeing death around me while in the army, the process of adjusting to civilian life and to some form of normal existence was still difficult and it took three months before I felt like I was in sync with civilian life, as such. I also realized, after nearly three years, how affected I had been by the whole experience. Even though I was out of the army, I found that my attitudes and perceptions of life were greatly altered from what they had been both before and during my stint in the service.

I wanted to kick back and take the summer off. I was discharged in June – the army called it separated – but my mother insisted that I have a job in place immediately so that when the fall came I wouldn't be hanging around the house with no job or prospects. She needed to 'chill', as the young folks say today. But since she didn't, I took the first job that I heard about to get her out of my hair and as a result ended up in a job that I would have never accepted under normal circumstances. The job was a teaching appointment in a small consolidated school system in southwestern Oklahoma, with a token music program and no prospect of anything more to come. Not exactly the environment you would hope for or the money that would allow for anything other than survival. That lasted for one semester. When I was offered the chance to move to a much bigger, more active and progressive high school in Graham, Texas, I jumped at it.

While I was at the school in Oklahoma I frequently went to Oklahoma City to find any kind of social life and certainly for musical activity. It was interesting to find there, just like in Enid, that the white jazz groups were reluctant to allow anyone to set in, and that when they did, they were full of comparisons and criticism. Conversely, in a black club or group I would be welcomed with warmth and sincerity. Now, to be sure, they would put you 'on the wall', meaning 'test your ability to play'. Once you were able to come off the wall, you were welcomed with all the warmth and comfort you could possibly want. This was how things were for me at that time in our country's history. I'm not proposing that they haven't changed in any way, just that my experiences were such. Inevitably, after finishing my 'wall' set, someone out of the group would buy me a drink and we'd begin to talk about music. That is when he, or they, would compliment me on some aspect of my playing and then offer, occasionally, a suggestion about how I could do this or that easier or with more definition or could handle certain changes with more confidence. It seems to me that I was always getting help from the black musicians I came into contact with during the years I was learning how to be a musician. I've told so many people, some of whom were my students, that I never had 'a' teacher – I had hundreds. Most of them didn't know they were teaching me, although some did, like the men I'm referring to here.

After I moved to Texas I began going to Wichita Falls regularly and occasionally to Dallas. Wichita Falls was closer, so naturally I spent more time there. It turned out to be the ideal place for me, as it was there that I met 'Big' John Hardee. John was a great alto and tenor man who had been on the scene in New York and around the country for years before he decided to get out of the business and return to his roots in Texas. He began teaching young people about this music and how to go about developing their talents in this direction, if that was where they, or he, thought they should go. At the time I met John he was teaching in Wichita Falls and working every night in a club over the state line in Lawton, Oklahoma.

He later moved his teaching skills to Dallas, where his father was living, and continued to play in clubs around Big D. John was the mentor of a number of jazz people who went on to have careers in music. Among those were James Clay, Marcus Belgrave and Leo Wright, as well as myself.

Leo was a student of John while he was in school in Wichita Falls. James Clay was a young man in Dallas when Big John became active around there. Marcus came under John's influence while he was stationed at the air force base in Wichita Falls and I was befriended by John while I was teaching in Graham. I spent all my weekends, and some week nights as well, in Wichita Falls just to be around John. I have a story about him that I must tell concerning his incredible musicianship.

We were working together at some university, probably in Texas and most likely either in Wichita Falls or Denton. We had finished the gig and were in the process of packing up to return home when I decided that I needed to go to the bathroom. Over the PA system in the building came an Art Tatum record. I was so surprised that when I got back to the ballroom I was about to say something about how hip the school was to have such taste in music. But before I got a word out of my mouth I saw John playing the piano. It was John I had heard over the PA and he sounded just like Art Tatum. I just stood there and listened, amazed at the command he had of the piano.

Many years later I was talking to Leo Wright backstage at the Newport Jazz Festival, which at that time was still in Newport, Rhode Island. We were both performing that night on the same bill, he with Dizzy Gillespie and I with Stan Kenton. We got to talking about John Hardee and Leo made the comment that he had been trying all these years to get a sound out of his horn that was to some degree like Big John's. He told me that when he was a student in school and was to play at a school assembly or on some such occasion, John would accompany him on piano. No matter what he played or what mistakes he might make, John would cover him so that he would sound good. The theme of helping others to sound good keeps coming through, as this is what I encountered time and time again from these men who were my mentors. It has been a privilege to know all of them. Their approach was in contrast to the attitude prevailing among so many musicians – whether students, amateur-professionals or major league professionals – of judgmental arrogance. Thus my growing association with African–American jazz musicians reinforced my view that collaboration was what making this music was about.

A recording was released some years ago featuring a collection of the works of John Hardee and Ike Quebec which had some classic John Hardee tracks on it. I wish I could spend a whole book on John Hardee but my association was so brief, only two years, that I don't have enough material on him to do the subject justice. I'm sure there must be someone out there who will eventually research his life and publish the results. John was an incredible musician, teacher and member of the human family.

While I was living and working in the Graham/Wichita Falls, Texas, area I observed something about music that was both a revelation and a curiosity. I was playing oboe with the Wichita Falls Symphony, a civic orchestra (which means you don't get paid), with some Dallas Symphony members joining us for performances (they got paid). It was a chance for me to keep up my oboe chops and play some challenging music. I remember this one night very well, as it was that night that I experienced this phenomenon.

We were rehearsing with the symphony, preparing the opera *Amal and the Night Visitor* by Gian Carlo Monody. We were working on the section of the opera called 'The Shepherds' Dance', which is primarily a duet between the two oboes. It was very demanding, technically, for me, since I was playing the second oboe part and much of the figuration was down in the bottom of the range of the instrument. It was very hard to manipulate the little finger of my right hand around the passages that were called for. Anyhow, it was a demanding rehearsal and I felt good about it when it was over. When I left the orchestra rehearsal I went across town to play with a big jazz band on tenor. It was then, as I began to play the chart that was in front of me, that I realized that the notation was the same quarter notes, eighth notes, sixteenth notes, half and whole notes that I had been playing earlier at the symphony rehearsal but that somehow or another they didn't look the same. And I didn't play them in the same way at all. It was as if they were two different sets of symbols having different relationships. I realized that even though the notation was identical, the conception of what it meant was altogether different and that the result was two very different expressions of musical art, of cultural diversity. It became clear to me, at that moment, that notes are merely a relative guide to what one might do. The rest is a result of our choice, based on cultural prerogatives.

Sometime during my stay at Graham, the Kenton Orchestra came to Wichita Falls for a concert with a package that included Charlie Parker and Dizzy Gillespie as well as the Errol Garner Trio. Of course I went and that was the first time I heard any of these people live, so you can imagine how impressed I was. In many ways it was comparable to my experience of hearing the Lunceford band so many years before. Hearing Charlie Parker live for the first time, it wouldn't have mattered whether anything else happened that night; hearing Bird and Dizzy was enough. It was one of the best bands Stan ever put together and they were impressive. This was in 1953. Later, in 1960, Stan and I had a revealing discussion about that band while I was in his band. Stay tuned, details to come later.

During these years my efforts to gain acceptance in the white jazz community began to wane, as each time I tried to be friendly and reach out, I was met with indifference or sometimes outright rejection. This does not mean that all white players I met were like this. As a matter of fact, there were a number of really great white players I came to know during these formative years who were experiencing very much the same thing that I was from our white peer group, particularly if the group was well established in the area. There seemed to be a need to protect oneself from others, especially from those who could see and hear from a wider perspective. It was almost as if they were afraid someone would find out that they weren't as much in touch with the truth as they pretended to be. On the other hand, the black groups didn't have a prayer of becoming one of the established groups and had nothing to lose by being open and honest about who and what they were, personally and musically. Funny, but I've known musicians, primarily black, who have been very successful in the business, who have worked with major orchestras and groups but who when they leave that lofty environment and return to a more simple surrounding lose all credibility with the local established folk. This, no matter how knowledgeable and skilled they may be. Fascinating! Dizzy said to me once, 'That's why I left South Carolina and came to New York.' I once asked Thad Jones, 'How come so many guys from Detroit got so good, and what was the common ingredient?' His answer was, 'They got the hell out of Detroit.'

After spending a year and a half at Graham, Texas, as a high school and junior high school band director and as the director of the high school choir, I decided that I had to try to do something with my music before I got too old, or at the very least, to find an environment where I might be able to grow musically. So I headed out for parts east, towards New York City. I knew that there was a friend of my family who lived in Columbus, Ohio, where I could make a stop – this was the army officer I ran into in Japan. If nothing else showed up for me I might at least start some graduate work at Ohio State University on the GI bill, since I qualified for this. The day I arrived in Columbus I got a call from my folks back in Chanute – of course they knew where I was going – informing me that a man from the Paul Neighbors Orchestra had called and wanted me to call him in Houston, Texas. I had just left Graham two days before.

To paraphrase my mother's words: 'We thought about not telling you about the call from this Paul Neighbors but your dad and I discussed it and we felt that if we didn't tell you and you found out someday later, you might not ever forgive us, so we decided that we'd take the chance and call you.' You see, my mother thought that the most wonderful thing I could do with my life and in music was to become a high school band director like Al Brown had been in Chanute those many years before. She saw no value in pursuing music performance as a career, particularly not in jazz. Dance bands, on the other hand, were a different story. She felt like so many others did who have asked, 'Well, when are you going to find a real job?' or 'What do you do for a living?' It was all right to fool around with jazz as a kid, during school and even in the army, where it served a good purpose by keeping me out of a more dangerous assignment. But then I was supposed grow up and get a real job.

Well, here I set, 70 years old, and I ain't growed up yet! I figure if it ain't happened by now, it probably won't. So I've decided to enjoy myself and accept what I've been and still am.

So I called the manager for the Paul Neighbors Orchestra. They wanted me to join the band on the tenor/baritone saxophone chair, doubling on clarinet. It seems that this came about because there was a trumpet man living in Chanute who used to play with Paul – he had been giving private lessons in Chanute while I had been away in the service. Apparently he had heard about me and what I had been doing as a musician from local people. He recommended me without ever hearing me play. I thought that was a little chancy on his part but he said that he had told Paul all that and Paul's need was great enough that he was willing to chance it. It turned out that there was a tenor man working for Paul at that time who had been at the Naval School of Music with me and had, probably, also endorsed the recommendation. I don't know for sure whether that's what happened.

5

A Real Professional Musician

I took the job and then began to try to put things in place so that I could do it. First, I had never considered the necessity of belonging to the Musicians' Union. There wasn't a Union, that I knew of, where I had been before, so now I had, somehow, to become an instant member. Fortunately for me, my friend Captain Scott Defebaugh was the director of the March of Dimes charities for the Columbus area and had many occasions to call on the resources of the Columbus Musicians' Union for activities that he was arranging. He was able to persuade them to bend their requirements a little to accommodate my need to be in the Union, which they did the next day.

The second obstacle was to find and purchase a baritone saxophone, which I did not own or have any hope of owning owing to the cost of such an instrument. I knew where there was one, or at least, where there had been one. During my last year at Graham I had begun to play baritone some. The school had one and the student who played it never took it home to practice, so I would occasionally play it at jam sessions in Wichita Falls.

Actually, the reason I started playing the baritone was to force myself to slow down the melodic ideas I had found myself gravitating to on tenor. After I got out of the service my playing on tenor changed. I began hearing chord changes as a supporting foundation for a free-flowing superimposition of a melodic composition that went beyond the restrictions and limitations that had always been imposed on playing over chord structures before, or at least on those I had heard from others. The result was a rather complex flow of melodic lines which was not only rapidly realized but utilized many areas and extended the harmonic vocabulary through this process. Since I was, again, trying to be more acceptable to my peer group of jazz musicians, I hoped the baritone would force me to play fewer notes and thus help me find melodic ideas that were more acceptable to the players I was associated with at that time. I still didn't want to be too different but at the same time my own inner ear was talking to me. I was in conflict with myself. Many years passed before I realized that what I had been hearing on tenor was not that far away from what John Coltrane had developed and had begun to show to the music world as a viable extension of the harmonic, melodic and rhythmic language. Please do not presume that I was on his level, no way; the direction was similar but without Trane's technical mastery. By the time I realized that I had been on the right track those years before, I had brought myself down to a more modest way of expressing myself musically.

Big John could hear what I was hearing and was trying to do. He encouraged me to ignore the cats around me and to keep on with what I was doing but my desire to be liked was stronger. Consequently I made a detour from the natural uniqueness of my playing to try and accommodate the practices that were current among my peers. I've done what I can to get back to that original naturalness without too much success; somehow the ability to hear the way I did back then has been relatively impaired. What's that old adage? 'Use or lose it.' Once in a great while I will feel that flow again but it doesn't stay with me like it did those many years ago. I wish I had had the confidence of character and spiritual awareness of the creative process to have been my own person and not sacrificed originality for acceptance. Besides I didn't, in the final analysis, get the acceptance for which I had made the sacrifice. DO NOT compromise on your God-given gifts, for they will be evaluated, just as it says in the parable of the talents from the Bible.

During that year before I left Graham, when I began exploring the baritone, I had the opportunity to try out a Selmer baritone with a low 'A', which was a Selmer innovation. I had found it at a music store in Wichita Falls. Since I was now confronted with the necessity of having to acquire a baritone to make the gig with Paul Neighbors, I called the store in Wichita Falls, found that they had not yet sold the Selmer and discovered that they were anxious to get rid of it. They offered to let me have it for $425, which was a very good price for that instrument in 1955. It was listed at $695. I later found out that I could have bought the same instrument in New York City for $375. Can you imagine that today? The list price for a low 'A' Selmer is now around $9,000. I wouldn't be able to get into the business today just because of the price of the equipment. The music store was willing to drop ship the baritone to Galveston, Texas, where I would be joining the Neighbors Orchestra. So within a couple of days I had resolved all the obstacles and was able to turn around and drive back to Texas from Ohio, where I thought I was going to begin a new direction in my life. As it was, I did.

I drove straight through to Galveston, which took me 32 hours of constant driving – there was no such thing as interstate highways then. I was fairly young and driving was, and still is, a pleasure for me. When I walked into the lobby of the hotel where the band was staying in Galveston, I was met by Bob Hill, the tenor man with whom I had attended the Naval School of Music in Anacostia. What a surprise and a pleasure to know that I wasn't going to be a total stranger to everybody in the band.

The Paul Neighbors Orchestra was a little better than the average hotel band. Its forte was Paul's renditions of cha chas, mambos, meringues and boleros, as well as the standard 'Mickey Mouse' material familiar to all hotel bands. The home base for the band was the Shamrock Hotel, which was then on the outskirts of the city. It was demolished years ago and where it used to be is now well inside the south central part of the city of Houston. Back then it was THE class hotel of Houston and the show room, where we worked, was the big show room for the area. Major acts and entertainers were regularly booked into the room throughout the year. It was a great opportunity for me to learn about backing acts and playing material by different writers for each show. I also became aware of the difference between the stage image presented by the various acts and the real personalities we had to put up with during the run of their booking at the Shamrock.

The band went on the road every three or four months and toured throughout the midwest, southeast and the eastern seaboard. This included one gig in New York City, where we played the Ed Sullivan show. It was my second time in the big city. Following each tour we would return to the Shamrock for an extended stay.

During the stays in Houston I got acquainted with some of the really good players who lived there and I was a regular participant at the sessions that were held throughout the city. Two places stand out in my memory. One was a club where the leader of the house group was Jimmy Ford, who had been in New York. A few years later he went back to New York where he gained a bit of recognition with the Maynard Ferguson band during the time when Maynard had a great big band, originally called the Birdland Dream Band. Jimmy was an excellent player and was always open to my setting in whenever I could come to the club. Jimmy was one of those exceptions I alluded to in my earlier reference to white jazz musicians. With Jimmy the doors were always open to anyone as long as he could 'play'. This club became a refuge for me from the musical inanity of the Neighbors Orchestra.

The other place that stands out was a black club that we used to go to and play on Sunday afternoons. I remember it as the Ebony Club, if I can trust my memory. It was a really good jazz environment for all of us, including Jimmy, and we were warmly welcomed to participate, with one condition: that we white players would leave the premises before the sun went down. If we were still there when the Houston police came around to check on the club, they would close the place down. It didn't alter the warmth of the reception that we got from the crowd and the owners but was just an acceptance of what would happen if we acted otherwise.

It was in that club that I heard 'Fathead' Newman play, as well as Arnett Cobb, and one night was the first of two times

I was to hear and see 'The Worm'. I don't know anybody who actually knew 'The Worm', who he was or where he came from. Apparently he would just appear from time to time and play some of the most incredible alto you could ever imagine.

The second time I heard 'The Worm' was while I was with Paul, working the Blue Room of the Ambassador Hotel on Canal Boulevard in New Orleans. I had found a little club down the street from the hotel where I would set in from time to time. One night the musicians in the group invited me to go with them to a concert at a black YWCA in another part of town on Sunday afternoon. A big band of New Orleans musicians occasionally got together to play charts written by some of the local cats or by someone who might have been brought in from other bands. This particular concert had Wallace Davenport in the trumpet section. He was at home in New Orleans, recovering from a very serious bus accident that happened while he was touring with the Lionel Hampton band. He had a badly broken leg and other minor injuries that kept him at home even though the band, in typical Hampton style, was back on the road. Years later I ran across Davenport at a jazz festival in Nice, France, where he was directing a gospel choir that was participating in the festival. Another name I remember from that time was Plas Johnson, who I later encountered in Los Angeles.

The concert was going beautifully when out of the wings of the stage strolled 'The Worm', playing his alto sax. The band immediately slid right in behind him and brought him into the piece they were playing. It seemed that everyone in the band knew him and was just as pleased to see him as I was. 'The Worm' finished his contribution, turned and strolled off the stage, just as he had strolled on, while the crowd went wild in appreciation. He never reappeared that afternoon and whether he was still in the hall or not, I'll never know. Such are my two experiences with 'The Worm', a legendary character if ever there was one and an incredible player. I've heard of him showing up all over the country and with similar responses and similar behavior. Who knows?

6

Jomar Dagron

On one of these tours away from the Shamrock we were working at Elyches Gardens in Denver, Colorado. While we were there I discovered a home boy (meaning someone from my home town) working in a club in the Five Points area of Denver, which was the center of black social activity in the city during those years. Ron Washington, my homey, had been an alto player when we were in high school. In the summers between school years he had toured with an uncle or some relative who was a traveling preacher and had played for this relative's religious services. Ron was a very good alto man but was never a part of the scene around Chanute, maybe because of his connection to his preacher relative.

After he left Chanute I understand that he went to Topeka, the capital of Kansas. There, as well as in Kansas City, he garnered a dynamic reputation as a stellar alto man reminiscent of Charlie Parker, or so they were saying around the city. Interestingly enough, when I ran into him in Denver he had switched from alto to tenor and I had switched from tenor to baritone. Every night after I got off our gig at the park, I made it a habit during the band's stay at Elyches Gardens to head straight to Sonny's Lounge where Ron was working and sit in with the group. I became somewhat of a regular attraction at the club and as a result I was offered a job to play at Sonny's from then on, if I wanted. After thinking it over for a few days, I decided to take the offer. The money wasn't nearly as good but the opportunity to play jazz all night, every night, was too appealing for me to turn down. I gave Paul my notice (two weeks – Union rules and all that), which would come into effect when the band returned to Houston.

When I returned to Denver I began my association with Sonny's Lounge and with the group that would soon call itself the Jomar Dagron Quartet.

Sonny's was an R and B joint that became an all-out jazz club shortly after I joined the group. This was not necessarily because of me but adding me in seemed to give the group a greater emphasis in that direction. The owner agreed with the new direction. Besides, he was having so much success at the door and at the cash register that he didn't care what we played. Sonny simply believed that he had his hands on a good thing and, as it turned out, he did.

In case you are curious about the name Jomar Dagron: The group was made up of Jo Jo Williams, from Wichita, Kansas, on drums, therefore the 'Jo'. Jo Jo had spent a few years traveling with a territorial band led by Ernie Fields which worked up and down the center of the country from Texas to North Dakota and back. Jo Jo was a lot better drummer than he thought he was; in fact, I did my best to get him to come to New York after I got established but he couldn't bring himself to take the chance. He was unquestionably the best drummer in Denver, along with Shelley Rhim, who had passed up an opportunity to play with Duke Ellington, or so the story goes. I was the 'mar' part of the name. Dag Walton was an ex-saxophone player who played a reasonable keyboard and wrote some arrangements for us that worked pretty well. Hence the 'Dag'. Ron Washington, as I have said, was an outstanding tenor man, having converted from alto, which had been the source of his earlier reputation. *Voilà*, the Jo-mar-Dag-ron Quartet!

The club had what was called an Organo. This was an electrical attachment placed under the keys of the piano throughout the middle range of the keyboard. This allowed for a separation of the left hand from the right, making it possible for the player to make the left hand play a bass line while chords and lines were played by the right. I know nothing about electronics, so don't rely much on my description, but it did work that way. This was a very cheap way of trying to get a little Hammond B3 sound out of a piano. It

wasn't even close. But that is what Dag played with us. We
voiced everything so that Ron and I would be the top two
voices and Dag would fill in the voicing on the Organo like
it was a full sax section. It worked pretty well for us and
established our sound as quite unique for Denver. If you can
imagine a sax section with a lead tenor and second baritone,
you can sort of hear the sound in your head. It also demanded
that I play in the top end of my horn on almost all of the
charts to get that close voicing sound.

When I got back to Denver from Houston after leaving the
Paul Neighbors band, I met the president of the black
Musicians' Union in whose jurisdiction the club fell, George
Morrison. He informed me that I would have to transfer into
the Denver local to keep on playing at Sonny's and that was
fine with me. He was considerate of the fact that I been hired
onto the gig, so waived the period of probation, which would
have meant waiting for a certain number of weeks before I
could take a steady engagement. Ron and I went over to
George's house the next day and while we completed the
transfer, signing papers and stuff, George told us the story
of his life in this business, which was fascinating. He had been
on the scene many years before when jazz really was a new
thing in the country. You can read it for yourself in the
appendix to one of Gunther Schuller's books on jazz entitled
Early Jazz.

One night after I had been on the job for three or four
months and we were becoming known throughout the city,
George stopped by the club to tell me that the white Musicians'
local in town was going to report him to the international
organization of the Union if he didn't get me to transfer to
the local white Musicians' Union office. I still can't understand
why they made such a fuss, inasmuch as they weren't offering
me any work or improving the money we got from Sonny. That
was George's business and his jurisdiction. But I had to join
the white Musicians' Union and pay three times as much in
dues. I was working in a black club, for black money, under
a black Union's jurisdiction but I was responsible for white
dues. Now that is a typical racial situation which blacks are

very familiar with, so it was my turn to pay some of that debt. To make matters worse, I don't think Dag, who was also white, was ever approached about his status with the Union. Go figure.

Anyhow, George was a sweetheart and apologized about this turn of events, agreeing with me about the injustice of it. He said how pleased he was that I had associated myself with his Union and that if he had had any clout, he would have considered disputing the claim but as he acknowledged that he didn't, we would have to live with the situation. His stories were great and he seemed to love telling them. I really didn't put up a fight about the whole thing because I was doing what I had always wanted to do: play jazz all night, every night.

This was during the time of the Clifford Brown/Max Roach Quintet, which was setting the standard for most of the small groups around the country. We copped as many of their charts as we could figure out. Sonny's went from being an almost exclusively black R and B club to the most successful jazz club in the entire Denver area. The crowds became a real mixture of black, white and Hispanics. The club became distinguished in Denver as a black and tan club, which honored the inter-mingling of all races and backgrounds. Most of the jazz fans in Denver came to Sonny's and some of the members of the Denver Bears AAA baseball team, a farm team for the New York Yankees, became regular customers. That was how we got acquainted with Tony Kubek, Jim Stafford and many other members whose names I can't remember and who became our regulars. Every time they came in we would play 'Take Me Out to the Ball Game'. Hey, it's not a bad tune to play on at all.

Very few of the guys we got to know went up to the majors, except for Tony Kubek and Bobby Richardson. One member of the Denver Bears did go to the majors but not to the Yankees; he went to the New York Mets during their early years. This was the infamous Marvelous Marv Throneberry. He was a great guy and made as much fun of himself as everybody else did. He did have great potential, which you could see when he was playing with the Bears, but it never seemed to completely materialize like Kubek's and Richardson's did.

I once got an invitation by the guys to practice with the team during their practices at the Bears stadium there in Denver but I never accepted it as it had been years since I had put on a glove and I didn't have that kind of guts.

The Jomar Dagron Quartet did do an album for the Golden Crest recording company out of New York – their headquarters was out on Long Island somewhere – which was called *Rocky Mountain Jazz* and that was our main claim to fame outside of Denver. The record went nowhere and neither did we.

We worked at Sonny's Lounge seven nights a week from 9:00 p.m. to 2:00 a.m. with matinees on Saturday and Sunday. In addition, we began to work in an after-hours joint Friday and Saturday nights from 2:30 a.m. until 5:30 a.m. after our gig at Sonny's. Add two hours for the matinees and you can compute the amount of playing we were doing every week. This was just like a day gig, hour-wise. Of course, then you have to add into that the time we spent each week in rehearsals, trying to develop new material all the time. You can see how I would have been getting into pretty good shape, physically, technically and musically. The association with Ron, Jo Jo, the people who welcomed me into the scene in Denver and into the life in Five Points, increased my awareness and sensibilities to the music and the culture so much so that I would, for long periods of time, forget that I was white.

The long hours we put in on the job really was a training for me in preparation for things to come that I knew nothing about at the time. Add to that, Ron Washington was a speed demon on tenor (like the stories you hear about Johnny Griffin in Chicago) and he wouldn't let up on me. He had been the leader of the group before I joined and was ostensibly our leader now – at least, he was the spokesman – and consequently he called all the tempos. That meant that up tempo was UUUUP and, I must say, that slow was also SLOOOOW. I learned how to burn either way because of Ron. There is no greater challenge to a player than to really take care of business in a SLOOOOW blues. Ron was masterful at it and he forced me to come up to him every night; he also put me on the wall every night. He might have been trying to get me into territory that I couldn't handle, thereby making him a winner or something. I really don't know. Besides, it doesn't really matter to me because as a result of his constant challenges I gained a greater capacity and confidence about my ability to play. As a result I was being prepared for 'Things to Come', thank you Dizzy, without knowing that things were coming.

We worked for Sonny for 13 months. After the first month we had standing room only from 10:00 p.m. from Thursday to Saturday and on the other nights we were always full. And this was seven nights a week. You could say we were doing a pretty good business for Sonny. But, true to the tradition, when we asked Sonny for more money, he decided that he didn't need us anymore. He was going to go big time with big name groups from around the country and cater to a more sophisticated crowd. So he fired us and remodeled his place, making it much bigger so he could make more money. Six months later he went bankrupt, a very familiar story in this business. We were only trying to go from $75 to $90 per man per week, which added up to a big increase of $60 per week for the entire group. We made no request for fewer hours or anything else because we were happy playing all that time. He made that $60 on any given afternoon from his regular bar crowd. Sometimes I wonder about the workings of the minds of club owners, as this happens all too often in this business, or it used to. Now it seems that a club's failure often comes from the owner/manager putting too much of the profit from the club up his nose.

Sonny's Lounge had become the place in town to go for straight-ahead jazz and consequently when bands or groups were in town for concerts, the musicians from those groups would show up at Sonny's after their gigs were over, just like I did when I was working at the Gardens. As a result we got to meet some very great musicians, such as Errol Garner and Keeter Betts. Joe Howard and Frank Beach were two other cats who came into town with Frank Sinatra for a series of concerts downtown and who came our way every night to set in and let their hair down, so to speak. Pepper would stop in whenever he was in Denver or passing through on his way somewhere and spend a day or two with us and hang out. One of those stops was a very important turning point for me and my future.

Pepper and Doug Watkins, a bass man from Detroit who, like Pepper, was on the music scene in New York, were on their way to L.A. to join Chet Baker for a tour, or maybe they were on tour and on their way to L.A. They stopped and spent a couple of days with us. We played together every night and hung out afterwards each night and talked about lots of stuff until the early hours of the morning. It was Doug who convinced me that I'd never know for sure whether I could make it in New York until I tried. I think his expression was, 'to see if you can swim in the big ocean'. And his follow-up comment was, 'You can always come back to the small pond and be the top man in town, if you find you can't swim in New York.' They both told me that it would be nothing to be ashamed of if I couldn't swim in the Big Apple because there were a whole lot of excellent musicians around the country who couldn't who were still functioning very well where they were. For some reason, as simple as it was, it made sense to me for the first time. So before the year was out I was on my way to New York City with a newly-acquired wife, a cat named Kitty and a dog named Mr Blue.

There was another jazz club downtown, the name of which eludes me. I know it doesn't exist any more, anyway. Sonny's was located on the border between Five Points (black) and downtown (primarily white) and one block up from Arapaho (Hispanic). During the last few months we were at Sonny's, this club, downtown, opened up with an excellent jazz group led by a young local trumpet player, Ed Klieger, I think his name was, who had with him an incredible tenor man from Pittsburgh, Booker Erwin. Booker went on to a great career in New York with the Charlie Mingus group of the '60s. The drummer was, often, a man named Billy. Booker and I used to set in with each other whenever we could and later did a gig or two together while in Denver. After we both went to New York, Booker and I kept in touch but never had another chance to work with each other. By the time I had an opportunity to work with Mingus, Booker had been dead at least a year.

The Jomar Dagron Quartet worked a couple of other clubs in town but not with the kind of success we had at Sonny's. The last gig we had before I left Denver was a strip joint downtown which was . . . interesting, to say the least. During those few months, before I took off for New York, a number of things happened to me that helped to formulate my understanding both of the music and of the social/political reality of the music business. The difference in white and black attitudes I had experienced in high school and college was reaffirmed in Denver. When I had an evening free to get around town, I'd be shown the same reserved, judgmental attitudes from local white groups that I'd known before. I really couldn't understand it, since we had always been open to them when they had come into Sonny's.

In defense of Denver as a city, given the social environment of the '50s, from a racial perspective, I found the city's openness quite remarkable for that time. Other than New York City, I hadn't been in a large city anywhere in the US that was as open to social interaction between blacks and whites. This provided a reasonably comfortable environment in which mixed couples could go to restaurants, theatres, clubs, hotels and so on without overt action being taken against them. You might get a look that would indicate some displeasure but that would be from an individual, not a general social barrier. We were able to come and go as we pleased, throughout the city, with a minimal amount of hassle. Yes, when I was by myself I didn't get the kinds of looks that I got when I was together with blacks but that was cool. I guess I should say that Washington DC wasn't too bad either but there were places where we could not go at all if anyone in the group were black.

A few years later I came through Denver with the Kenton band and a pretty good contingent of my old friends came to the ballroom where the band was playing to say hello. It was great but I missed many old faces who I realized weren't there because they couldn't afford the price of the ballroom for that engagement. I'm afraid a few felt that I was, somehow, now big time and they shouldn't bother me, or so I was told. I wanted so much to hang out in town to try and find at least some of them, somewhere in Five Points. But the Kenton band was not staying in Denver that night and we were on our way to another city immediately after the gig. We didn't stay in town long enough even to eat. I almost begged Stan to schedule the stop so that we could stay that night in Denver but to no avail.

At this point I want to tell you about the title of this book. I think it is becoming obvious that my life's experiences have given me a unique insight into the differences between white and black societies. There were many occasions where I met white folks as well as white musicians who sincerely cared about the injustices of racism that were around all of us and they were as appalled about it as I was. Having said that, let me add that I had become as distrustful and guarded of the white community as were my friends in the black community. We were always aware of it, even when we lived in the relatively comfortable and liberal social environment that existed in Denver. Even with our awareness of the racial differences that existed, which was kept in check by those who might prefer to address those issues differently, we were always open to anyone who appeared to be genuine. But we were never too surprised when that person turned left on us or backed off from the relationship.

It is not the way you would choose to be with your fellow man. However, after repeated disappointments it becomes second nature to guard yourself against being taken advantage of and in some cases abused, not so much physically as emotionally and psychologically. It really is a trip to know someone with whom you feel you've made a meaningful contact, with whom you assume that you have established a friendship, and then one day meet that person, accidentally, in a different environment and have him, all of a sudden, not know you or be embarrassed to acknowledge he knows you or to pass you off to other people he is with as a passing acquaintance.

My first reaction when this happened was to get angry and to want to retaliate in some manner. It was at these moments that I began to recognize how caring the people I was living with were, as they would calm me down with gentle and mature advice about the injustice of the situation. It was like being with a grandfather who, when you are small, gives you his wise counsel and makes the hurt and pain go away by being there for you. My family was the black community and I was a white man they had embraced as one of their own.

As I look back with that famous 20/20 hindsight, I realize that what had happened to me was for my friends the normal reality that they had to deal with every day. This made the way they responded to me even more important. That is not to say that I never ran into any difficulty with anybody in the black community. That would be unrealistic. However, those occasions were relatively few and far between and mild in comparison.

Here's a story to document some of what I'm trying to say. I was dating a young lady whom I had met when she and her friends had come to Sonny's while, in her words, 'they were out slumming one night'. We met and one thing, as they say, led to another and we became each other's significant other shortly thereafter. Her father, who was a retired air force bird colonel, had absolutely no use for me, even though we had never met. Therefore he decided to use his influence to harass me into breaking off my relationship with his daughter. He did have some clout in the city from his years as a major player at the air force base in Denver and as result he got the D.A.'s office to send plainclothes men to the club where I was working and inquire about me. Apparently they came during the daytime because I never saw them there at night and I was there seven nights a week and then some, as you may recall. When the D.A.'s men asked about me, the community associated with Sonny's and the Jomar Dagron Quartet said they didn't know anything about me. They thought they could remember some white kid coming around at one time or another but they hadn't seen him for some time; however, they certainly would keep their eyes open for him. The community simply closed around me and I became invisible. Of course, it is also possible that the D.A.'s office may not have been all that keen on finding me but was just fulfilling the request of this pushy old man who used to be important when he was a power in the air force.

It didn't really matter because Joanne, Jo, the lady in question, found out about it and made a deal with her father that he could live with. After spending six months in isolation in Tucson, Arizona, a time she agreed with her father, she returned to Denver. When I later decided to leave for New York, we stopped in my home town in Kansas and left there as a married couple.

The bottom line of this experience for me was the comprehension of the depth and effectiveness of the protective curtain that could be drawn when necessary. The circumstances of life for the average black person during those years – and still today, to a greater extent than should be – made this imperative for survival. To have had the opportunity to experience it from that side of the social spectrum was not only illuminating but humbling.

Another story that was very important for me, personally, also illustrates the general ignorance of the white community about the reality of the black community. During the time I was in Denver, I invited my parents to visit me, which gave me an opportunity to show them the beauty of Denver and the Rocky Mountains, to show off the music I was playing and to demonstrate the sense of self-worth that I was acquiring as a musician because of it. Whenever I wrote to my folks or talked to them, I would place a great deal of emphasis on the group and the musical experience that I was having and how I was developing as a musician. Since my mother had decided for us, my sister and I, that music was going to be our vocation and avocation in life, I figured this would be of singular interest to her, particularly since I was excited about what was happening to me developmentally.

I made arrangements for my parents to stay at a motel in town and to spend an evening at Sonny's Lounge, to have dinner, hear the group and hopefully realize, first hand, how their son was progressing. The staff at Sonny's were great. They reserved the very best table in the house for them, which was a booth directly back from the bandstand in clear view, yet away from the bar and the action that was always going on there. The attention the staff gave to making the environment as warm and cordial as possible was beyond anything I had seen before at Sonny's and we had had some real celebrities in the room from time to time. But these were Marv's mom and dad and that made a difference. The cook at Sonny's could COOK some chicken! The only place I've ever had fried chicken tasting that crisp and moist and delicious was at Minton's in Harlem. (Before she left Denver, for somewhere in Pennsylvania, the cook gave me the secret to her fried chicken. No, I ain't givin' it up.)

Mom and dad came into the club and were escorted to their booth. The chicken, with all the trimmings, was ready for them and the wait staff made a subtle but gracious fuss over them to make them feel comfortable. We played our first set and Ron, who was our spokesman, introduced them to the crowd, many of whom went over and introduced themselves to my folks. I'm sure I have conveyed the fact that the crowd in Sonny's was always racially mixed, with a slight majority being black, so the people who were going out of their way for my folks were both black and white.

You might expect the evening to have been a grand success for my parents as well as for me. Sorry – it was a disaster. It was just like the first time Smitty had walked in the front door of our house in Chanute those many years before but this time my mother had no place to escape to. By the end of the second set she was nearly in tears and couldn't get control of her feelings, though I know she tried valiantly, just as she had with Smitty. All she could see was her little boy in a black club, with black musicians, playing a black kind of jazz, which she couldn't hear because she was so ashamed and afraid for her little boy, for whom she had had such great hopes and who she wanted to be a high school band director. Realizing the situation, my dad suggested that they really should get to bed, as for them it was getting pretty late. Well done, dad, but we all knew what had happened. The saddest part about the whole evening was that everybody in the club, including Sonny (which was certainly not his style), had gone out of their way to make my folks as comfortable as possible. But . . . most of them were black, except for Sonny.

There is a counterbalance to this event, which, in a way, undoubtedly added to my mother's consternation and which probably compounded her reaction. When I had been with the Paul Neighbors 'Mickey Mouse' Orchestra on one of our tours in the midwest, we had had an engagement at the Park Sheraton Hotel in St Louis, Missouri. We were, among other things, backing a show that featured Nelson Eddy, the heartthrob of the movies my mother so adored. While we were there I made arrangements for my folks to come to St Louis, stay at the hotel – no mean feat, as the cost of staying at the Park Sheraton was up there – and to see the show with Nelson Eddy. Remembering my mother's fascination with Eddy, I was able to arrange with the *maître d'* of the room to sit them at a table ringside. Now that I think back on it, I sure did have an awful lot of support and help from the people I was working with through the years. I had spoken to Nelson, who was a genuine person and not affected by the usual Hollywood arrogance that I had found with so many. I told him about my mother and asked if he would autograph a picture for her. He not only autographed the picture, he gave it to her himself while she was sitting at ringside following his show. I thought she was going to pass out in sheer ecstasy from being directly spoken to by her long-time screen idol. So you can see why the contrast, for her, was just too much to cope with. Her boy had gone from the heights of what she would consider success to this pit of despair. Poor mom. In a way, that was probably the hallmark of my life: always to be the incorrigible black sheep of the family.

7

The Big Apple

The trip to New York was great, especially when you consider that it was also a honeymoon, of sorts, with all the hopes and dreams of a new marriage filled with prospects and expectations for a life of meaningful professional activity and even possible financial success. No different from any other newly-married couple at the beginning of a life together. We were not in a rush and therefore stopped whenever and wherever we felt like. I'm embarrassed to say that I have no recollection of anything having to do with that trip except that we were not in a hurry to get there.

Our arrival in Elizabeth, New Jersey, and our decision to locate there, was predicated on the assumption that it would probably be cheaper to live there than in New York City which, of course, it was. What I didn't know was that the New York Musicians' Union did not include New Jersey in their jurisdiction. That wasn't too bright of me but served us well in getting a start in making some connections in New York. After we moved into a small efficiency apartment for which we had signed a one-month lease, I immediately called Pepper, who had been in New York for a few years by then, as well as Jimmy Sedlar, who I had known at the Naval School of Music. Jimmy, as I expected, was friendly but distantly so. Pepper was, as usual, glad to hear from me and happy that I had decided to come to New York and try my wings, so to speak, or I guess I should say my flippers, since I was supposed to see if I could swim in this ocean.

Pepper invited me to meet him at a recording session that he was doing the next day in Englewood, New Jersey, as he felt I should get to meet the musicians that he would be working with on that session. You should have noticed that Pepper was in no way concerned or protective of his turf and, quite to the contrary, felt that if he could help me get connected he would be happy to do so. The importance of this is that Pepper is white and, therefore, a major exception to what had become almost a standard expectation from my other experiences with whites. He gave me the address and a few directions to help me find the place. The next day I left early enough to allow for some difficulty in finding the studio, which turned out to have been a very good idea, since it wasn't that easy to find and I was not familiar at all with the area or metropolitan traffic.

When I did finally get there they had already started the recording session, so I waited for that 'take' to be over before I went into the room where the group was set up. The studio, if you could call it that, was a converted living room. The equipment – tape decks, monitors and control board – was set up in what would have been the dining room. It had been enclosed with a large glass window looking out into the living room to separate the engineer from the musicians.

This was the original Rudy Van Gelder studio, his house. Later he was to build a beautiful cathedral ceiling recording studio in Englewood Cliffs that was a part of a huge house that he had built behind it – sort of like a house with this huge appendage attached to its front. This studio became legendary for it was the venue of many equally legendary recording sessions. I also had the pleasure, a few years later, to record in that cathedral.

This particular session was under the leadership of Gene Ammons and he had on that date Paul Quinichette, tenor; John Coltrane, alto (yes, I do mean alto, not tenor); Jerome Richardson, flute; Pepper Adams, baritone; Art Taylor, drums; and I'm sorry to say I don't remember the other two rhythm section players. The piano man may have been Walter Davis Jr, I just don't remember. The session was great. I knew who I was hearing being recorded in Gene Ammons (remember Shabootie), and I had heard of Paul Quinichette. Of course, I knew Pepper but the other guys were all new to me. Pepper did make sure that I got to meet everybody there, including Van Gelder, and let them know that I had come to town for the purpose of getting into the business. You could not ask for more than that for your first day in town. On top of all that, you must realize that Pepper knew that I had switched from tenor and was now playing the same instrument as he was. He still wanted to help me get started in New York if he could. Talk about separating the men from the boys!

After the session I drove Pepper, Paul and Coltrane back into Manhattan, since I was the only person there with a car. Jerome had grabbed a cab earlier, when he had finished the tunes which were using flute, so that he could get back into town to the Roxy where he was a part of the house band; he had to make the next show. The others seemed to have their own transportation worked out for them and their equipment, drums and bass, etc. On the drive into Manhattan we shared some observations about music and Paul got all bent out of shape over something that was said about some classical composition or something having to do with the classical music scene. He was really unloading on classical musicians and their music and Pepper and John both tried to show Paul the error of his thinking and gave examples and tried to justify the discipline. I've known very few jazz musicians who didn't have a very good working knowledge of classical music, from its discipline to the great composers and their musical priorities. They also tend to own fairly extensive record libraries of classical as well as jazz performances. John and Pepper were no exceptions to that. Paul, however, most certainly was.

Pepper shared with me a story about Charlie Parker's love of European classical music, particularly of the modern composers, that he had told Pepper. It seems that while Bird was in Europe for a period of time, he heard a piece by Honegger at a concert that had knocked him out. He shared his impressions and analysis of the composition with Pepper since they had established, early on in their relationship, that common interest. This was at a time before Honegger was recognized in the US, with a few rare exceptions, of course. Yet Charlie Parker had not only heard Honegger's music but was extolling his virtues as a composer. It was some time later that Honegger became a known entity in the classical music world of the US, having been 'discovered' by the classical musicians there.

We dropped Coltrane off uptown. Actually, it wasn't really uptown but around 92nd and Riverside Drive on the West Side of Manhattan. I then drove Pepper down to the Lower East Side where he lived and so had the opportunity to ask him about John, who he was and what was he doing musically on the alto. I had never heard anything quite like it before with, possibly, 'The Worm' as an exception. Even so, John's playing was even more profoundly different. Pepper's reply was that John was still putting it together and he felt sure that it wouldn't be long before it was all going to fall into place for him. Boy! Was that ever prophetic. Before the year was out John Coltrane was recognized around the world as the new giant on the scene. From then on we were all affected by 'Trane's' direction.

Jo, my wife, found a job as a secretary on Staten Island through a temporary service and I went into New York to begin to find my way around. As I said before, it was our good fortune that we had only taken a one-month lease on the little efficiency apartment because the first thing I found out, after trying to submit my Union card for a transfer into #802, the New York City local, was that I couldn't transfer unless I was living in New York City proper, which meant Manhattan, Brooklyn, the Bronx, Queens or Staten Island.

Even though Jo had a job on Staten Island, moving our residence to Staten Island would mean that to get into Manhattan I would have to take the ferry, which really restricted scheduling. Or I would have to drive back through New Jersey and into Manhattan through one of the tunnels, which would have been worse. And there was no reasonable access to public transport – it all took hours to get anywhere. So moving into the city was our only alternative. I immediately began to look for someplace within the New York jurisdiction that we could afford to live. Manhattan was out of the question for us financially. I then discovered Queens and found a nice little place in Jackson Heights. So we moved into Queens after we finished up our lease in Jersey, which by then was just about used up anyway.

I started going to different clubs and setting in when I could, much like I had done in every city I had ever been in before. And, as a result, I was, eventually, invited to join a rehearsal band at the Juilliard School of Music on the Upper West Side of Manhattan. This gave me another opportunity to meet more musicians in the city.

It wasn't long before I got a call from an alto player, Joe Lopes, who had been made the contractor for the Tommy Dorsey band, under the direction of Warren Covington, the first of a series of ghost bands to hit the road out of New York. He had first approached Pepper, who wasn't at all interested but who recommended me as being a good prospect for the band. The Dorsey family had decided to re-form the band and to send it out on the road to maintain an income for the family. It had chosen Warren as the leader of the band. Warren had for years been a regular studio musician in New York and played quite well. I think he saw this as an opportunity to make a bigger name for himself and get out of the City for a while. At any rate, I was offered the job on baritone and took it.

I had by that time been in the city for just a few weeks and the Union had a restriction that anyone who was on transfer probation was not to go out of town with any group for more than a weekend. The probation was for six months and I had only been in town for a few weeks. The Dorsey band was going on tour, which was *verboten*, but I took the job anyway and just hoped that they wouldn't catch me until I got back into town in a couple of months.

These ghost bands became the rage during that time and the Tommy Dorsey band was the first of that genre to be formed. Then came the Jimmy Dorsey band, the Glenn Miller band and, more recently, the Woody Herman band. Also the Count Basie band, the only band in my estimation that has retained the quality and content of the original band and this largely because of the expertise and musicianship of the band's leaders, first Thad Jones and then Frank Foster.

There was also the Duke Ellington Orchestra, which didn't stop on Duke's death but continued under the leadership of his son Mercer, maintaining, for a while, the same personnel who had been on the band when Duke died. The older men began, one by one, to leave the band and Mercer decided who the replacements would be, which assisted in the decline of the quality of the orchestra. The Ellington orchestra had always been the result of the unique voices on the band and the genius of Duke in writing these different voices into the orchestrations in a way that expressed that collective uniqueness. The men who were responsible for creating the Ellington sound through Duke's compositional genius were now either dying off or had left the road because of advancing age or infirmity; one had entered, some years before, the priesthood. Mercer simply did not have the ability to hear in a musician that unique voice which his dad could hear and had used to determine his choice of musician.

The Dorsey band had rehearsals every day for about a week at Nola's, a midtown studio on 7th Avenue, just above 52nd Street. This studio became rather famous as the rehearsal studio in midtown that was used for years by many orchestras. I realized very quickly that I was in a different circle of musical professionalism. The technical and musical exactness was more critical than anything I had experienced before. The phrasing and even the breathing was disciplined, the use of vibrato and when not to use it at all – this was more demanding than any musical organization I had ever been a part of. So another lesson was in progress.

I will repeat that I've learned from every person that I have ever worked with, whether he knew it or not. I had to do some woodshedding to keep up but before long I got pretty comfortable with the demands that were being made and from then on got along very well with everybody musically. There were situations on the band, of a personal nature, that were less than what I would have preferred to have around me. But I was beginning to learn how to close it out and either go into myself or hook up with someone on the band I could feel at home with. Another lesson that I learned while in Denver.

On this tour the band was going to go through Chanute on its way to Tulsa, Oklahoma, after leaving the previous night's gig in Kansas City, Missouri, and traveling through the night. Consequently we would be going through Chanute sometime early the next morning. I had told my mom that we would be coming through at that time and that if I could I would call as we went through town.

This was enough for my stage-struck mother. She insisted that we stop at my folks' house for breakfast on the way to Tulsa. When I shared that request with Warren he was most agreeable to the stop. That was all my mother needed. She got all her friends and the neighbor women to work for hours preparing a huge breakfast for the entire busload of musicians. When we got there the newspaper for our little town made a big thing out of the event and my mother was in hog heaven then and for some time after. Remember Sonny's in Denver? Well, the Dorsey band was all white, so I had redeemed myself in her eyes, for a while. I wasn't a band director but I was with a musical organization that she could relate to.

The Dorsey band was a very good dance band and a very professional musical organization but it wasn't playing what I understood jazz to be. So there was an empty place in my soul for what I felt right about both musically and personally. Well, the Union took care of that. I got an urgent call from Jo in New York and when I got back to her she informed me that the Union expected me to appear at the Union offices personally the next Monday to discuss what I was doing. Jo had tried to excuse my not returning their calls but after a while they pretty well knew what I was up to so they sent a letter demanding my appearance.

There is a clause in the Union rules that will allow a member on transfer to be on tour with a band but the leader has to prove that there is nobody available in the Union who could do the job. I was told that some effort was made to invoke that clause but to no avail, as there were many baritone players in town who were available and the demands were not terribly unique on the Dorsey band. So I was off the band.

Here I was, back in New York after only six weeks of being out on the road, which was not long enough to qualify for unemployment, and no gigs. So I went back to setting in and making rehearsal bands. Man! I made every rehearsal band in town that I could get into, and as far as playing was concerned, I had found Basie's on 132nd and Lexington every Monday night. Monday nights at Basie's was jam session night and it seemed like every young cat in town was there. The musicians who wanted to play were organized by a trombone player whose name was Plummer, I think, and he'd set up who was going to play on what set and with whom. So each night different people would be playing together on every set. Despite this, or maybe because of it, the music was heavy, as you only got one shot each night and you made the most of this moment on a bandstand where everyone offered the very best they had to offer musically.

What a highly charged and fertile musical environment! Some nights I heard guys play so much stuff that I was almost too scared to even get on the bandstand following such great playing. On occasion I would find myself on the bandstand with these same great musicians. Now you want to talk about the moment of truth? That was it! Somehow, and God only knows how, I said my say as best I could and, more often than not, what I got was encouragement from both the musicians and the people in the club. Very reminiscent of all the other black clubs where I used to set in. The difference was the quality and level of musicianship.

Those Monday nights put me in the environment and influence of every major young player to come out of the New York City scene in the next 10 years: Horace Parlan, Wayne Shorter, Clifford Jordan, Herbie Hancock, Walter Bishop Jr, Walter Perkins, Bobby Cranshaw, just to name a few, and all of us were trying to get a start in the City. You want to go to school? That was school like no other school you'll find and there is nothing like it today anywhere and certainly not in the institutions of higher learning. As I have said a few times now, the reality of 'Let's see what you've got' and the subsequent, 'Yeah! man, you can play!' is what it's all about.

Possibly the most important element of this music, which is lost on most musicians today, is the meaning implied by the musician who used those expressions. He'd be referring to the musical and melodic content of your improvisation, not the speed and accuracy of your ability to manipulate a set of chord changes. This mistaken but widely-spread definition of improvisation has forced some of us to change the identifying label from 'improvisation' to 'extemporaneous composition', which more closely approximates what we understand to be improvisation.

The discipline of chord manipulation, which gives you the ability to run patterns derived from the scales relating to a specific chord and even those patterns derived from alternate scales which can be superimposed over that same chord, is the craft of improvisation, not the end result. Once that craft is finely honed and all the related scale structures are absorbed into your consciousness with the accompanying 'mind to ear to finger' recall immediately at your disposal, then you are ready to begin. Learning how to express a melodic and thematic exposition, with a compositional command of the development of those melodic or thematic statements, and to allow that melodic line to embrace the underlying chord structures as wind flows across trees, is the ideal. If you think I'm just waxing poetic, listen to Bird and Dizzy, Clifford Brown, Sonny Rollins and John Coltrane, Pepper Adams and Monk – the list goes on. For those who may have difficulty accepting that the old cats weren't hip to today's way of playing, may I suggest Mulgrew Miller, Joshua Redman, Chris Potter, Branford Marsalis, Wallace Roney, Terence Blanchard and Nicholas Payton for openers. They are not just playing the craft and calling it improvisation. Therein lies my contention with the majority of college jazz studies programs around the country. The great young musicians who are coming out of these colleges remind me of something Clark Terry once said to me, that he had become what he was, not because of his education, but despite it.

By the time I arrived in New York I had more or less given up on the idea of trying to set in with the stereotypical white jazz musicians simply because I didn't need to go through those kinds of changes, that is, to deal with unpleasant and usually arrogant attitudes. Besides, there were plenty of places, groups and opportunities during those years in the City to find nourishing environments in which to explore your musical skills and artistic development without the jive you might have to deal with in the other places. Here again, I'm not suggesting that the only place or the only musicians you could set in with and be nourished by were black but black environments were more likely to welcome your participation. Of course, after I had developed to the point that I was recognized and respected by most jazz musicians in town, finding a place to play was not a problem.

All of my observations here are with regard to my efforts to get my playing to the level that others in town had achieved and were thereby able to use throughout the city in a professional capacity. That DOES NOT happen in a practice room. Or in a class of improvisation at a university, though it should. I once had a graduate student in one of my improvisation classes complain to me after class one day, early in the semester, that I wasn't teaching him or the class improvisation; we were just having a jam session. I chuckled and replied that he was right and that jam sessions were where you learned how to improvise. After a few more weeks the student began to realize that the assistance he was getting was coming from those jam sessions and through them he recognized what it takes to express oneself more clearly through this medium. One of the greatest accolades a student of ours could receive was to be invited to one of the teacher's basements for a jam session; then he knew he had arrived at another level.

After my return from my short engagement with the Dorsey band, I found that I needed to bring some kind of cash into the household, to help support our dog and cat at least. Since the City wasn't knocking my door down to get me to play for them yet, I took a job as a stock boy at G. Schirmer Music Company in midtown Manhattan. It didn't pay a great salary but it did allow me the freedom to take any call that might come my way. I was free to make a rehearsal or a gig or anything that would lead to work in the industry. The boss of my department gave me that flexibility up front when I applied for the job. As he said, I was not in New York to work as a stock boy at G. Schirmer's and I should take advantage of every opportunity available. Many of the men working in the store had either been in the business and realized their personal limitations or had retired from the business after their edge had begun to diminish. All of them were very encouraging to me, even those who had tried and hadn't quite made it. Now, there were some exceptions; they were all white as I remember. Of course, none of them were playing either. Who knows? New York City has often had a bad rap for its inhumanity. In my opinion, and having experienced both New York and Los Angeles, I'll take New York any day.

Here's another old false image that was destroyed for me in New York in a very meaningful and empathetic way. There was a Jewish delicatessen in our neighborhood in Jackson Heights, which was essentially a small mom-and-pop deli where pop worked – I never saw mom there. It was about a block from our apartment. The owner was Jack Felsenfield and he and his sons ran the deli. It became a practice for us to buy odds and ends, milk, cigarettes, bread, etc. from Jack. He set up an account for us so that we could purchase these little bits when we didn't have the cash available and he would run a tally that we would pay when we could. Sometimes that tab could get pretty substantial when there was no playing work coming in and we had to survive on Jo's salary and my little $50 from Schirmer's. Jack never bothered us about the size of the tab or even inquired as to when we would be able to pay something on it.

On the occasions when I would get a weekend gig out of town with some band, I would often write Jack a check for some cash to get through the weekend and ask him not to cash it until Monday. When I got back in town from the weekend gig I would have the money to deposit to cover the check. After I had used this method for a while to cover my expenses for the weekend gigs, Jack confronted me. I fully expected that he would let me have it for using him like that, maybe even demand that I pay up my bill and probably cancel our right to a tab at his deli. Instead, he chastised me for wasting the ten cents every time I wrote a check and told me that from then on I should ask him for what I needed to get through the weekend. 'I'll give it to you and put it on your tab, then you can pay me back when you get back from your work out of town. No more wasting ten cents on writing a check.'

Add to that, when I would come back from a financially successful trip Jack would say, 'Look, you kids take that money and go to the supermarket and stock up on what you need. Its too expensive for you to try and buy everything from me. I know that I'll always get your business when you need me.' Don't ever talk to me about tightwad, penny-pinching devious, scurrilous Jews. Jack Felsenfield kept us alive for months with no reservations or concern for his own well-being. A more caring, benevolent soul I've never met.

I asked Jack one day how he could afford to give this kind of support and trust to people. Didn't he ever get burned by some of those he had trusted? His reply was rather profound.

'I know that sometimes people need to be helped to realize their dreams and I feel it a privilege to help, in my small way, by doing this for you and others. I've never been cheated. It may take a long time for it to come back to me but eventually it does. And if it doesn't, it is probably because it became impossible. Even if it was intentional, am I to quit trusting and caring for my friends? It is better to accept a loss than to lose my humanity. But it doesn't happen to me, inshallah.'

I became pretty busy on the weekends with bands that would go out only for the weekend or maybe for a short tour of a week or two. In those bands were some very good musicians who were in a similar situation to mine: leaders like Sonny Land, Ray Eberle, Larry Elgart and a few others whose names I can't remember, probably because I didn't meet them very often. Larry Elgart was the band I ended up working with the most – I even did some recording with his band. His tours would often take us out for weeks at a time, though mostly it was just weekends. Larry wanted to have a kind of commercial jazz band with a musical approach along the lines of the

Basie band but didn't have a clue about how to accomplish that within his personal playing style. That style was unique to say the least.

Here we go with lessons again. As a side man it was my responsibility to figure out how to complement the style and distinctiveness of the leader's musical comprehension. Larry had a very distinctive way of playing alto and soprano saxes. It was an experience being able to adapt to his style and approach to sound production and phrasing. He began to appreciate my ability to get into his approach and I gave him the kind of bottom to his sax section that he was looking for. I didn't particularly care for the way he played but I certainly respected his ability to produce on his instruments the sound and concept that he perceived. I feel I expanded my under-standing of the diverse ways to create a sound and my concept of melodic phrasing as a result of being in his section with him over those many months. When I listen to the recordings I made with him, I know that I succeeded. Since he wanted the band to be a kind of club date jazz band, he allowed those of us on the band who were jazz players to have as much opportunity to play as he could and still keep the style of the band intact. Consequently Wayne Andre on trombone, Howie Collins on guitar and myself on baritone would get the call to play on various tunes during the night and sometimes he would let us stretch out for a couple of choruses, particularly if we were playing a blues.

Larry and his manager Bob Bonis – actually I think it was Bob who first discovered her – found a girl singer in a small club in Providence, Rhode Island, they really liked and soon had on the band. She had some great jazz chops and was a definite plus to the appearance of the band. Her name was Carol Sloan and she eventually went on to do some very good things on her own. While on the Elgart band she would often sing the jazz heads with us, adding her voice as if it were another voice in the ensemble, which was very effective. It was a little reminiscent of Ivie Anderson with Duke Ellington. We recorded that sound on the band's rendition of 'Walkin'', on an album we did with Larry called *New Sounds at the Roosevelt*, which was recorded while the band was doing an extended engagement at the Roosevelt Hotel in midtown Manhattan. Having a steady gig in town, working with a weekly salary and having the same money coming in every week was something to have. I almost felt successful.

After we had been at the Roosevelt for a few months I got a call from Nat Pierce, who was calling for Woody Herman, offering me a gig with Woody's band. Many months prior to this I had heard about Woody having auditions for a tenor chair that was open in his band and I decided to take a shot at it, even though I hadn't played tenor in years. I rented a tenor from Charlie Ponte, one of the music stores in midtown that I had been trading with since I had been to New York. Charlie and I became good friends over the years and he was always helpful to me with any of the needs I had in the business. He passed on some years ago but my feelings of gratitude still remain.

I made the audition on tenor. Woody did not audition in the manner of classical orchestras with the artist behind a curtain and playing alone. He would put the person audition-ing in the band as a part of it and rehearse a tune, seeing how well that player could fit in. He would have him take a chorus at some point in the chart. I have followed that example in my auditioning process ever since and have found that it is a good way of truly evaluating the capabilities of the auditionee, who needs to work under that kind of pressure.

Following the auditions Nat came over to me and told me that they knew I wasn't a tenor man and that Woody wanted me to know that when a vacancy came up on the baritone chair that he would give me a call. I took that as a nice way of saying I didn't cut it in the audition and I accepted that because I knew that I hadn't played as well as some of the other guys. I did give it my best shot and what else can any-one do but that?

When Nat offered me the gig I knew what my answer would be but I also realized that I would have to discuss it with Jo. We discussed the advantages and disadvantages of taking the job with Woody, particularly in light of the security of the ongoing gig at the Roosevelt with Elgart. I do not recall how that discussion went but the end result was that I took Woody's offer. I have no doubt that there was some reservation on Jo's part, since the gig with Elgart was the first steady engagement that I had so far held in New York City. But on the other hand Jo was fully aware that my reason for being in New York was to find out if I could swim in this ocean and going out with Woody was definitely a step in the direction of finding that out.

I took the job with Woody and I left town. The band rehearsed at Nola's – yes, it is the same Nola's from the Dorsey and rather famous or infamous, depending on the story being told. I understand it has since moved to another location in Manhattan. After a week of rehearsals I was on the road with one of the best white jazz bands in existence. Working with Woody was a ball, even though his facial expressions could be intense if directed towards you during the performance. He would sometimes stand in front of you while you were playing to let you know that he was specifically listening to you and that he might or might not be happy with what he was hearing. He never said anything to me but when he stood in front of me I knew I was being listened to and evaluated. Pressure does two things: it either causes you to get so paranoid that you crumble or it forces you to dig in and bring more out of yourself than you had any idea was there.

One very good example of this characteristic of Woody happened to me one night. The band was playing its chart on the Horace Silver tune called 'The Preacher'. The chart, which was essentially a 16–bar blues in the key of G, which put me in E, had a solo for baritone in the arrangement. I could skate in any key for a couple of choruses but didn't feel confident to really play anything of substance in that key. Woody, recognizing my inadequacy, would stand by me while I was down front playing my solo on 'The Preacher'. Two choruses later I'd be through and ready to sit down but Woody would stand there with his index finger extended, which meant that I had to play another chorus. I would have to try and find some way of keeping a musical line of thought going for another chorus, which I knew I couldn't pull off. Chorus after chorus Woody would stand there with that God-awful finger extended, in my face, and my soul in absolute fear and doubt. This went on night after night, until the challenge began to have its effect by making it possible for me to hear musical ideas in that key and I began to elaborate on what I heard. Just about the time I began to become comfortable with 'The Preacher' and felt I could really begin to stretch out, I'd finish the second chorus and start to open it up. And here would come Woody, blowing into my next chorus as if to say, 'OK, now that you've learned to play what you should have known to start with, I'll take over and you've now learned to play in the key of G.' That's a teacher!

There were some really excellent jazz players on that band. We used to call it the 437th Herd because they used to refer to the original Four Brothers Herman band as the 2nd Herman Herd. There had been so many different Herman bands over the years that we decided we must have been somewhere around the 437th Herd. We had Paul Fontaine out of Boston on trumpet along with Bill Chase. Paul was out of the Miles Davis school but with his own voice, while Chase was a bulldog and an incredibly good lead man. Don Lanphere was playing the lead tenor chair and was probably the best all-round soloist we had on the band as well as being the right sound and conception for the band on lead. Since the primary sound of the band came from the collective sound of the sax section, it was imperative that the lead tenor express the Herman Four Brothers sound. The other three of us had to match that concept while still retaining our own individuality of sound that would show each of us as unique – which is what the challenge of being in that band and at that level of musicianship was all about. Don was a great teacher, though he said absolutely nothing to me about what or how I was playing; it was there in the way he led the section throughout the entire tour. It becomes clear that your ears are more than an asset: they are an essential ingredient to your very existence. 'If you can't hear it, you can't play it' is more truth than platitude.

The tour with Woody took us all over the east and south-east and into the midwest but we didn't get much further west than Chicago. Chicago turned out to be the second home for all the bands I toured with, inasmuch as we would work out of Chicago throughout the midwest, making forays out for different venues but always returning to Chicago as a home base. Consequently, one became very familiar with Chicago and the Chicago scene, which wasn't a bad deal as Chicago has been, and still is, one of the most vibrant cities in the US, culturally rich and plentiful.

That gave us an opportunity to develop friendships with the Chicago jazz community that would last, for most of us, a lifetime. You would find Chicago musicians moving to New York and New York moving to Chicago for periods of time. Either was acceptable to the other and we all began to realize that the quality of musicianship was quite comparable and, for the most part, interchangeable. Of course, you will find those who feel they have to be provincial in their judgment. Too bad. I like the other perception better. Los Angeles is another city that has had a similar compatibility but it is not as comfortable and familiar as Chicago, for me.

One of the exciting things about being on Woody's band and associating with men at this level of musicianship was the energy and commitment to the music that issued out into the towns and cities where we played. Any time we could, after our concert or dance had finished, we would go out into a local club and set in with the local group. This would frequently be nearly the whole band, since everybody on the band was committed to playing jazz in every form. This did not exclude Woody either. He often would go with us to the local clubs after our gig but he never played. Sometimes we would split up and go to different clubs but that was more often the result of our host's preference or of the young ladies that the guys may have met on the gig. The bottom line here is the musicians on Woody's band found every opportunity to play, in addition to playing as the Woody Herman Orchestra. The purpose of being on this band was not just to make money – and if you knew the salaries most of us got paid, you would really understand that it wasn't for the money.

The tour was great but, as far as I was concerned, way too short. That was another learning and growing time for me and it did much to encourage me to realize that there were white jazz musicians who knew what the music was about and who had respect for and even revered their black mentors. Many of our individual stories had similar scenarios in them. After the all too few weeks had passed, we returned to the Big Apple and I was again unemployed. However, I was as happy as I could be because I was beginning to realize that what I had thought of as only a remote dream and questionable desire was becoming, instead, a real possibility. To be a real, functioning, jazz musician. I'll let others decide the extent and quality of that accomplishment.

I was home for about two days when I got a call from Stan Kenton, who wanted me to join his band that coming weekend in Boston. I had hardly unpacked my suitcase and was already being asked to go right back out with a band that had been one of my teenage dreams and fantasy imaginings. The decision to go or not to go (that is the question) was made almost immediately by both Jo and me, since it meant steady employment and continuing to be a functioning jazz musician with a reputable jazz organization. So I packed my bags and caught a flight to Boston to join the Kenton Orchestra.

The day I arrived was also the first night I played with the band. No preparation for the gig, no rehearsal, not even a peek at the book, just on the bandstand that night. Stan kicked the band off and I was immediately an integral part of the Kenton band.

The most important teacher I found on this band was the alto player Charlie Mariano and, again, I learned from him by example and by having to adapt my playing to his, thereby supporting the way he conceptualized the music and the sax section's responsibility to the music. Charlie was also the most beautiful and commanding soloist in the entire band. I can honestly say that almost every night he would play something so beautiful that chills would run up my spine. This lasted for the remaining year that he spent on the band. Years later,

I was working with Charlie as a part of the Charlie Mingus small band at the Village Vanguard. During one intermission I was having a conversation with Mingus, back in the kitchen of the Vanguard, which was the only place you could go to get off by yourself unless you wanted to go outside on the street. During this conversation Mingus said to me that Mariano was the best blues alto player that had ever been on the stage at the Vanguard since Charlie Parker. He did make that distinction of 'blues' alto player, which left room for Eric Dolphy to still be one of Mingus's favorite alto men. Make no mistake about it, Mingus says only what he means and he did not pass out compliments easily or often.

The Kenton band I joined was an excellent group of musicians. The saxes, in addition to Charlie, were John Bonnie from Philly and Bill Trujillo on tenors with Jack Nimitz and me on baritones. Kenton had been carrying two baritones, two tenors and one alto for a few years by then, which, of course made the sax sound a little heavy on the bottom but that was his choice. I think the first words out of Nimitz's mouth when we were introduced were, 'Were you able to hold the low C♯ on the end of "Early Autumn" without having to take a breath?' Jack had been on Woody's band some years before I got on it and was referring to a chart in the Herman library that demanded a low C♯ on the baritone with a hold on it until the solo tenor finished his cadenza on the end. My answer was an honest no. Jack's reply was, 'I haven't met anybody yet who has.' A very interesting and unique way to begin a relationship, don't you think? Jack and I did become friends immediately but unfortunately our wives took an immediate dislike to each other and as a result, I'm sorry to say, kept Jack and me at a distance for the rest of the time we were on the band together.

Someone once said to me that a road band is not a place for wives and that you are better off if you fly them in for a weekend now and then rather than have them traveling with you regularly. I don't know that I necessarily agree with that view but it certainly applied to the situation that developed around Jack and me. I am happy to report that the distance between us was not terminal. While I was in L.A. on business a few years ago, Jack and I got together for an afternoon at his home and had a very nice visit. We even broached satisfactorily the subject of our former wives. We had both found it necessary to leave our former relationships and had subsequently found new spouses. Jack was one of the most excellent musicians in the band and I admired, and still do, his command of his instruments. If you've ever heard Super Sax you will clearly know what I mean since Jack has been the bottom of that group since its inception.

One of the musicians on the Kenton band at that time who I felt was outstanding was Archie LeCoque on trombone. The choice of gigs he made after he left the Kenton band did not afford him the exposure he needed to garner greater recognition, which I always thought he should have had. Then there was a great trombone man who was on the band for far too short a stay, as far as I was concerned – Jimmy Knepper. I think Jimmy was using the band to get himself to New York and he shortly thereafter became very well-known from his association with the Mingus bands during their years of major impact. He can still be heard with the Mingus Dynasty Band at the date of writing. Bud Brisbois, trumpet, was the high note specialist on the band and of course Stan always had to have one of those. Bud, however, had a faculty for being able to play up there and in tune, which was a rarity in those days. Neither Maynard nor Cat Anderson were all that well in tune up there but, of course, Cat went so high beyond everybody else that it didn't really matter, since only dogs could be critical at that altitude. Duke, at one of his sacred concerts, is recorded as having made the comment, after Cat had worked his way up into the stratosphere, 'We don't get any closer than that', obviously referring to heaven. It was always good to hear Bud putting a top on the trumpet section, and the band as well, that was musically sound and not just a screech. As I quickly learned, this was not the Woody Herman band.

The style of playing required to satisfy Kenton was almost the flip side of Woody's concept. Even with the excellent musicians who were on the band there was no rhythmic groove, which had been so essential to Woody's style. Jack said to me one night before we started a dance job somewhere that I would love the dance book as it was the only time the band got to swing and the charts were fun to play because of it. The rest of the book was Kenton's pseudo-classical/symphonic affected jazz. I came to understand what Jack was saying, with the exception of the Johnny Richards Afro/Cuban charts from the 'Cuban Fire' suite. I found the Richards charts to be some of the best in the entire library at that time. As I said earlier, shortly after I joined the band Jimmy Knepper left, which he had planned to do after we had finished playing Birdland in New York for a week. This was about the second or third week after I joined the band in Boston.

Another story about my introduction to playing on the Kenton band would be very appropriate here. During the first week I was on the band, after playing around Massachusetts for a few days and basically working out of Boston, I began to have chest pains that really hurt. They were bad enough that I became worried about what they might mean for my health. I was telling John Bonnie about this pain and how I was going to have to see a doctor when we got back to Boston. I was seriously afraid that my lungs were collapsing, or worse, that some kind of a heart problem was about to take its toll. My concern was heightened because we were arriving back in Boston on Sunday and I didn't know how I would get hold of a doctor on a Sunday. So I asked John about it. He just laughed, which didn't make me too happy, and said, 'Don't worry about it. Wait a few days and it will go away.' That was not a good answer for me, with the pain I was experiencing, so I said, 'No man. This is serious. My chest hurts and sometimes I'm not sure that I can get enough breath to play.' I could just see my gig coming to an end because of a major illness or, worse, a heart attack that would put me out of the business for who knows how long, just when I was getting off to such a good start.

John stopped laughing and said words to this effect. 'I don't mean to make fun of your discomfort but what I said was true – it will go away in a few days. You see, you have never played this loud before in your life. I went through exactly the same thing when I first came on the band and I thought I was going to die. Your lungs have never had to work so hard to get that much air in them and out again. It's because of the ridiculous volume that this band plays at. You will get used to it and it won't bother you anymore.'

He was absolutely right. By the time we got back to Boston the pain had gone away and never occurred again.

By this time Jack had switched parts with me on a chart on 'Frenesi' which had a baritone solo in it. I really appreciated the offer and the opportunity to show what I could do as a soloist. As it turned out, 'Frenesi' was a good vehicle for me and I suspect that in a small way Jack may have regretted the choice he made because I ate that chart up and began to garner some rather enthusiastic audience response. I'm not sure but it did seem that after that exchange Jack's wife and Jo began having a serious conflict which spilled over into Jack's and my relationship. The only purpose in bringing this up is to show the atmosphere and attitude I found with this band, in contrast to Woody's band, and how that differed from what I had found among the clubs and musical environments I had experienced before coming to New York.

All of a sudden, here I was on a band that I had admired for years as a kid, having realized what had been just a dream. And then to find that I was back in those clubs where the guys were into cliques and attitudes about the other people they were working with. Worst of all was that it carried over onto the bandstand. Of course, there had been guys in Woody's band who clearly had preferences about who their friends and buddies were going to be. That's normal, whenever you get more than two people together in a living situation. But you should never see or feel any of that on the bandstand. You should sense nothing but the love for the music and absolute support for the players in their efforts to be expressive. Woody's band was the blackest white band I ever worked with.

The Kenton band left New York with a new trombone player who had been on Maynard's band, Don Sebesky. His future was going to be very bright because of his great skills as a composer/arranger but he was also one hell of a trombone player. We toured across the US by bus, of course, and many of the men on the bus had their wives with them. Jo was with me, as we were going to make the move to Los Angeles to see if there might be a career for me there, as many men associated with the Kenton Orchestra had done before. As a matter of fact, a great number of the successful studio and recording session musicians in L.A. had come through the Kenton band and subsequently made very good careers for themselves in the music business there. So we were going to seek a similar success for me.

I must interject at this point that traveling with us on this particular trip was our dog, Mr Blue, and our cat, Kitty. To try and make a very long story short, Mr Blue became the band's mascot and his regal self (he used to stop pedestrian traffic on Fifth Avenue in New York), gloried in the attention. However, that was not the case with Kitty. Without going into the gory details, it became imperative that we leave her in Grand Island, Nebraska, as the result of a very disturbing and unpleasant accident on the bus. Here is my opportunity to praise all the men on the band, for as unpleasant as the accident was, the guys were really cool and never, ever brought it up to me or Jo afterwards. After we arrived in L.A. and found a place to live, we were able to send for Kitty, who was shipped from the kennel where we had left her.

On the way to L.A. Charlie Mariano left the band for a few weeks while he went to Las Vegas to get a divorce from his wife from whom he had been separated for a number of years. He had recently found a lady who made him feel the need to be legally available for a future commitment. While Charlie was in Vegas, Stan acquired the services of an alto man, who had been on the band many years before and, in fact, had been on the band when I had seen them in Wichita Falls all those years before. His name was David Schildkraut and he was a joy to play with. He brought a new life to the band just by his musical presence. He wasn't as strong a player as Charlie but he had a great time feel and conception that were immediately a balm for me. I shared with him my appreciation for him and we then talked about his association with Charlie Parker and about the mentors he had had in New York during the great days of jazz on 48th Street and around Broadway and 7th Avenue during the '40s and '50s. Here I was, in school again. What a wonderful two weeks that was.

During the time that Davy was with us the band played the Playboy Jazz Festival in Chicago. It was at this festival that I got to meet Coleman Hawkins, who was getting pretty old by then but who was just as gracious as he could be to a young player he knew nothing about except that he was here to play at this event. His acceptance of me as a fellow jazz musician was just what I had experienced so many times before by so many: they had embraced me just because I was a young, serious, musician who obviously loved the music.

During the Kenton portion of the evening's show Stan decided to do a number from the 'Cuban Fire' suite and, since Charlie was not with us that night, he asked me if I would play the solo on 'La Suerte de Los Tontos', which had been written for alto. It wasn't even a question for me. I said sure, though I had never played it before or even thought about it, how it was formed or what the changes were to support it. It was going to be my ears and the Good Lord! It must have been OK, from the reaction of the crowd and the other musicians around the backstage area. I could never figure out why Stan asked me to play that solo, though I sure did jump at the opportunity.

Shortly after Charlie's return the whole band was invited to the wedding reception of Charlie and Toshiko Akiyoshi at the Hickory House in Chicago. It wasn't long after his marriage that we lost Charlie to their own quartet. Yes! I know that Toshiko is now married to Lew Tabakan and to her music and her orchestra. But she and Charlie were together for a number of years before eventually going in different directions.

After Charlie left, Stan brought Lennie Neihaus back on the band to finish the tour. By the time we got to Vegas, where we stopped only to let Archie LeCoque and Bill Trujillo off the bus, I was very familiar with the peculiarities of the men on the Kenton band. I hated to see Archie and Bill go because I knew that they would not be coming back. They had made it very clear to me that they had no intention whatsoever of going through that experience again.

8

City of Angels

We got ourselves settled in L.A. and I began to look around to see what I could get into there. The first thing I found out was why, if you wanted to do anything in L.A., you had to have a car. The public transportation was at that time horrible to non-existent, particularly late at night. One night I decided I wanted to go to Shelley's Manhole (Shelley Mann's club in Hollywood). It took me nearly two hours to get there from where I lived, which was also in Hollywood; later, after the night was over, I got a ride back to my place with someone who had a car and it took 15 minutes. All my activities were predicated on the availability of a ride from someone who also wanted to go where I wanted to go. You can imagine how often that happened. I'm not really sure but I think it was after another tour with the Kenton band that we were able to purchase a Volkswagen Beetle so that we could move to a different part of town and I could start getting around the area to make contacts for future work.

It was sometime during this stay in town, after that tour, that I was invited by Joe Howard and Frank Beach (remember them from Sonny's in Denver?) to meet them at the Universal Studios in Burbank where they were working that day. They took me around the sound stages and introduced me to more people than I would ever have remembered and then told me that if I would stay in town and not go out, even with Stan, that they would have me on staff at the studios within the year. One of the advantages they thought I had was my ability to double on oboe and English horn, as well as bass clarinet.

I was studying again with the oboist who was then with the Los Angeles Philharmonic and I was practicing to keep my

chops up and hopefully make some progress on my instruments. My teacher was good and didn't insist on my exploring
the classical repertoire since he knew that my interest was in
using the instruments as a double in studio work. The study
exercises that he gave me were to aid in developing the skills
that would address the demands that I might encounter. Joe
and Frank's proposal was a great offer and I seriously
considered the option of not going out with Stan again and
getting into the studios through my connection with them.
They were kind of like the godfathers of the studio scene in
L.A. at the time, so my future would be secure through their
influence.

I spent every night I could trying to find places to play but
it was like being back at Phillips University in Enid, Oklahoma,
or Denver or everywhere else that I have tried to play in the
clubs of the established cats in town. 'Wait until the last set',
'well, not tonight', 'its my gig and the club owner doesn't want
guys setting in' or whatever excuse they found convenient.
So I decided that if I wanted to play I would have to find a
black club or a club that used black musicians to keep that
part of my music alive. I found Dynamite Jackson's Lounge
on West Adams, which is in the Watts area of Los Angeles.
What a surprise for me when I went in there the first time
because, lo and behold, there was Plas Johnson working with
a Latino organ player and a drummer. After introducing
myself to the guys, they invited me up to play. As time went
on I had begun to realize that the music was the most
important thing to me and that playing music was my life, not
making money and becoming a music-making machine –
which is exactly where I figured the studios were or would
become to me if I accepted the offer.

My heart kept saying, 'Get back to New York, to where you
know the music is and you also know how to operate. This L.A.
scene will do you in if you don't.' Everything happened in
somebody's backyard with a swimming pool or at a barbecue
out at Balboa at a beach house with the yacht tied up at your
dock – like at Joe Howard's place, where he invited Jo and
me to spend a weekend. For whatever reason, Jo just could not

bring herself to go there for that weekend and I would not go without her, so it became the beginning of the end of our stay in L.A. I don't think I would have gone along on the deal with Joe on joining the studios because by that time I was sick to death of what I felt was an L.A. attitude. That was not what I had come to believe music was about and certainly not what my many mentors had instilled in me through their affection and appreciation. So when Stan went out again, I went with him to work our way back to New York City – Jo, Mr Blue, Kitty and me, with all our luggage and my horns in a Volkswagen following the bus across the country.

There were some good times with the Kenton band, just as there were the not-so-good times, so to be fair to this account of my experiences they should be identified. One of the tours with the band, after time off in L.A., was through the midwest; the culmination of the trip was a short tour of Mexico. For the most part it was a new band: as I indicated, all the really good players jumped ship as soon as they could, either on various locations around the country or after getting back to L.A. This included the only man I ever had as a roommate on the band. Having a roommate saved you a little money since we all had to pay for our own lodging and food. That's also different from today: now it is expected that those things will be taken care of by the leader.

Picking a roommate requires that you find someone with whom you feel a real compatibility. I was more inclined to want to be by myself when I could. I saw enough of the guys on the bandstand and on the bus, so when I had a chance to get off by myself at a hotel, I cherished those few hours. Consequently, for me to even consider a roommate, that compatibility had to be real. The one man I knew on the Kenton band during my stay with whom I found myself to be compatible was Don Sebesky. We had similar responses to the music and had the same priorities about what the important elements to successful representation of the music were. Also, we were both married (I knew his wife from my days on the Dorsey band; she was one of the singers.) We weren't into the womanizing that was rampant among most of the band. This meant we didn't always have to worry about wanting to go to bed and finding that our roommate was occupied in the room, forcing us to hang around the lobby until he was finished with his 'conversation'. Our love for the music generally filled our conversations during the time we spent in our room. Or one of us would be on the phone to his wife.

Sebesky and I must have become roommates . . . right after we arrived in L.A.? . . . but I can't remember how this came about. I do know that Sebesky was on the band during our move to L.A. because he was sitting in the seat right behind us on the bus and took the brunt of our cat's accident. He was just as sweet as he could be about it. So it had to be after that. Or it was when we were still working around the east coast before we headed out to the west. That seems likely because I know that Sebesky had said thanks but no thanks to Stanley, shortly after we arrived in L.A. He also had written some great charts for the band, one of which was a beautiful showcase for Charlie entitled simply 'Mariano'. Now that I think about it, Charlie was sitting in the seat just in front of us on the bus that fateful night. Don was also on the band when we recorded 'Mexican Jumping Bean' and 'Standards in Silhouette' and those sessions took place in New York and Atlantic City before we headed west. That had to be the sequence because sometime during the New York area days Bill Chase and the drummer Jimmy Campbell, who had been on Woody's band with me, joined Stan as well before we headed west.

Well, that gives you a glimpse into the convoluted mind of Marvin 'Doc' Holladay, previously known as Marv Holladay. It sometimes is very strange living in here. Now I remember. It was during the 'Road Show' tour, which Stan had put together in L.A., with the Four Freshman and June Christy. It was on the return from that tour that everybody jumped ship. I shared a room during that tour with Don Sebesky.

Return to the tour of the midwest and Mexico. As I said, the only remaining members of the band for this tour were Bud Brisbois, Jim Amlotte, Dalton Smith and, I think, Bobby Knight. Two trumpets, two bass trombones and me. Gabe Baltazar joined us on the alto chair as well as two new tenor men and another baritone player, so I was the only returning member of the sax section from the old band. The rhythm section was all new except, now that I remember, the bass player, Peter Chivily, who had also joined us in New York. One situation stands out in my recollection of Pete and that was the time when his calluses all came off his fingers and he had to play using other fingers entirely until his calluses grew back. What a sight to see! Those big holes in his finger tips. The bass players in those days did not have amplification and consequently had to produce a sound big enough to anchor the rhythm section of the band. To get that kind of sound out of an acoustic instrument meant that the quality of the instrument was essential. It also meant that you had to work at producing the sound by pulling the strings with a great deal more force than bass players do today and still lock into that rhythmical pocket. That is what separates the Ray Browns and Ron Carters from all the rest as far as the pocket is concerned.

The band itself was pretty good and above all seemed to want to play with as much feel as it could generate with the charts we were playing. Which meant we were trying very hard to find a groove for each piece, so that it would swing. Whenever we would start to groove, the next time we played that chart Stan would kick off the chart with a faster tempo to get the edge that he wanted back. He could not feel comfortable with a groove of any kind. That might be why his best musical renderings were the Afro/Cuban charts we would play. There was nothing he could do, and since he had no way of altering that kind of a groove, it stayed. If he tried to play them too fast the chart would simply fall apart because of the complexity of Johnny Richards's writing.

To make another long story short, Stan didn't care much for that band, which put us in company with the best bands Stan Kenton ever had. I asked Stanley one night what he thought of his '51 and '53 bands – the '53 band was the one I had heard in Wichita Falls. Stan's reply was that they were OK but not the bands he liked the most. The '53 band had possibly the best complement of jazz players that Stan Kenton ever assembled but he didn't like them.

There is a story to go with the '51 band which included Zoot Sims on tenor and other really good jazz players who went on to acclaimed careers. The story goes that Zoot reportedly told Stan one night while Stan was waving his arms, as usual, in front of Zoot's stand, to go away and quit waving his hands, that the band would take care of the music.

The tour of Mexico, however, was a delight for the guys in the band and the people really liked what they heard from us. That was apparent everywhere we went, so we just enjoyed the response instead of worrying about whether Stan was upset or not. Let me give some credit here to Stanley because even though he didn't like the band, he did not get hot about it like some band leaders did. (Oh! The stories that abound around Buddy Rich.) Rather he would voice his displeasure but resign himself to the inevitable. The exception was when he found a few of the new guys smoking pot. Then Stanley did go off on them, threatening to send them back to L.A. immediately and all that. Even though the use of pot had been prevalent on the band all the time I was on it, the older cats were much more discreet and it went unnoticed or undiscovered. Stan was very jealous of his own image and having guys on his band caught doing something illegal like smoking pot was something that he could not tolerate. All of this is to Stan's credit except that he cared more for his image than he did about the integrity of the music.

If he had been able to justify his musical priorities from a sound musicological foundation, he might have got what he wanted. The problem was that he continued to promote the band as a jazz orchestra without any accommodation of the basic roots of the idiom. Had he promoted the orchestra as a symphonic orchestra incorporating elements of the jazz tradition, he could have realized his vision. In fact, he had one such orchestra back in the late '40s, with a complete string section, French horns, tuba, some double reeds, etc. as well as the instrumentation of the jazz orchestra. It truly fulfilled Stan's ideal, in my opinion. It was too bad that he couldn't afford to keep that orchestra functioning, as it was his most successful venture. You could accurately say that Stan was a frustrated symphony conductor without any credentials to fulfill his quest.

There was one other mistake Stan made during the height of his popularity in the business. Stan decided that he didn't need Joe Glaser anymore. Joe Glaser was the man who had managed the band and built its fame throughout the world. Stan felt that he was so big that he could do it himself. That was the beginning of his decline, gradual as it was, and I'm happy to say that I got in on the tail end of that good era and therefore enjoyed the remnants of what had once been. But then I watched the rapid decline.

Stanley and I had had many discussions about the importance of TIME and the groove that would be realized from this as an essential ingredient of any good jazz band – my position. His position was that TIME and the resultant groove had nothing to do with jazz, that it was sound and the building of sheets of sound that were the important ingredients. These discussions would go on for hours and, unfortunately, usually in the back corner of a bar somewhere with Stan blasted and me in no pain. I really didn't like booze but shared in its abuse from time to time. You can well imagine the lunacy of two characters, neither in his right mind, trying to convince the other that his position on the subject had to be validated by the other person. Pointless, but very humorous if you were watching, I would imagine. Stan was simply dead set against a groove and would destroy it every time it would rear its head.

The quest to convert each other came to an abrupt halt one night on the bus, with all of us stone cold sober. We were on a different tour, which I can only identify as the next to the last one I ever took with the band. I do remember that Sam Donahue was on the band, a tenor sax man who had been reasonably active in jazz circles around the country out of, I think, Detroit. The subject again was time, groove and swing as it applied to jazz and jazz performance. Since the discussion – argument really – was not going anywhere constructive or towards any real conclusion, I said, 'I suppose you're going to tell me that the Basie band don't swing.' To my amazement, the reply was, 'Yes! it never swung and besides it was nothing but a nursery rhyme band that didn't play anything more musically demanding than that.' Well folks, that ended the conversation and I knew that it was time to go back to New York City. There would never, ever be a time that this band would play with the integrity of the basic essence in which this music is rooted. I knew at that very moment that the next tour out of L.A. would be my passage back to the Apple and whatever might lie in wait for me there. I was going home.

When we played Guadalajara, Mexico, a group of Mexican musicians came to the concert and wanted me to hang out with them afterwards. Since I had decided, with a few other guys on the band, to stay overnight in Guadalajara and catch a flight to Mexico City the next day instead of riding the bus all night through the mountains, I said sure. We must have hit every joint in town that had any music and much of it was very good and surprisingly varied. The musicians just wanted to show me what was going on musically in their city, not impress me with their version of American jazz. I had a ball. Of course, they wanted me to see some very beautiful Mexican ladies who were in their city, which we did in multiples. Now I did say 'see'. Remember that. After we had used up the clubs and closed them all down we went to a corner café to get something to eat. After taking our seats they offered me some peppers as an appetizer. While they were watching with that gleeful look in their eye, I began to eat the jalapeños that were offered with gusto. I'm sure that they were disappointed – I had been eating jalapeños for years and they have some real Mexican restaurants in L.A. I have a picture of all of us at one of the clubs which I still cherish as a memento of my visit to Guadalajara.

We played two concerts in Mexico City, one at the National Auditorium and the other at the Belles Artes, which was the prestigious concert venue in the city and the home of the Mexican National Symphony. The acoustics at the Belles Artes were comparable to the acoustics at Carnegie Hall. It's my understanding that the concert was recorded by a Mexican recording company. After our return to L.A. I tried to locate the company but I could never find it or get any information about it. I'm sorry I couldn't find it because I played one of my best performances of the tour that night and would love to have had a recording of that evening's concert.

Stan had begun to present me as a featured soloist and one of the showcase charts that I did most often was an arrangement by Bill Holman on 'Stella by Starlight'. Holman had originally written this chart, I think, for Lee Konitz and I had played it many times with Charlie Mariano as the soloist. I played 'Stella' that night as well as I ever had and experienced that rare event when you play to your own satisfaction. Most of the time you are disappointed with your playing or are hypercritical of what you have done. That's par for the course for most musicians I've found. Roy Eldridge was reported to have answered a question posed to him in his later years: 'What keeps you playing at your age?' He replied, 'That one night a year when it all happens.' I know what he meant. I received many glowing reviews of my playing with Kenton from place to place and you usually don't pay much attention to them and shouldn't, either, whether good or bad. If you start to believe your press you can end up going one of two ways, neither of which is going to do you any good.

The overall feeling I had about the Mexican tour was that here was a band that could really become a positive example of what could be done with the Kenton library. The next time the band was put together we had a whole new complement of musicians, with the exception of Gabe Baltazar and myself and a few of the others who had sort of made the Kenton band their musical careers, like Jim Amlotte.

Before I finish with this segment on Kenton I have a couple of stories to share that should help put the whole experience in perspective, if the others weren't enough. The tour before we headed back for New York brought a new trumpet player on the band out of North Texas State University in Denton, Marvin Stamm, a brilliant young player and a committed student of the music. His favorite band at that time was the Ray Charles band. I made reference to the quality of this band earlier in this treatise. Even before Marv came on the band I had been talking to Stan about me doing an album under the auspices of his 'Kenton Presents' series on Capitol records. He agreed that it was probably about time for me to do that. I contacted Don Sebesky, who had left us long before, and we chose tunes for him to arrange or compositions of his own that he might like to contribute to an album. It would be Marv Stamm and myself as the front line for the group. The title of the album, I thought, would be appropriate for release that year. Mickey Mantle and Roger Maris were chasing each other for who was going to be the home run king for that season. Hence the title, *The M & M Boys*, for Marv and Marv. Corny, maybe, but it would probably have marketed well anyhow.

Sebesky sent the charts and Stamm and I began to work on them whenever we could. We were out every night of the tour playing somewhere together. Sometimes it was just him and me in some room or club. We were beginning to develop a level of communication, musically, that was almost at a level of ESP. We could pretty well play in each other's heads at any time and in any environment. We were ready! So what happens? We're on our way into L.A. at the end of the tour and as we reach the outskirts of the city Stan calls me up to the front of the bus. He then informs me that he has changed his mind about the date of the recording and would like me to spend another year with him to get a little more seasoning.

I hadn't planned on staying with the band anyhow but this was just another incident that further confirmed my decision to return to New York and get off this band which had been such a great disappointment in every aspect of this music. Then take into account the social consciousness that kept showing up: bigotry, jealousies, overt racism, back stabbing, petty bickering. And to top it off, Stan's need to have every boy on the band look to him as the great counselor. I couldn't get away quickly enough. It was truly one of the unhealthiest environments, musically and personally, that I had ever experienced.

The highlight of the tour on the way back to New York was a three-week package tour, with the Basie band and the Kenton band splitting the evening's bill in venues around the midwest and northeast. Jo and I, with our animals, traveled in our own car on this tour. We spent more time during those three weeks with the Basie band than we did the Kenton band, except at our lodging, as we were booked into a hotel as a part of the Kenton band. I still feel that the Basie band of those years was quite possibly the best band in its history. It is hard not to say the same thing about the band with Lester Young and Herschel Evans. That's the problem with a band of this historical greatness. I'm just happy that the Basie band was always the closing act of the package because that band blew us away, night after night after night. Only a deaf person would not have noticed that the charts the Basie band was playing were as complex and demanding technically as anything the Kenton band played. I know that Stan kept searching his library, trying to find some chart that would show us in a comparable light. Let me leave that alone – you've already heard all about it.

That Basie band had Marshall Royal and Frank Wess on altos, Frank Foster and Billy Mitchell on tenors and Charlie Fowlkes on baritone. Snooky Young (the greatest lead trumpet player I ever heard or worked with), Thad Jones, Joe Newman and Sonny Cohen made up the trumpet section. Al Grey and Henry Coker were on tenor trombones with Benny Powell on bass trombone. Sonny Payne, drums; Eddie Davis, bass; the 'Rock' Freddie Green on guitar; and his eminence Mr Basie on piano made up the rhythm section. The band featured the vocals of Joe Williams. That was one heavy-duty roster of musicians and, despite what my fellow Kentonians thought, one smokin', groove makin' band. With all the names that have entered the annals of history who were part of that band, how many of the Kenton band of those years can anybody remember? Maybe Gabe Baltazar, who deserves every accolade that comes his way. Beyond that, forget it. Nonentities all, except Stan.

As a result of that three-week tour I have enjoyed a lasting friendship with many of the Basie band members and still do with those who are yet with us. The last night of our package tour with the Basie band I experienced what was the most satisfying, yet unbelievable and humbling happenstance that I have had to this day. The concert was at some midwest university. After the Basie band finished its last tune of the night, everybody, including us, came back on stage to receive the appreciation of the audience. We went back to our dressing-room, which was a locker-room, since the concert had been held in the gym. We were putting our equipment up and changing clothes when the Basie band's road manager came into our dressing room – this had never happened at any time during the three weeks – and asked the first person he met where the baritone player was who had played 'Stella by Starlight' each night on the tour.

They pointed me out to him and he came over to tell me that the Count wanted to speak to me. Whereupon he left the room, came back in with Basie and walked directly to where I was standing. Basie walked up to me and stuck out his hand to shake mine. I was dumbstruck. He then proceeded to tell me, in his gravelly voice and in his characteristically few words, how much he and the guys on the band had enjoyed my playing every night. He said that his guys would come to the gig early just so they could listen to me playing 'Stella' and that after I finished they would all go to their dressing room to get ready for their turn to go on. I can't tell you what my response was. I was so overwhelmed that if I said as much as thanks, I can't remember because it was too dream-like. I can say that the smile I had on my face will probably be there when I die.

One other engagement does stand out. It was towards the end of that tour at a concert scheduled for Carnegie Hall in New York City. When my feature of 'Stella by Starlight' came up I played it as usual and felt really good about it; I was home and in Carnegie Hall. I brought the chart to the ending where I was to play a cadenza which was to be followed by the last chord by the band and which I was to cut off by bringing my horn down. Only this time, when I got into the cadenza, I could feel the warmth of the crowd – my people, New Yorkers, who know jazz and appreciate the exponents of that idiom. So, after I had done all my cadenza type stuff I got into a blues groove with the audience, just them and me, and when they started to clap in time with the groove I was playing, we went for it. Stan was going crazy on the side, off-stage, and I could feel him walk on, then walk back off, then back on and back off again. The audience and I were having a ball. I finally began to feel that Stan might have a heart attack or something and thought I'd better bring this to a stop. So with another flourish of stuff I brought the band in on the last chord and did a couple more flourishes and cut the band off. The crowd went bananas and poor Stan didn't know how to react, which was cool with me. For that one moment I was able to show him just what I had been arguing about with him for those two-and-a-half years I was on his band. He never knew.

9

The Big Apple Again

Quincy Jones! I had been back in New York for a week or two when I got a call to make a recording session with Quincy Jones, for some kind of jazz station breaks for a radio network somewhere in the country – nothing big musically. He was putting together essentially the same band that he had used in Europe with the Free and Easy show but since Shahib Shahab had gone to Sweden or Denmark, someplace up there, and Pat Patrick was back in Chicago working with Sun Ra, they needed a baritone player and I got the call. This was the beginning of a new, richly-rewarding, nurturing, spirit-restoring and musically wholesome return to my musical roots.

I was like a kid in a candy store at that recording session. Jerome Richardson and I were having so much fun and enjoying what we were doing that Q said to us, between takes, that we ought to pay him for this gig since we were having such a good time. It was, of course, in jest. If there is anybody who has fostered that kind of joyful appreciation for what this music brings to us as purveyors of it, it is Quincy. That band was like being with one great big family, whose love and respect for each other knew no bounds. We were all related by a common bond and that bond was the ability and desire to express this music with all the depth of its joy and meaning. When you put 17 people together with that strength of commitment to a common goal and sprinkle in their love and respect for one another as one family, you've got an untouch-able, unbelievable and unstoppable force of energy that will sweep away any obstacle, difficulty or shortcoming it may encounter. The audience is the recipient of this unity – it impacts on them through the music. I'm not referring to the high voltage adrenaline rush that comes during a contemporary pop music concert but rather the warm nurturing and uplifting of the spirit as you allow the music to embrace the depth of your being in contemplation. I will, in a later chapter, discuss more completely the power of music.

Q's band did several isolated gigs around the New York area and made short tours along the eastern seaboard, some of which I will tell you about. We did a number of benefit concerts for SNCC and other civil rights organizations during that time. One I will not forget anytime soon. It took place at the home of Jackie Robinson up in Westchester County. Having been a baseball player as a kid, you can well imagine the interest I had in being in Jackie Robinson's home. We actually played under a tent outside by a pond in what would normally be identified as a backyard but there seemed to be no end to it. During our breaks I would go into the house and admire Jackie's trophy case, which pretty well filled up the whole room – I was told that there were more trophies that were not on display at that time. For an ex-young ball player they were fascinating to view. On top of that, I had been a teenager when he and the Brooklyn Dodgers had broken the color barrier in professional baseball.

This family of musicians who made up, at that time, the Quincy Jones Orchestra included Phil Woods and Jerome Richardson, altos; Budd Johnson or Billy Mitchell and Bennie Golson, tenors; me on baritone; Snooky Young, Joe Newman, Bill Berry and Clark Terry or Richard Williams or Donald Byrd or many others as a sort of turnstile chair, trumpets; Jimmy Cleveland, Quentin Jackson (aka 'Butter'), Billy Byers and Melba Liston, trombones; The Phantom (Julius Watkins) on French horn; and a rhythm section of Patti Bown, piano; Martin Rivera, bass; Mickey Roker followed by Grady Tate, drums. I know that while the band was in Europe with the Free and Easy show they had used Les Spann on guitar but there was no guitar used while I was on the band. At this concert at the Robinson home, Wes Montgomery and his group were playing as well, so for that day we would occasionally have a guitar player and with that addition we truly had a dream band.

Every musician on the band was not only a good musician but an exceptional soloist as well. Not a weak link anywhere and even I could hold my own, though when it came to the likes of Phil Woods, Benny Golson, Clark Terry, Jimmy Cleveland, etc. I was not in that league. But I wasn't an embarrassment either and I got my 'turn in the barrel' along with everyone else. From the Quincy Jones band on, every band I have played on has been made up of jazz players, all of whom could play their ***s off. By the way, this was also true of Woody's band. Everyone on the band could play and play well. All of the other bands I had worked with up 'til then had had a specific soloist who played the solos while most of the rest of the musicians were section players with no ability to play jazz, or at the very best, could do so only moderately. The great jazz bands of history – Fletcher Henderson, Chick Webb, Bennie Moten, Benny Carter, Duke Ellington, Count Basie, Jimmie Lunceford, Dizzy Gillespie, Earl 'Fatha' Hines, Billy Eckstine, Lucky Millander, Don Redman and on and on – were bands full of jazz players all capable of going down front and playing. True enough, these were also bands whose members were either all or predominantly African–American. But then again, that is the jazz tradition and these were some of that tradition's greatest exponents. The best white jazz bands of that period – Benny Goodman, Artie Shaw, the Casa Loma band (in a later chapter I will relate a story about this to you from Taft Jordan of the Chick Webb band) and Stan Kenton – followed the dance band format.

Quincy did another benefit for – I think it was SNCC again but I'm not sure – a civil rights organization unquestionably, at Carnegie Hall, which was only the second time I'd played in that hallowed hall. The first, you may recall, was with Kenton and was my swan song with that organization.

Q did some gigs around New York with the band and we made a couple of runs to Philly and Baltimore before we went with the Billy Eckstine show to Washington DC. I will never forget the concert in Baltimore, for a variety of reasons, only one of which was the backing of Dinah Washington, who absolutely loved the band and had more than a passing interest in Q, to his obvious discomfort. That was worth the trip all by itself, as Q was always the ladies' man and had every situation well under control. But Dinah put it on him so heavy that for once Q didn't know how to handle the situation at all. Suddenly Q was like a teenage kid trying to cope with a mature and very sophisticated woman, who was just wrapping him up. His suave, debonair, man of the world persona simply vanished under Dinah's dynamic and straight forward manner. Dinah Washington was somethin' else!

That night our drummer, Mickey Roker, couldn't get to the gig for some reason – I don't think I ever knew what – but the end result was that Quincy had to find a drummer in Baltimore. Through the Musicians' Union, either in Baltimore or DC, I'm not sure which, he was able to find a drummer. When the time came for the rehearsal that afternoon this young, good-looking man showed up to fill the chair of possibly the best big band drummer around at that time. He was quiet and rather self-effacing and I know that some of the guys weren't too sure he was going to be able to cut it and I'm sure he didn't either. He set up his drums and as we were getting ready to start the rehearsal many of the guys told him not to worry, that they would cover him and help him if he needed it – all with the good intention of making him feel a bit more at ease. Quincy called the first tune and kicked it off, when POW! This young drummer nailed the time, the chart and everything else and literally set the band on fire. From that first tune on, the band, to a person, shouted encouragement to him while we were playing. That was how Quincy Jones found Grady Tate! After the concert that night, Quincy told Grady to pack his bags and come to New York, that he had a gig with Quincy from that moment on. Which, of course, he did and the rest is history.

The third event of that gig in Baltimore was more personal and had to do with the love and family feeling that was so pervasive on that band. Ole' Dude [Budd Johnson] loved his booze, like many other musicians I've known, but didn't always handle it too well. In Dude's case it was exacerbated by his American Indian ancestry mixed in with his African–American ancestry. The American Indian, or so I've been told, has a fairly low tolerance for liquor. If that's true, that is another whole book, exposing the use of alcohol to undermine a people in this country.

After the concert we were taken to a restaurant lounge in the black area of the city to eat, relax and unwind from the concert. The host was very hospitable and generous to us all and we had excellent steak dinners with all the trimmings and, of course, all we wanted to drink. Well, by then I was finding liquor less and less appealing and pretty well restricted my consumption of alcohol to beer and wine and then mostly in a social context. My drinking on the Kenton band had an entirely different motivation usually. That particular night in Baltimore, I really didn't want anything to drink. I was exhilarated from the music we had just played and didn't feel a desire to lose that feeling to booze, so I just sat back and enjoyed the atmosphere and the camaraderie with everybody in the band and our host community.

By the time the band was beginning to gradually filter out to the bus, Ole' Dude decided that he and I should go over to this corner coffee shop and integrate the place – this was sometime in '62 or '63. That area of Baltimore was not too welcoming for a white man, even if he was with a black man but certainly not if he was with an intoxicated black man. I tried my best to persuade Budd to pass on the idea but he was far enough along that he not only didn't care but wanted to show everybody that there were white folks who were cool and I was going to be his example. You do not stop Budd Johnson from doing anything once his mind is focused on it, so I agreed – there was no other choice – to go with him to get a cup of coffee. He could use the coffee anyhow. Besides, he needed someone with him under those circumstances. Well, I don't remember too many times in my life when I felt as vulnerable and in the wrong place as I did in that coffee shop. There wasn't a friendly face in the whole joint and when Ole' Dude started telling everybody what he was doing and that I was the one he was going to do it with, I truly feared for our safety. Thank God, there was a black policeman setting in the coffee shop at that moment who saw what was taking place and though he wasn't any more happy about us being there than the rest were, his presence kept everything under control. We finished our coffee and I was able to convince Budd that we had to get back to the bus right away before it left for New York. Getting out of that coffee shop without incident was one of the greatest reliefs of my life. Whenever we looked back on that occasion, we shared a great laugh about it; however, while it was taking place, I was truly in a sweat.

The bus ride back to New York was also one to remember. For one, Cleve (Jimmy Cleveland) and Ole' Dude were standing toe to toe in the middle of the aisle of the bus, each just as out of it as the other, arguing over some insignificant issue that no one remembers but both with the necessary amount of alcohol to be totally unintelligible. It was funny, as neither one of them would actually start anything because they loved each other too much but that didn't diminish the volume or the intensity of the argument. The rest of us sat back and enjoyed the drama which came to a close when another discussion of a more serious nature unfolded which finally penetrated their consciousness.

Melba Liston was a sweet, kind and compassionate person, one of two women on the band, the other being Patti Bown. Melba was going through a very difficult time with her husband, soon to be ex-husband. As I said, the seriousness of the discussion about that cut through to Cleve and Ole' Dude and their spat came to a halt, their attention being directed to Melba, as was that of many others. It became a family affair where everybody converged on the one member who was in anguish. She was surrounded by her brothers and sister comforting and counseling her. Patti was a very strong lady and very independent and could, and still can, hold her own with anybody or anything that comes her way. Which is not to say that she didn't need or want care and nurturing but rather that if it was necessary she could, and would, take care of business. Melba on the other hand was very sensitive and sweet to the point of self-sacrifice and consequently set herself up for injury and abuse emotionally by those she opened herself to. Her old man did a number on her during their years together by manipulating her psyche through what we came to perceive to be his jealousy of the respect and admiration she attracted and her ascendancy in the musical world. He was an educator with a PhD and felt that what she did was of little or no importance in comparison to his stature in the community and berated her with it.

While the band was on tour with Free and Easy, Melba had 15 big brothers at all times whether she wanted them or not. (This obviously was a story conveyed to me since I wasn't a part of the band then.) Consequently, should some dude outside the band decide he was going to try and hook up with Melba after the gig, and Melba was not particularly interested, the dude would have to go through all 15 men on the band to get to her. A rather safe and secure place to be for a lady. On the other hand, if she found a dude that interested her, he had better do right by her or again he would have 15 big brothers to contend with. It's interesting, now that I think of it, as that was never the attitude towards Patti, primarily because of her strength of character and personality. Any fool who wanted to mess with Patti had best come prepared to cope or find the nearest exit. Assertive was not just a word for Patti Bown.

There is one more story about Melba Liston. We were backing Ella Fitzgerald at Basin Street East. That was always joyful because the music was so good and the band could swing as hard as we wanted to. If there was anything required when backing Ella it was for the band to swing, as that was her thing. The band was most certainly up to the challenge as it was composed primarily of musicians from the Quincy Jones Orchestra. The first couple of nights of any show the band would always be at its best. And since this was Ella, it was smokin'. But as the week went on we would kind of relax into a comfortable groove. The audience would still categorize this as smokin' but obviously there was a slight difference between us in this regard.

We were well into the gig, probably the second week, when one night POW! The band lit up like it was the first night and we were poppin'. We all began to look at each other, wondering what had happened, and then we discovered that the difference was Melba Liston, who was subbing for Henderson Chambers on the third trombone chair. She had lit up the entire band from that chair. We knew that she was there as a sub for Mr Chambers but didn't pay much mind to that, as having a sub from time to time was rather usual, as I have said before.

I think the trombone section on that gig was Quentin Jackson, Britt Woodman and Mr Chambers. The infusion of renewed energy and vitality into that evening's performance was recognized by the entire band and was the stuff of which legends are made. That such an influence might come from a first or lead part could be imagined but to have it come from the third part of the trombone section was startling. However, it was characteristic of the musical presence of Melba Liston. She was special.

By the way, everybody called Henderson Chambers 'Mr Chambers' because of his extreme dignity and decorum. One never heard an expletive or even a negative word from him. He was truly a unique figure in that world.

One of the most memorable tours with the Quincy Jones band for me was our tour with the Billy Eckstine show. Dig this line-up: Billy Eckstine as the star with Redd Foxx, comedian, and the dance team of Coles and Atkins (Honi Coles and Charlie Atkins), all accompanied by the Quincy Jones Orchestra. At this time Honi was the manager of the Apollo Theatre and Charlie had one of the most successful dance studios in Harlem and was responsible for the choreography of many of the famous groups to come out of the Detroit 'Motown' scene. Neither had danced on stage in years since both had retired from active performance. Honi wasn't dancing at all and Charlie's dancing was pretty well limited to setting examples in his studio. Quincy and Eckstine talked them both into putting their old dance act together just for this one tour, which was only going to be the Howard Theatre in Washington DC and the Apollo in Harlem. Somehow or another Q and Billy were successful in their efforts.

We rehearsed the show in the basement of the Apollo before taking the show to the Howard in DC. Those rehearsals were a ball and watching Honi and Charlie put their dance act together was an experience I won't forget. They were so professional and smooth, each would say, 'Hey! I'll do *** and then you do *** and then we can do *** together and follow that with ***.' You get the picture. By the second rehearsal you'd have sworn that that was all they had been doing for years, and in a sense, that actually was true.

I believe that they were the highlight of every show we did. Redd was possibly the funniest man I have ever been around and, if you can imagine, even funnier outside the show. It would get so bad on the bus that the band would beg him to shut up so we could survive. My stomach would hurt to the point of being painful and the funniest part about it was that he wasn't particularly raunchy, as was his stage show. Sometimes I wonder if that raunchy reputation was more for the entrepreneurs than his own personal sense of humor. Eckstine's voice was beginning to go, even though he was still a consummate entertainer and showman. He really didn't sound so good anymore and it got worse as the show ran on, partially because he ran with the 'old gang' in DC and New York, more notably in New York, hanging out for old times' sake and all that that usually entails. As a result he went steadily down from there.

The band, on the other hand, was dynamite and had plenty of spots during the show to do its thing. One of those spots was an Al Cohn chart on 'Air Mail Special', an old tune which really showcased the saxophone section and was at a tempo that you could not count. Each man in the section would have a 16–bar piece of a chorus to play and we'd work it right down the section, each one going down to the microphone. It went as follows: Billy Mitchell, tenor; Jerome Richardson, alto; Phil Woods, alto; Bennie Golson, tenor; to me and back again to Phil for another 16 and immediately into a sax soli that was a smoker, with all of us down front on the microphone. The soli was unreal but laid so well under your fingers that it almost played itself. More accolades for Al Cohn who I don't think ever got the recognition of his musical genius that he deserved, except among the musicians who knew him. We would come out of the soli and go into the out chorus with the rest of the band. We had a little choreography that we added to our sax line, down front, which set the crowds off and brought the chart to its climax.

There was plenty of space in the other charts that we would do that showcased all the great soloists on the band and gave plenty of opportunity for the band to show its wares during each show. This was in quite a contrast to most shows that we would work and most artists who we might be called upon to back. That was a major advantage to doing a Billy Eckstine show. He was the leader of one of the most influential jazz bands of the early bebop days and had that kind of love and appreciation for the men he was working with.

The Quincy Jones band was possibly the most fun band I have ever worked with and I've already described the family relationship that existed there. Musically the charts were so well written that the apparently difficult charts were not hard to play technically and yet the content of the music was superior and the musicianship on the band was stellar in every department. The writing skills of Billy Byers, Al Cohn, Melba Liston and Bennie Golson as well as Quincy were incredible and were the source of the greatness of the band's sound. These charts should be in the repertoire of all jazz repertory orchestras that are preserving classical American jazz art music, along with those of Duke Ellington, Fletcher Henderson, Jimmie Lunceford, Benny Goodman, Chick Webb, etc.

The personnel of the Quincy Jones Orchestra became the nucleus for a variety of orchestras on the New York scene and were probably the hottest group of musicians on the recording circuit around town. One of the mainstays for us was Basin Street East on East 48th. It would contract bands for each show that came into the club rather than have a set house band that would play each show. This gave the band a new look for each show and created a vitality that was always fresh and new. The guys who would usually get called for the gigs were members of what had been the Quincy Jones Orchestra. So it was like old home week whenever you went to work at Basin Street East, with a few new faces added to fill out the roster as needed. This offered me an opportunity to get to know such musicians as Danny Stiles, Jerry Dodgion, Seldon Powell, Britt Woodman (I actually worked once with Britt on the Ellington Alumni band, that story yet to come), Garnett Brown, Donald Byrd and other new faces. In addition to coming together for these gigs, these musicians also became the nucleus of the Thad Jones–Mel Lewis Orchestra. That orchestra went on to become the most dominant musical force in big bands during the '60s and '70s. More about that band later, as it deserves at least a chapter of its own.

During those years in New York there was, I think, a beer company, maybe Schaeffer, I don't remember, it could have been anybody, who sponsored the Jazzmobile. A group of us would travel by trailer through Harlem playing and drawing a crowd to a park or a recreational area where a stage of sorts would have been set up for the full band to play a concert. This was done throughout the summer with various jazz orchestras performing for the event. The most frequent association I had on the Jazzmobile was with the Frank Foster Orchestra which provided the only opportunity I had, during those years, to play with Howard Johnson (tuba/baritone sax player, probably best known as a tuba player). Frank's arrangements often had the tuba part (Howard) and the baritone sax part (me) playing together in a line contrasting the rest of the band, which gave us an opportunity to express that line rather emphatically, which we did, with gusto! Howard was a bit of a character, which I found enjoyable.

Howard had a couple of occasions to get some on-camera exposure in a commercial or two, one of which had him playing his baritone sax to advertise something. Fos' (Frank's more familiar shortened nickname) was an incredible arranger and composer and another Ellington-influenced creator. It seems that most everybody I worked with fit that category in one way or another. You would probably be more familiar with the work he did for the Basie band in those years I've expressed great admiration for, the one I describe in association with my sojourn with the Kenton Elephant Horde. 'Blues in Hoss'es Flat', 'Shiny Stockings' and 'Down for the Count' were just a few of many great charts that Fos' contributed to that organization. Between Fos', Thad Jones and Ernie Wilkins, the Basie band of those years had exceptional material to work with. My particular favorite was a chart Fos' called 'Disapproachment', which Basie seldom played but was recorded later by the Duke Pierson Orchestra. I had the privilege of subbing for Pepper Adams one night at the Vanguard with Duke after I had left New York and gone back to graduate school in Connecticut. More on that later. 'Disapproachment' was the chart that I frequently used to challenge my student ensemble when they began to feel like they had achieved an advanced level of performance skills. It was always a quick way of bringing them back to reality.

During those years, before Basin Street East closed its doors, we played some of the great acts and artists of the day and certainly some more than once: Ella Fitzgerald, Sarah Vaughan, Tony Bennett, Peggy Lee, Dionne Warwick, Vickie Carr, Buddy Greco, Chris Conners, Damita Jo, Don Ellis, Gerald Wilson and comics by the dozens, with Myron Cohen being one who has a special place in my memory.

Myron didn't have us bent over in pain like Redd Foxx did but he would have us waiting for his shows with great anticipation. Every show would somehow be different, even after we learned all the jokes. He would deliver the punch lines in a slightly different guise that would somehow be fresh to all of us and would have us laughing as if we hadn't heard the line before. All this consummate skill of communication and mirth without ever resorting to even an intimation of raunchiness. He could give you a line that would allow you, if you chose, to perceive it as risqué but it was just as funny whatever way you might choose to hear it, so your sensibilities were never compromised. On top of that, he was a wonderful human being and a true gentleman of incredible stature and integrity. This I came to know because of the contact we had, occasionally, living in the same part of New City, New York, out in Rockland County. Here I'm getting a little ahead of myself.

During these years Jo and I were having many difficulties as a marital unit and I had moved out twice to try to get some peace of mind and give myself the opportunity to pursue music in the manner I felt it deserved. During our second separation and attempt to start over I found my life take a 180 degree turn as the result of an off-the-wall, improbable – no, inconceivable – encounter that took place during the run of the Vic Damone show at Basin Street East in April of 1963.

10

Sid Bulkin and the Bahá'í Faith

We had a band room on the mezzanine floor of the Lexington Hotel on 4th Avenue, just above the lobby entrance into the club, where the band would spend its off-time between shows. We'd play cards, read or just talk and, of course, warm up before going on stage for the show. During one of these breaks between shows Vic's drummer, Sid Bulkin, came to the band room to get better acquainted with the guys in the band and to get into a conversation with whomever he could engage.

Sid was from Los Angeles but had started his musical career in New York City some years before. In fact, he was more of a New Yorker in personality and style of communication than he was Californian. He had been born in New York, so the characteristics of his personality came to him quite naturally, as did his Jewish mannerisms which were clearly from New York and, more specifically, from the Lower East Side or Brooklyn. He began talking about something to do with religion and how something special had taken place in recent history, etc. This subject matter abbreviated the group of musicians who had been listening to him by a substantial number and I was inclined to follow suit inasmuch as I had had my bellyful of holier-than-thou church folks trying to save me over the years.

I had been raised in a fundamentalist Christian church, as I made reference to way back at the beginning of this book, and had enrolled in the university in Enid, Oklahoma, which, you may remember, was sponsored by the same church. By the time I had reached my junior year at Phillips I was so disillusioned with what I had come to expect from that rather myopic view of religion – what I had perceived to be its hypocritical and egocentric practices – that I had backed off from all association with what one friend called churchianity.

During my sophomore year at Phillips I had come across a book entitled *The Glorious Koran*, which was an introduction and explanation of the holy book of the Islamic faith from its prophet Muḥammad. After reading the book and reflecting on its premise, I had more difficulty in justifying the fundamentalist Christian idea that every other religious teaching was heathen and therefore all of its adherents were damned to hell.

The spiritual teachings of Islam and Christianity were exactly the same. In addition, the Qur'án made even more of the importance of Mary and Joseph than did Catholicism and had more references to the divinity of Christ than did the Bible. True, there were major differences in social teachings but then there were many differences in the social teachings of the Bible between Moses and Christ as well. After looking into Buddhism a little and from what I already knew about Judaism, I was even more convinced that the rather egocentric, isolationist position of fundamentalist Christianity was off somewhere in left field. Even as a young person I was aware of the hypocrisy in the church and it became more pronounced to me as a teenager and was flagrantly demonstrated in my associations at Phillips University.

As a result of these experiences and my evaluation of them, I completely turned away from all association with any church. My belief in God did not lessen nor did my understanding of Christ's role in relation to God and to man. But I did not find anything resembling what made sense to me in the churches, particularly recognition of the validity of Islam, Buddhism, Native American Indian belief in the Great Spirit and others. What I did find in my search for a people who could be trusted to be what they said they were I found in the jazz community.

You will realize from this tome that what I mean by the jazz community is somewhat different than what some might understand from the popular viewpoint. Historically, I contend, you will find that the jazz community was the first in America to embrace racial unity as a given component of its social consciousness. We were very comfortable living together, dating across racial lines and marrying across them as well. Raising families with values and respect for each other was a normal approach to life and was, therefore, carried on by another generation. No, not everybody in the jazz community married someone from another race but neither was the choice predicated on what race the spouse came from. It simply was not an issue.

Consequently, I was convinced that no other group of people on the earth had a clue about the universality of man and that amity between people had nothing whatsoever to do with skin color or physical differences but rather depended on quality of character and trustworthiness. I had found that the most trustworthy of all the people I had come to know were those in the black community who had nurtured and accepted me for being who and what I was, with no expectations other than that.

Let me be clear. I was not treated that way by every black person I encountered along the way nor was I welcomed without reservation by the community until a thorough investigation and observation had been satisfactorily completed by those questioning my person – which, in my opinion, should be the criterion for evaluating one's character rather than skin tone. I am not going to bother detailing the different criteria used for evaluation by the majority white community; too much is superfluous and based on appearances rather than the quality of essential humanity. Again, let me clarify that this is the predominant view and not that of every white person you encounter; unfortunately, however, it is more the norm than not. It is a great advantage to have been afforded the opportunity to travel the world and be embraced by the wide diversity of humanity that exists on this planet, an opportunity that resulted from my gift for expressing music.

There was one incident in this area of my search for meaning in my life that I would like to share with you. It took place in New York before my second separation from Jo. I was beginning to feel a need to find some spiritual connection in my existence and felt it might make a difference in our marital life as well. I made the suggestion to Jo that we go to church for our spiritual health, at least to try and see if it might help us in some way. She agreed. So we got up on a Sunday morning, got appropriately attired and went to the church on Park Avenue that was of my parents' denomination. It was the same place that I had been billeted those many years before while representing Phillips University in New York City under the sponsorship of the International Lions organization.

When we arrived we were greeted by members of the congregation who had the responsibility of welcoming folks to the church. They asked us where we were from and all that with the social graciousness that one would expect. They were so glad to know that I had been there while a student at Phillips and said how they admired the university, etc. Then they asked what I did for a living. I answered that I was a musician, which was met with even more interest and enthusiasm until they asked what my field in music was and what orchestra I was associated with (obviously alluding to a symphony orchestra). When I answered that I was a jazz musician you would have needed a chain saw to cut through the ice that formed immediately. The next words were, 'You can find a seat inside.' End of social graces and conversation. We sat through the service with that pall over us and on our way out we were given the same, less than warm, response, confirming yet again that this was not the kind of religious association I could be a party to. In addition, I didn't see one black face there, which underscores the statement that the most segregated time in America is at 11:00 a.m. every Sunday morning.

The jazz community wasn't the perfect environment. We had our difficulties with booze, drugs, sex, etc. that were doing many of us harm, physically and psychologically. But these did not have the emphasis that the rest of society has presumed them to have. We helped each other when we could and kept open the warmth and love of the community to those in need without considering a person's racial background.

Back to Sid Bulkin and his conversation in our band room at Basin Street East. Sid held my attention and piqued my curiosity by one statement that I felt challenged my sense of integrity.

Integrity was a quality that I had come to admire in others and had subscribed to as the hallmark of my own character. One of the men I had met on my first gig back in New York after my return from L.A. and with whom I had been working regularly since my return was Jerome Richardson. Years had passed and I had presumed that we were 'tight', as the expression goes, referring to a long and close relationship. One night we were driving home after the gig at Basin Street East – we were then living relatively close to each other up in the '90s on the West Side. Jerome said that he wanted to talk to me at his apartment. I said sure, drove to his place on 91st and found a space to park in outside his building.

'Marv, I have to tell you something.'

Now I'm wondering, have I done something to offend him? What could account for the serious tone in his voice?

'I've been waiting for three years for you to show you're a *** like every white cat I've known who appeared to want to be my friend and I finally have to admit to you that I'm convinced that you are exactly what you seem to be. I can't tell you how much that means to me. Let me explain why this is so important and a bit of the history that goes with it.

'Years ago, all the way back to when I lived in San Francisco, when I was coming up, I would believe the overtures of the white cats and open myself up to them, excited by the prospects of having that kind of relationship with them. That is the way I felt it should be, only to have them, down the road, turn left on me [show themselves as treacherous, untrustworthy and devious users of my friendship]. It happened time after time and each time it hurt worse. I decided that it all had to do with the fact that I was a local boy. So I left Frisco and moved to Los Angeles, hoping to find a more hospitable environment. It wasn't long after I got there that the white cats in town opened up and welcomed me onto the scene in L.A. Now I really felt vindicated and this was going to be the way it should be. I immediately opened up, as I knew that I was one of them. It wasn't long before I found the whole thing go left there, just like it had in Frisco. So I stopped believing anything a white person said to me about his attitudes and beliefs and would therefore not put myself in a position to be hurt again by any white person, ever. But I have to admit to you that I'm truly convinced that you are what you appear to be.'

This was one of the most significant moments of my life. I heard for the first time the reality and depth of the suspicion that is experienced by African–American people in their relationships with the larger white community and which is even more pronounced on an individual level. This endorsed for me the value of the integrity that I had come to cherish and adhere to in my life.

As it happened, Jerome, Butter (Quentin Jackson) and I, along with Warren Smith, a great percussionist, were the only ones who stayed to listen to Sid and pursue the conversation about religion. All the rest of the guys had gone down to the bar for a taste and to get away from us. Sid's challenge to us was that if he were to tell us that the event that the entire Christian and Islamic worlds were waiting for – the return of Christ – had occurred and we had all missed it, would we immediately respond by saying to ourselves, 'Here's another California nut' or would we check it out for ourselves first, before classifying him as a nut. He couldn't have picked a better challenge for me since there was no way that I would ever allow myself to go back on that sense of integrity which had been a hallmark of my actions over the years. So our response to him was certainly not – we would investigate what he was proposing and then call him a California nut after we found the truth of the matter, whatever it was. He then began to tell us about Bahá'u'lláh and the Bahá'í Faith, its teachings and its history. He left us with a multitude of questions formulating in our minds and something for each of us to read about this religion and its Revelator. Without going into the step-by-step details of the journey of my investigation, let me just say that I have never studied anything as intensely as I did this subject. Graduate school, which I undertook some years after this event, was a piece of cake in comparison.

Night after night I'd come home from the gig and read with astonishment until I would fall asleep. When I woke up, more often than not I would read again. Then armed with what I knew would be the ammunition that would permit me to identify Sid as that 'nut', I would assail him with my question that would prove him in error, only to have the answer to my question be so simple and obvious that I often felt rather foolish that I hadn't seen it by myself since it was so logical. I could put away most anyone who approached me on the subject of Christian theology, since I had a solid academic foundation in both New and Old Testament literature from my undergraduate days. Inevitably, when confronted by my arguments the protagonist would go into hiding behind blind faith and literal interpretations of the Bible, regardless of the improbability of the position.

To keep this book from becoming overwhelming in size, let me say only that after intense investigation – meeting the Bahá'í community, calling out all the objections I thought I had found regarding the teachings of Bahá'u'lláh, discussions of various points of view with other members of the New York Bahá'í community and generally immersing myself in the investigation – I found myself early one morning confronted with the proverbial moment of truth.

We had finished the gig at Basin Street and I had offered to drive Willie Dennis, an excellent trombone man, home after the gig. He lived up in Washington Heights on the Upper West Side of Manhattan. I started to tell him about some of the amazing things I was finding out from my search and he suggested that we stop for a beer at Charlie's on the way. I agreed but I was still full of my investigation and didn't drink but about half a glass of the draft I had ordered. Willie finished his glass and we started on our way up to his place. I continued to share my findings with Willie and was really getting into it as we sat in the car outside his apartment building until the sun was about to come up. It had been raining all night but had now slacked off. Because of the late hour Willie said that he'd better get in the apartment quick because 'Mo' (Morgana King) would never believe that he had been setting out front all this time listening to Marv Holladay talking about some new religious revelation from God. So Willie got out and said goodbye and that he'd see me that night at the gig. I turned the Volkswagen around and started back down Riverside Drive when it hit me like a ton of bricks. I had better get off this thing I was on because here I was running my mouth about all this stuff on my friends and what did I think I was doing? Then I realized that I couldn't turn away from this, it was the TRUTH. I stopped the car on Riverside Drive in upper Manhattan and all I could think was, 'Why me?' My old Volkswagen had one of those pull-back sunroofs that covered almost the entire roof. I pulled back the roof. The rain had completely stopped and the morning stars were shining as the sun began to lighten up the sky and I repeated my thought out loud, 'Why me?'

When I got back to my room at the residential hotel where I was living at Broadway and 92nd, I called Sid, woke him up and said, 'OK Sid, now what do I do?' And that is how I became a Bahá'í. It's hard to believe but that was just about three weeks from my first encounter with Sid Bulkin. Sid suggested that we get together for breakfast the next day, so we met at his hotel for our breakfast at 12:00. What did you expect? The gig wasn't over until 4:00 a.m. and by the time you get to bed it's almost always close to 6:00 a.m. Noon was good.

At the restaurant Sid began to tell me what would be expected of me and when I should meet with the Spiritual Assembly of the Bahá'ís of New York City – what I should bring with me when I met with them – and then he began to share with me the laws of the Faith which I had already known about but hadn't really talked about. I said, with great confidence, 'I won't have a problem with that law, or this law, and that law, but I'm not sure about how I'm going to handle this one.' Sid's response was 'Don't worry about it.' This is not a 'you must be perfect' kind of teaching. It is a process of two steps up and one step back but the goal is to keep moving upward. No one is expected to suddenly become that ideal human being. That is illogical. We are here to acquire these attributes, one by one, in preparation for the next world, just like we did when we were in the womb world of our mothers in preparation for this world. Who needed fingers and toes or ears and what was that mouth for? Now we know, don't we?

The Spiritual Assembly asked me to meet with it on 20 April at 6:00 p.m. I had called Sid only a few days before that. The Assembly insisted that I come at 6:00 even though I knew it would be meeting throughout the entire evening and I didn't have to be to work until 9:30 p.m. That meant I was going to have to hang around in midtown for two or three hours but the Assembly insisted. OK, I'll be there.

This brings to mind a story that I think is very relevant to what brought me to this point in my understanding and to my recognition of what was for me a phenomenon. I've already identified why I thought that jazz musicians were the only people in the world who understood what God was really all about. In essence these were people who practiced what they preached. Well, Jerome and I decided one night while we were studying the Faith that we would drop by the Bahá'í Center and check it out. At that time the Bahá'í Center was in the Great Northern Hotel on 57th and its entrance was off the back of the hotel on 56th. We walked in around 8:00 p.m. with our horns in our hands and found that there was a meeting going on. We stood in the back of the room for a while with nobody noticing our presence and we began to feel like this may have been a mistake. We were beginning to think 'Oh yeah! here we go again, the draft is in' and we were about to walk out and say, 'Forget it – this is just like all the rest', when the gentleman who was giving the talk looked up, saw us and stopped mid-sentence. He started walking back to where we were with eyes that, I can still remember, looked like the landing lights of an airplane on its approach to La Guardia or JFK. That kind of froze us in place and all the people who were there stood up, turned around and began to welcome us into the room. That was neat enough but what blew me away was that there were blacks and whites, Persians, Arabs, Asians of all nationalities, Native Americans, Latinos and even some Africans. Even more amazing, as I was to discover, there were men and women who were college professors, stevedores, truck drivers, even an executive of a major New York insurance company, salesmen and students, all in an environment of unified humanity. I could only have dreamed about or imagined such a diverse group of people consorting with such unanimity. This was special!

Back to my meeting with the Spiritual Assembly. I arrived at the Assembly meeting as directed at 6:00 p.m. on 20 April 1963 and was welcomed by all nine members. They proceeded to ask a few questions, nothing unexpected – they just wanted to be sure I understood what I was declaring my belief in. Then they explained their insistence on the early hour. At sundown, which would occur shortly, the Faith would be entering its second century from the time of the declaration of Bahá'u'lláh's Revelation. They felt it so important for me to declare in the first century of His Revelation that they imposed this early meeting. I'm still not sure why this was so important but I fulfilled their hopes by responding to their request. Yes! My life changed on that day in April when I first met Sid Bulkin and it has continued to change ever since but with a clearly delineated path to recognize and follow.

11

The Big Apple Continued

Basin Street East holds a very special place in my heart both for what took place there and for all the great artists I had the privilege to play with, for and behind. It is also a special place because of all the different musicians in New York who from time to time played on the band and who I will always respect and admire for their musicianship and their humanity. These bands were always mixed racially, not by intention or affirmative action but as a result of musicians' abilities. Sometimes there would be more blacks and sometimes more whites but the determination was made on the availability of the individuals to make the gig. Oftentimes we would have to send in a sub for one night or two during the run of the show. That was agreed to by the contractor because she wanted to have the best people she could get for the show and understood that to get that quality of person and to have those she really wanted, she had to be flexible with the musicians' schedules.

For example, the opening night of the Gerald Wilson Band at Basin Street East was also the Monday night at the Village Vanguard for the Thad Jones–Mel Lewis Orchestra and also the same night as a major concert at Town Hall with a big band backing Bill Evans. The core musicians for all three gigs were the same. As a result, the opening night of the Gerald Wilson Band was nearly 60 per cent subs and the first set at the Vanguard had probably 40 per cent subs since a good 50 per cent of the personnel at Town Hall were supposed to be at both of the other gigs that night. One thing you did not ever do was to send in a sub who wasn't at least as good as yourself to cover for you. Consequently, I actually spent more money on subs for that night than I made. That was cool, since I got to play all that good music with Bill at Town Hall and finished the concert in time to make the rest of the night at the Vanguard. And I still had a whole week left of playing the Gerald Wilson book at Basin Street the next night and on to the end of that week. This was one time when I knew I was in the mainstream of the jazz music scene in New York City.

The Thad Jones–Mel Lewis Orchestra began as a rehearsal band that met on Monday nights to read through music written for the band by Thad and a few others who were mostly on the band. People like Bob Brookmeyer, Jerome Richardson and later Tom MacIntosh and still later yet Cecil Bridgewater and, finally, Jerry Dodgion contributed some extremely beautiful creations for the band during the later years of the orchestra. But the main writer for the band was Thad. Anyhow, the musicians would gather at the A and R recording studios, thanks to Phil Ramone, who owned the studio. This meant that the rehearsals would start around midnight following the day's regular schedule of recordings. We would rehearse the charts and read through new ones that were always there each Monday night. Yes, I was the original baritone saxophone player on that band and was with them until I left the city to do a gig at Kutchers Country Club in the Catskills for the summer before going back to school to do graduate work.

When Thad and Mel decided to start a rehearsal band, Thad called Pepper Adams to join the band. Pepper never really liked playing with big bands and avoided them as much as he could, although he certainly did his share with Stan Kenton, Benny Goodman, etc. When Thad called him, Pepper declined the offer and suggested that he call me, as Pepper knew that this was something I enjoyed and was good at. So I was with the band during its formative years and loved every minute of it. Unfortunately for me there is no recorded evidence of my participation since the first recording was made after I left New York to pursue graduate studies. Now that I think about it, there was a live recording made during my tenure on the band, while we were at the Vanguard one Monday night. I wonder what ever happened to that.

We rehearsed in the A and R studios from, I think, October of '65 until Mel set up a deal for us to begin our Monday nights as open rehearsals at the Village Vanguard for Max Gordon. Max agreed to the venture and that we would take the door (meaning that the money collected at the door as admission would be given to the band to divide up between the musicians who were playing on the band that night). No advertising was done to let people know that we were going to be there, so the notice was all word of mouth. In this case that wasn't a bad deal since the word had already gone out around the city that Thad's rehearsal band had been at Phil's studio for the past months and its reputation was already becoming common knowledge among many who closely followed the jazz scene in the Apple.

Anyhow, the first night came and Max was going to charge $2.50 per head – keep in mind that this was 1966 – at the door for us and he was going to get the bar action. By 10:30 the place was pretty well filled up and stayed that way the rest of the night. Now Max Gordon didn't get rich by being a philanthropist for down and out musicians. He saw a good thing brewing the very first night and during the first break we took he made a deal with Thad and Mel to pay everybody in the band $20 every Monday night whether the people came or not and they went for it. Musicians are not business people and as a result consistently find themselves on the short end of almost any good deal. The next week Jerome and I shared a cab from our area in the 90s on the West Side, primarily because it was raining like crazy and we didn't want to have to walk in the rain with our horns from the subway station on 7th Avenue to the Vanguard.

When we pulled up to the club we couldn't believe our eyes. People were standing outside of the Vanguard waiting to get onto the stairs leading down into the club – standing in the pouring rain, some with umbrellas and some trying to share or get somehow under the very small marquee. One of the most amazing things about this was that many of the people standing out in the rain were musicians from all over the city, waiting to get in like everybody else. Many of those musicians were of such a stature in the business that they would normally be allowed to bypass the line. But there they were.

Jerome and I had to push our way through the crowd on the stairwell to get into the club to get ready to play. Well, needless to say, Max was sitting on a gold mine from the second night that the Thad Jones–Mel Lewis Orchestra appeared at the Village Vanguard. From then on and into the '80s that success continued. Even after Thad left the country, Mel continued the Monday nights at the Vanguard until his passing in February 1990. Most of you know the Thad Jones–Mel Lewis Jazz Orchestra as the most important and influential big band in the country during the '60s and on into the '80s.

It was during these years that I had a second or third opportunity to work with the Ellington Alumni band. The first time was as a sub for Jerome, which began my association with that orchestra for the rest of the time I spent in New York. This band was made up entirely of alumni of the Ellington Orchestra. The only chair in the whole band that never had an alumnus was the baritone. Harry Carney joined the Ellington band right out of high school in Boston and Ellington himself was probably no more than in his early twenties. This was before the Cotton Club days. Harry was the baritone player from that time on until Duke died in 1975. Harry passed about four months after Duke. This is why there was no baritone alumnus on that chair. This made being asked to fill that chair on that band even more of a challenge and privilege.

As I said, the first time I worked on the band was as a sub for Jerome. The second and future times it was me they asked for. I have no reason for that except that I was usually identified around town by the sound I produced on baritone, and if you wanted that kind of sound in your sax section, I was the one you would call. Pepper, on the other hand, was always called because of his incredible ability as a soloist. Apparently the band and Mercer Ellington liked the way my sound fit which, by itself, was an extreme compliment. Harry Carney had, without peer, the most commanding sound on baritone saxophone in the history of this music.

The first time I went to rehearse with the band was like being transported into a parallel universe of sorts. I was surrounded by the most illustrious musicians in the music world who were associated with the most esteemed orchestra in the history of the idiom, an idiom which personified the evolution of American indigenous classical music. Duke would not use the word 'jazz' in reference to his music; it was, rather, his music. His was also the most revered American jazz orchestra in the world and probably the most well-traveled in the world as well, which could only have increased its acclaim.

At this rehearsal were Hilton Jefferson and Harold Minerve on altos; Harold Ashby, tenor and a tenor/clarinet man who I cannot remember; Britt Woodman, Quentin Jackson and John Sanders trombones, with Bill Berry, Clark Terry, Ray Nance and a fourth trumpet player who might have been Richard Williams. I'm drawing a total blank on who the rhythm section was on that day. There was a gig later and I remember that section very well. The point of this story is that we began the rehearsal and here I am playing Harry Carney's notes, which are often the fattest notes in the voicing.

I'm roaring out that part almost as if I were playing lead. I couldn't help myself. I had heard the sound of that band for so many years and realized the dominant role Harry's sound played in the overall sound of the band that I was doing my utmost to make my sound approximate his. We took a break after about an hour and I became a bit self-conscious about my playing during that part of the rehearsal. When I got up from my chair, I turned and started talking to Butter Jackson, Britt, John and Bill Berry, who were standing near me. I made the comment about what fun it was to play all those great notes that Duke had given to Harry to play and asked Britt and John, who were setting right behind me, to pull my coat tail (let me know if I got to playing too loudly). They all started laughing and Butter and Britt both said, 'That ain't possible. Harry's sound covered the whole band. In fact, you are, more often than not, playing lead on baritone in the Ellington band. Get used to it and let it all out.'

From that moment on I began to learn about the Ellington sound and how it was generated. One thing I would have to do was to listen for Hilton on alto and try to play as if we were playing duets, with my role being equal to his in terms of the balance of sound. As I listened to the way the alto, trombone and trumpet leads were meshing their respective lines, the whole process through which this orchestra created its unique composite of musical synergy began to become clear. It was like no other musical experience I have ever had, before or since.

The other gig with that orchestra I would like to recall for you was during the years I was working at Basin Street East. This was during the holiday season, December to New Year, when they had hired the Ellington Orchestra for an extended engagement at the club. Ellington had a prior commitment to do a concert somewhere outside of the city, in Jersey or someplace, and we, the Alumni Orchestra, were asked to sub for Ellington that night on the gig at Basin Street. We were called to rehearse that afternoon at the club.

The people for the gig were the same with the addition of Billy Strayhorn on piano, John Lamb on bass and Sam Woodyard on drums. Now this WAS the Duke Ellington Orchestra. When 'Sweetpea' sat down at the piano along with Lamb and Woodyard, everything not only sounded like Duke Ellington but felt like it as well. The people in the club that night heard the Ellington Orchestra without its regular piano player but replaced by the most important and familiar person possible, one who was equally responsible for the orchestrated sound of the band. Most of the audience probably assumed that Duke was not feeling well enough to make the gig that night as Sweetpea had filled in for him on many occasions.

Hilton Jefferson taught me as much about what it took to play Ellington as anyone possibly could and, just like all the times before, he did it without knowing it. I'm still going to school on the men I'm working with.

Isn't it funny how some of us just can't ever seem to be in the right place at the right time when the boat comes by that will take us to paradise? The expression I've used for that is 'a day late and a dollar short'. I decided to go back to graduate school because by this time Monday night was the only music I played all week. The rest of the time we would be setting in some studio playing the most indifferent music imaginable for hours. Repeated takes of the same old and tired riffs. Meanwhile Gene Orloff, with a collection of symphony caliber string players, would be playing goose eggs for umpteen bars at a time and a rhythm section of great 'poquette' players going boom, chink, boom, chink, for 30 takes while they had some jive singer in the booth who had to repeat himself or herself that many times to get enough usable material for the producer to patch together one track that would sound presentable for the marketing people, who would then make him a star. Anyhow, I left for graduate school in the fall of '66 and that fall the Thad Jones–Mel Lewis Jazz Orchestra went to the moon with recordings and tours, and the rest, as they say, is history. They also had the greatest jazz soloist on baritone saxophone in jazz history (my opinion, of course) on the band, so you see things are as they should be.

Thad and Pepper had grown up together in the Detroit area. Actually, Thad was from Pontiac and Pepper from Highland Park but they were both considered to be a part of greater Detroit. Thad kind of leaned on Pepper to come on the band; as I said earlier, Pepper didn't particularly like playing with a big band, so Thad used their home-boy association and his mother's relationship with Pepper during their varied activities as young men on the scene in Detroit. That story is very convoluted, so I think I'll leave it there. I consider my time on that band as another highlight in my career and feel honored that I was a charter member of the organization, even if I wasn't able to reap the benefits of its great success.

It may have been the most demanding, technically, of all the bands I ever worked with. Quincy's was the most enjoyable from the aspect of a loving family of musicians playing excellent music together while Ellington's was the most demanding music to realize in its musical essence because the language was so unique and required you to become one with it. As Butter once said to me, 'When I first got on the band I couldn't hear my part right. It seemed like I was playing wrong notes and everything sounded weird to me. It took a few weeks before I could hear things right. It was then I knew I was working with a musical genius because once I began to hear it I realized that this was like nothing else in this world.' Dizzy comes later, oh yeah!

Butter related another story about Duke's compositional mastery. He said that he had been bothered about how Duke got the sound that he did with the sax section on the arrangement of 'Caravan' (a composition of Juan Tizol and Ellington). So one night, during a break on the gig, Butter decided to look at the saxophone parts to try and figure out how Duke got that sound. He said that he found that Duke had written the melody for each saxophone player but each in a different key, creating the unusual sound that had been bothering him for weeks. For those technically-minded folks, it was a stack of fourths, i.e. a series of 6/9 chords voiced in parallel motion with the melody.

Ellington was a painter – he actually was – and had been encouraged by his parents to explore his art in New York. But before he did so he found himself in the music scene and went from the Kentucky Club to the Cotton Club rather early on. The quality of his perception carried over into his music: he treated the respective sounds of his orchestra members as pigments of color on a palette that he could blend and utilize in his own unique, creative manner. This gift separated him from every other composer/arranger in this business.

I've come across musicians who've thought they had discovered the 'Ellington' voicing. My question to them is, 'On which arrangement?' Which is followed with, 'You may have discovered his voicing on that arrangement but it won't work on the other arrangements because they are each unique unto themselves.' Duke did not write by formula but by using his palette, the unique qualities of sound of each member of the orchestra. That's why he often rewrote arrangements as the membership of his orchestra changed, which didn't happen very often, or he heard a different coloration that he could achieve by combining different qualities of his palette. Genius may be too mild a term to adequately describe this consummate musician.

Thad's writing, Monk's writing, even Mingus's writing show themselves to be extensions of Ellington although Thad's writing, I believe, most closely approximates what Ellington might have done in a newer generation of his own evolution – Brookmeyer's writing as well, although it was not as demanding as Thad's. I found that Thad used the men in the band as a palette from which to paint his pictures very much in the Ellington manner. The men Thad had at his disposal were all so accomplished he really didn't have to hold back anything and could be sure that whatever he wrote would be played and played well. It must be very satisfying for a writer to know that no matter what he writes the musicians in the band can and will play it as he conceived it. I'm not talking about notes here but the expression of the musical thought. Being a part of such a consummate collection of musicians and being considered a peer is a cherished part of my musical life.

In addition to achieving this level of musical accomplishment, the other human component of the band was also realized at a very elevated level of consciousness. The band was always mixed racially because Thad's attitude was expressed quite openly: he was not willing to sacrifice his music for any kind of political expediency. This was another standard that was held by others at that level of excellence. There is a story of Quincy's experience with this political phenomenon that happened to circle around my association with him.

Not long after we had finished the Eckstine show Quincy was booked to go back into the Apollo Theatre for a two-week engagement with just his band as the headliner. I heard about this and thought to myself, 'Great! this will be a nice gig for two weeks in town playing with that group of musicians again.' I waited to get a call from either Q or Jerome to let me know when and where to go for rehearsal, etc. The call never came and the band went into the Apollo without me. You can imagine how much that hurt and how confused I was over what, I thought, was a mutual appreciation, both personally and musically. After the band had been into the gig for two or three days I heard from Jerome, who had a message to pass on to me from Q. First, he said, Quincy wanted me to know that he was terribly sorry for what he had done regarding my chair for this gig. He wanted me to know that he had knuckled under the pressure of a 'brother' who had been bad mouthing him about using an 'Ofay' on the band while he wasn't doing anything. He 'called' out to Q's responsibility to stick together with his brothers and so on and so forth until Q finally told him, 'OK man, you got the gig.'

When the Apollo job began, the band again used Al Cohn's chart on 'Air Mail Special' in which the sax section is featured down front with the solos and the sax soli, etc. Well, it seems that this dude who got my gig would go out to do his solo when his time came but would then go back to his seat while everybody else stayed down front for the soli and the rest of the chart. Quincy said that this cat wouldn't even try to memorize the part for the sax section so as to present it the way it had been designed by the rest of us. He said he was stuck with the cat because by the time his notice would be up (the Union required a two-week notice before a man being fired could be cut) the gig would be over. From then on Quincy's position regarding the personnel for his band was the same as Thad's. Later Jerome told me that even after being on the gig for the whole two weeks this dude never made any effort to be a part of that chart and pulled the same thing each time.

A second story directly relates to this incident but was not conditioned on or by it. My wife Jo used to hang out with her drinking buddies at Charlie's – that's the one on 48th Street where predominantly white cats hang out. One night during general conversation regarding the business – since they were all drinking together I guess she felt confident enough to broach the subject – she asked, 'How come Marv doesn't do more work with you guys?' She got her reply, apparently without much hesitation. 'If Marv wants to work with the black cats, let the black cats hire him!'

If you have followed the underlying theme of this reminiscence you will further realize why the title of this epistle is *Life, On the Fence*. This has been a reoccurring reality that began, as you have no doubt noted, in about junior high school.

I hope this doesn't appear to be a 'poor little ol' me' posture. What I'm trying to share is the recognition of who and what shaped my understanding and comprehension of this societal paradigm. And what really existed during this one unique life. How easily we could have got beyond it had there been a willingness to see and come to know. Also, I am not trying to propose that our current societal paradigm can be altered through the same approaches that were possible at an earlier time. I am saying, however, that having the strength of one's integrity so that one does not compromise with the forces that are battering us to take sides and join in with other forces bent on exorcising others from our lives, is one of the most positive steps that an individual can take. Finding those who have embraced the oneness of the human family, without exception, and whose deeds are complemented by their words, will assist us in establishing a life that can be real to every person with whom we come into contact.

I could not deny or turn away from those who had taught me and nurtured me until I reached the stature of the jazz musician that I had become. My attitude to ethnocentricism made it difficult for me to continue to participate in that sphere of activity, while at the same time the other faction would have nothing to do with me because of what they perceived to be my preference. I'm only interested in truth and accountability.

Putting together my life's experience – as a child, as a young man and later as an adult and an accomplished professional – I knew that the assistance I received in achieving that stature, as a musician, would not allow this artificial racial distinction to become anything other than what I perceived it to be, a chimera. Because of my life's experience, which was confirmed by the teachings of Bahá'u'lláh, I knew that this was not the way for us to bring about a world of unity which will be the hallmark of this age and which will be realized with or without our participation. It makes sense to me that being a participant in this reality can only help to defuse the severity of the calamity that humanity must endure to arrive at that summit, regardless of those who might oppose such an accomplishment.

Do you remember an earlier reference I made to a story told to me by Taft Jordan regarding his days with Chick Webb and the Casa Loma Band at the Savoy ballroom? Well, here it is. Taft told me this story one night between shows at Basin Street East when, I think, we were backing Ella Fitzgerald. I'm sure of that because it was on that run that I saw Taft and Gus Johnson take Ella all the way back to when she was a teenager singing with the Chick Webb Orchestra. They would tease Ella something awful on the bandstand and before we would get too far into her show you could see her respond to the teasing just as if she were again a little teenage girl on her first gig. Now, let me interject here, that the teasing was not cruel or mean – it was more like the embrace of older siblings with a cherished younger sister and the loving tease that would come from that. It was a beauty to watch as they collectively revisited their youth.

Now to the story regarding the Casa Loma Band. Taft shared with me that the Chick Webb Band, being essentially the house band at the Savoy, was so good that the members never worried about any band coming into their turf and blowing them away. On several occasions the Savoy would have two bands in the ballroom, which was true of many of the old ballrooms around the country, particularly in the big cities like New York and Chicago. Taft said that the only band that made them work was the Ellington band, of course, and that the rest – like the Goodman Band and the Dorseys – they could blow away without much effort; even Basie they never worried about. However, he said there was one white band that made them reach to the bottom of the book and that was the Casa Loma Band. Taft said that when they came into the Savoy ballroom they would open up a book (library) that they never ever used anywhere else and would make the entire evening a real contest to see which band would come out on top. For those of you who know nothing about the Casa Loma Band, it was known in the industry primarily as a commercial, almost sweet band, that played most of its engagements in the big hotels around the country.

Taft went on to say that Chick would never know what to expect. The Casa Loma Band, following the first set by Chick's band, would begin its set. On these occasions the guys in Chick's band would stay around the ballroom and often go near the band to hear what they were coming out with. He said that they never did this for any band except, of course, the Ellington band.

One incident had stuck with Taft all those years. There was a chart that had been written for Chick that featured Taft on a tune I can't now remember. One night after Chick finished his set, Taft said he walked over to the other band-stand to hear what the Casa Loma Band was going to play. He heard them playing the same tune that had been his feature when Chick's band had played at the Savoy against the Casa Loma Band the time before. When they got to the place in the chart where his solo had been, Taft said that the whole trumpet section stood up and played, note for note, right back at him and in harmony, the entire solo that Taft had played. As you can imagine, this blew Taft completely away. He went on to say that that was what they had come to expect from the Casa Loma Band whenever they came into the Savoy. They were the best and baddest white band on the scene during those years but you never heard them play up to their real capability except there at the Savoy ballroom in Harlem. Taft's respect and admiration was very apparent.

Before I leave this time period there is one other story that I would like to share with you. It's about my association with 'Moondog'. Many of you who are from New York or have visited the city often enough will have seen an unusually clad, blind, bearded gentleman of distinction on 6th Avenue, usually between 54th and 55th Streets, recognizable by his helmet with horns, a six-foot spear and accompanying garb which created a very distinct Viking appearance. That was Moondog. You could find him there almost every day selling his music,

With my parents, Joseph
and Gladys Holladay, 1953

The Tommy
Dorsey Orchestra
on tour

The Tommy
Dorsey Orchestra
at my parents'
home in Chanute

At the Jazzmobile concert, uptown in Harlem, probably with the Frank Foster Orchestra

Photo by Raymond Ross Photography, New York City

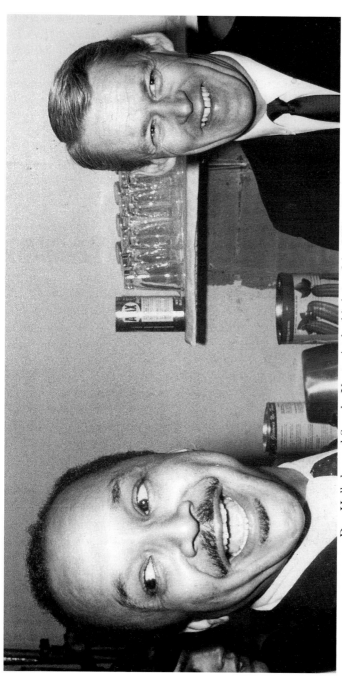

Doc Holladay and Snooky Young in the kitchen of the Village Vanguard
Photo by Raymond Ross Photography, New York City

Moi with the Thad Jones–Mel Lewis Jazz Orchestra
Photo by Raymond Ross Photography, New York City

Sax section of the Thad Jones–Mel Lewis Jazz Orchestra
From top left: Joe Farrell, Jerry Dodgion, Jerome Richardson,
Eddie Daniels, moi
Photo by Raymond Ross Photography, New York City

Oakland University Jazz Ensemble

Oakland University Jazz Ensemble with Thad Jones conducting

Diane and moi

The J.C. Heard Sextet at the North Sea Jazz Festival, The Hague

poetry and writings. I used to walk by him regularly, since I lived on the corner of 6th Avenue and 58th Street. Having passed by many times and considered him to be, more or less, a rather strange apparition, as did many who saw him, I decided one day to stop and see what he was about. To my great surprise he was very talkative, telling me who he was, why he was there and most clearly about his music and poetry. I acquired some of both from him and began to look forward to greeting him each day as I went by.

One day, probably a year or so after I began to know him, I got a call from him with the request that I join him for a concert that he was performing at a small theatre on 41st Street between 6th and 7th Avenues. He had gotten my number from a friend of mine who was also a baritone player, Danny Bank. Danny had been doing performances with Moondog but couldn't do this one and had recommended me to replace him. I agreed to the engagement and Moondog asked me to come by his place to discuss the performance and to rehearse some of his material. I found the address on West 43rd Street. As I entered this small hotel, I saw that it was run down, dilapidated and funky, one step away from being an out and out flop house. I wasn't at all comfortable even walking into the place but I made my way to the elevator, of sorts, and went up to his floor. As I walked down the hall the environment was almost too much. However, I had committed myself to this encounter and I pressed on to Moondog's room. I knocked and was greeted by Moondog dressed in casual, rather loose-fitting clothing, obviously homemade, as was his street clothing. The difference between his room and everything else in that hotel was incredible. He welcomed me into the room. It had one small window looking out onto a brick wall about three or four feet away so the room at midday was very dark, which, of course, didn't matter to him as he was blind. He turned on a light, which was a single bulb hanging from the ceiling, and to my amazement I saw a room so immaculate that you could have eaten off the floor. Everything about him and his immediate environment was absolutely pristine. The cleanliness of his person and his environment was in stark contrast to everything around him outside of his room. How he was able to maintain such a level of purity with all that around him still boggles me.

After we had discussed and rehearsed elements of the music we were going to play at the concert, we began to discuss our lives, values and beliefs. We talked about our common origins in Kansas, which had not held a lot for either of us other than that our lives had started there. I shared with him the Bahá'í teachings and he shared with me his commitment to Odin and Thor. His religious orientation was in no way a pretense. He was a serious student of Viking lore and I'm certain he continued that study until his passing in 1999. I came to admire and respect his beliefs and the purity of his life, as I knew it to be. He had had a short period of notoriety in the '50s but that had somewhat diminished by the time I got to know him. I was extremely glad to see, a few years ago, that he had been discovered by a patron who sponsored him, making it possible for Moondog to go to Germany where he would have been that much closer to his heart home and his Viking ancestry. He also began to receive recognition for his compositional talent and had an opportunity for his creative gifts to be heard once again. I will cherish my moment with him and the lovely 'Lament for Bird' that he had written and dedicated to Charlie Parker.

Ah! New York City, a place of never-ending stories and monuments seen and unseen.

12

Grad School, Yale

My summer in the Catskills wasn't much musically but did provide me an opportunity to be with my son for weeks at a time and got me in touch with the administration at Yale University. As a result, I was able to garner a tuition-free year at Yale as a special graduate student of music. I had just had a 20–year career in the performance of music and they were, ostensibly, preparing me for a performance career, which made no sense. So I attended Yale while I looked for another school that would allow me to grow in a new and different direction.

It should be clear by now that Jo and I had got back together, actually as a result of my finding the Bahá'í Faith. And after many years of infertility we miraculously conceived a child, a handsome little boy. At this juncture Jo was pregnant with a second child, which turned out to be a lovely little girl. The ideal family picture, don't you think? The second pregnancy was the catalyst for our departure from New York City – and, by association, the music scene that I loved so much and still do, even though I'm not a part of it now and haven't been for some years. I doubt that my feelings are much different from those of anyone else who was that much a part of the music scene in our beloved New York City.

During the year at Yale I supported the family by teaching at a junior high school in New Haven, Connecticut, which, as most of you know, is where Yale University is located. This was not a highlight of my career as an educator but it does have one significant story associated with it. During the '80s when I was personally associated with Dizzy, I was visiting with him and his group on some gig he had in the area (Ann

Arbor/Detroit) and think I may have broached the subject of where his guitar player Ed Cherry was from. When Ed responded with 'New Haven, Connecticut', I mentioned that I had taught there for a year while attending Yale. Ed said, in so many words, 'I knew you looked familiar but couldn't place you from anywhere. But now I know – you were my junior high school teacher in New Haven.' What a surprise! There is no way I could have recognized him from those days, as he was now six foot three or four, carried himself well and weighed in at probably close to 225 to 240 pounds. Ed was so big that the guitar looked like a large ukulele in his hands. He really had growed up!

I continued to play but at a rather retiring level of activity. I did get a call to sub for Pepper with the Duke Pierson Orchestra at the Vanguard one night. It was a joy but also a realization that the fine tuning of my skills on the instrument had slipped and that my performance at that level of musical competence had diminished since leaving New York. What is that old expression? Use it or lose it!

One of the more positive experiences from my year at Yale was meeting Firuz Kazemzadeh and Howard Gary who were at that time sharing an office in one of the colleges at the university. Actually, it was my philosophy professor who introduced me to them, as their office was across the hall from his. I had come to speak to him about a proposal for my research paper for his philosophy class. When he realized that I was a Bahá'í, identified from the subject of my research paper, he told me of these two Bahá'í professors in the office across the hall and proceeded to take me there and perform the introductions. As fate would have it, this philosophy teacher moved to Wesleyan University the year before I began my graduate studies there.

Howard Gary was living in North Haven, the next suburb north of Hamden, where I was living. He was a very accomplished amateur flutist, so it was kind of natural for us to begin a closer relationship. He knew I was discontented with my Yale experience and, consequently, introduced me to Wesleyan University, about 35 miles away from New Haven in

Middletown, where he had discovered a music program that was most unusual. Because of my interest in music of cultures around the world, he suggested that we go to one of the evening musical activities that were held each Friday. What I found there was not only a surprise but a clear indication of where I could get the kind of education I had been searching for.

In my undergraduate days at Phillips I had seen the movie *King Solomon's Mines* and was fascinated with the music I heard on the sound track. From that moment on I had the desire someday to learn about traditional African music. My interest in that tradition provoked an even greater urgency in me to discover the relationship of that music to what I had learned from my many years of association with African–American musicians. When a professor at Wesleyan informed me that they were going to offer graduate studies in African music and bring in an artist in residence from Ghana the following year, I knew that I had found my school.

I did not return to Yale the next year but waited a year for this new program to begin at Wesleyan. Wesleyan agreed to accept me on a probationary basis for graduate studies in African music and after the first year, if I qualified, I could become a candidate for a PhD in ethnomusicology. I antici-pated the arrival of the African artist with great enthusiasm, which carried over into my teaching.

After that first year with the New Haven school system I applied for and got a teaching job at a high school in Stratford, Connecticut, a town much closer to Bridgeport than to where we lived in Hamden. It provided a substantial increase in salary over what I had been receiving in New Haven, so that made the commute quite tolerable. It was also rather convenient to stay in Hamden, since Wesleyan was about the same distance from Hamden in the opposite direction.

The year after I joined the faculty at Stratford they hired a new vocal teacher and between us we developed quite an impressive music program for Stratford High School, which culminated that spring in a concert of a quality unprecedented in that community. As usual, the academic administration of the school would have preferred a greater emphasis on the marching band. When an offer came from his old school, the vocal teacher decided he would rather return to it than stay. So mediocrity continues to reign supreme as a norm in the land of music education with, of course, some rare exceptions. Clark Terry's observation keeps rearing its ugly head in my educational experience.

13

Grad School, Wesleyan

Sometime during 1968, before I enrolled at Wesleyan and during my first year at Stratford High School, I received a telephone call from a friend I had known quite well in New York City. When I moved to Connecticut to pursue graduate studies he had accepted a position as a psychiatrist in New Jersey. He seemed rather strange on the phone and I was curious to know what he was being so mysterious about. He said that as the secretary of the Bahá'í Spiritual Assembly of Englewood, New Jersey, he had received a Bahá'í declaration card from Los Angeles from a person he thought was a friend of mine. He finally went on to say that the name on the declaration card was a John 'Birks'. . . I finished for him, 'Gillespie?' He started laughing and said, yes, it was Dizzy and that he had just received the declaration card in the mail that day and had to call me immediately because he knew how excited I would be. I assured him that he was certainly right about that! As soon as we hung up I called Butter in Brooklyn to tell him, since his relationship with Dizzy was longer and closer than mine. Oh, yes! Butter had become a Bahá'í about two weeks after me. Butter got so excited that he almost hung up without saying goodby and immediately called Dizzy. As a result of this, Dizzy's path and mine began to cross more often and he became an important ingredient in my life and most certainly in my academic pursuits.

While pursuing graduate studies at Wesleyan University I was afforded the opportunity to become conversant with many cultures including African, which was my field of concentration. Goro Yamaguchi was in residence at Wesleyan and was a master of the shakuhachi, a Japanese flute. At the same time there was a Korean master of taegeum, a flute of relatively epic proportions in that tradition, whose name was Cho. In addition we had a Javanese gamelan as well as a gamelan master in residence from Jakarta who was accompanied by master dancers from the Javanese tradition. From India we had representation from both Hindustani and Karnatic traditions with a slightly more pronounced emphasis on the Karnatic because of the artists Vishwanathan and his brother Raganathan. Vishwa and his brother came to us from India with most impressive credentials, having toured extensively throughout the US and the western world. The North Indian artists were Laxmi Tewari and Gosh.

Laxmi, Russell Hartenberg, Robert Becker, Daahoud Haroon and I, along with others, participated in the West African drum ensemble under Kobena Adzinyah's direction. Laxmi went on, after graduation, to become an artist in residence at a university in California. Besides Tewari there were two artists in residence at Wesleyan who were also graduate students in ethnomusicology: Asante Darkwa and Ampofo Duodu, who were both from Ghana. Darkwa was a master of the Ashanti flute tradition and Duodu was a master of traditional dance.

With these artists all in residence at Wesleyan at the same time, how could one not become familiar with these diverse cultures? Wesleyan University is the only university I know of that has a music department called the Department of World Music. It includes all the western European traditions, i.e. symphony orchestra, wind ensemble, early music consort, choirs, choruses, liturgical groups, etc., as well as traditions from around the world. This awareness of the validity of all cultures and the equal attention given to the serious study of all these different disciplines created the most exhilarating musical environment that I have ever experienced in an academic institution.

In 1972, after I had finished my courses and had passed the preliminary examinations for a PhD, I was offered an assistant professorship at Oakland University in Rochester, Michigan. This left me with a difficult choice: on the one hand

I had an opportunity to stay at the university and spend my time working on my dissertation, which would include doing further research in Africa to support my thesis, and on the other I could accept the appointment and the accompanying income that went with it. I took the job for a couple of good reasons. First, I had two growing children and a wife to be concerned for and, secondly, I had worked and become friends with so many great musicians from the Detroit area that I surmised that there must be a very fertile environment for jazz in and around that city. As it turned out, there was.

14

Thesis: The Evolution
of American Indigenous Classical Music

I began my studies at Wesleyan University under the tutorage of Abraham Kobena Adzinyah, a master drummer from Ghana who was a Fanti. Ghana is a geographical construct of colonial origin that has nothing to do with the cultural reality of the people living there, so being a Fanti was a greater distinction for Adzinyah and a better way to identify him than saying he was Ghanaian. He was new at trying to communicate with Americans and even more unfamiliar with the American student population. Despite this, he gave us, in his unique manner, all he could impart. We were, in turn, instrumental in his becoming comfortable and confident in teaching American students about Africa and African culture, particularly an appreciation of its music and, even more specifically, of the drums in that traditional culture. This was the beginning of what was to become a lifelong friendship.

The graduate students in the African studies field were from an interesting collection of backgrounds and professional associations. Two of our group were members of the percussion ensemble Nexus: Robert Becker and Russell Hartenberg. As a part of their graduate studies at Wesleyan they were also students of North Indian Tabla and South Indian Mrdngam, respectively. The group also had two students from a jazz background – one was a drummer from the Dominican Republic and the other a trombone and conga player, Daahoud Haroon – as well as others with less professional performance credentials. And then, of course, there was moi.

The more success we had assisting Abraham to communicate

with his American students, the further he was able to take us into his culture and sensitize us to an experience none of us had ever been able to explore before. What a revelation for us! I began to understand why I felt so intensely about the elements and functions of the music I had been performing all my life. Though I had tried to emphasize my points about these fundamental elements in some of my previous associations, I didn't have this level of comprehension and theoretical documentation to support my sense of what was important and why, to make myself clear in my arguments.

Let me share with you a possible scenario for the process of acculturation and evolution that has occurred organically over many generations. This phenomenon took place in the United States, was largely recognized throughout the world, and is now even more pronounced in the US itself: it is American indigenous classical music. It has had a major impact, musically, on the rest of the world.

African music has been studied and analyzed by many musicians and people with personal interests – some seeking personal gain, some on cultural quests, others on journeys of self-discovery – as well as by musicologists and ethno-musicologists from around the world. The result has been treatises of widely varying degrees of comprehension and reliable authenticity. One of the more authoritative voices to come to the forefront over the years is J.H. Kwabena Nketia. He is not the only one, just one of the more understandable and reliable exponents. (For a reliable and accurate account from the viewpoint of a non-African I recommend John Chernoff's *African Rhythm and African Sensibility*.) Nketia has written numerous studies of African music, as well as a more intricate and detailed analysis of his native Ghanaian cultures which include Ashanti, Ewe, Ga, Adangme, Hausa and some Malinke. I believe Nketia's treatise on African music to be the best overview of continental African music that has thus far been written. If I had felt the need to document my expositions I would have undoubtedly used Nketia as my resource. But since this is not a scholarly tome, I have not bothered with any of it and have left it to you to decide for yourself whether what I say makes any sense.

We know from all the research that has been done on it that African music has an emphatic and fundamental rhythmical foundation and is predominantly centered in a drum ensemble and/or the master talking drum, with many variations on that theme. The voice, stringed instruments of all varieties (chordophones), flutes, whistles and horns also of many varieties (aereophones), rattles, bells, chimes, gongs, xylophones, etc. (idiophones) and the previously mentioned drums of great variety (membranophones) have as their structural foundation an emphasis on that fundamental rhythmical pulse of African life. This rhythmical orientation cannot be truly understood by the mathematical subdivision of pulse that delineates meter in western European music theory. The basic meters of duple (2), triple (3), quadruple (4) and the compound meters thereof – 6, 9 and 12 – or the combinations of meter, i.e. 5, 7, 9, 11, 13, 15, etc., really don't apply to African rhythms.

Instead, what exists in traditional African rhythm is a very sophisticated use of a variety of ordered rhythmical orientations or patterns utilized concurrently which do not imply a meter but a continuum of rhythmical flow which coincides at given points in the order. This results in what has been musicologically identified as cross rhythms because of the natural expansion and contraction of the overall relationship of this rhythmical flow. For example, western theory explains the use of duple and triple meter occurring simultaneously as a subdivision of a single unit, or two against three. The African feels this same relationship as two distinct and separate rhythmical entities that periodically coincide by virtue of each rhythm's continuum. Consequently the tendency of the western version is to realize this complexity as 'pulse, pulse subdivided into two, pulse' or, in musical notation, 'eighth note, two sixteenth notes, eighth note' or 'quarter, two eighths, quarter'.

In contrast, the African use of a similar combination results in an independence of a two pulse and a three pulse over a common space in time that coincides in a relative manner as each progresses along its path adhering to its own speed and rhythmical dimension. This results in a sound that you can hear only in African traditional music. I ran into a brick wall trying to find some way to make this more clear but I have finally realized that it is so subtle that you have to hear it for yourself to be able to truly comprehend the distinction. You recognize the difference quite quickly if you are in the process of producing it in an ensemble of drummers, while being able to discern it just by listening is much more difficult. It will be more felt than heard even for the listener. Another explanation has been to think of African meter, if I can use that term, as additive, not subdivided. This is also true of an Indian tala.

In addition to the rhythmical sophistication of African music, the most glaring misconception, often postulated in jazz history textbooks, is the idea that African music is pentatonic in scale structure. It is not. Nketia identifies three predominant scale structures throughout Africa: pentatonic (five tone), hexatonic (six tone) and heptatonic (seven tone). These are found throughout the entire continent, often within neighboring tribes of a given region. In his book *The Music of Ghana* Nketia goes into detail about the way that melody is generated from each scale structure employed by a particular cultural group and how, as a result of that melodic generation, the melodic material periodically ends up in a harmonic interval that varies depending on which scale structure is being used. This is a bit too much of a generalization but it is, nonetheless, the norm more often than not. This results in pentatonic scales ending up in the intervals of fourths or fifths, hexatonic scales ending up in intervals of unisons or octaves and heptatonic scales ending up with intervals of thirds and sixths. Musicians will understand that these intervals are the inversion of the others – perhaps the rest of you can ask a musician friend to show you what I'm talking about.

Let me give you a brief example that might make this a little more comprehensible for those of you who do not know music. I'll use both 'do, re, mi, fa, so, la, ti, do' and a keyboard orientation of 'C, D, E, F, G, A, B, C'. Let's start with 'do, re, mi, fa, so'. If you count up those scale degree symbols you will see that 'do, re, mi, fa, so' encompasses five scale degrees or 'C, D, E, F, G'. We call that a fifth. To invert that means to start on the fifth scale degree and count up so that you get 'so, la, ti, do' or 'G, A, B, C'. Hence the inversion covers four scale degrees or the interval of a fourth. Following the same orientation you can see that an octave inverted becomes unison and a third – 'do, re, mi' or 'C, D, E' – inverts to 'mi, fa, so, la, ti, do' or 'E, F, G, A, B, C' or a sixth. But looking at this from an African viewpoint, the inversion business is totally unimportant. The African analysis is based on whichever pitch is on top. Traditional African music does not see the theoretical concept of inversion as having any particular importance.

What on earth does this have to do with the evolution of African music in America? We need to realize that the slave trade, which brought this music to America, was an entrepreneurial activity and that to protect their merchandise the businessmen who engaged in it needed to control certain elements of the environment of their cargo even prior to its shipment. For many, delivery of that cargo must have been viewed in the context of animal husbandry. Unfortunately, this was, apparently, more often than not the mind set of those who dealt in the trade and of those who valued receipt of the shipment.

So the first thing that these businessmen had to do was to eliminate anything which might unite the slaves – which would give them strength – particularly those things which would permit basic communication between the constituent members of the 'herd'. To accomplish this goal it was absolutely necessary to separate partners from one another and from their children and to mix them, more or less randomly, with those whose language and social habits were as different as possible, thereby reducing the possibility of any unified action among them. This wasn't always completely successful but the idea was to achieve as much disunification as possible. The construction of slave pens on the islands just off the west coast of Africa served more than one purpose: not only did they contain their consignment but they effectively protected it by getting rid of individual renegades and culling out the infirm, the uncontrollable and the diseased. All this was simply a part of the responsibility of the agent in preparation for the transport of the consignment. As barbaric, inhumane and offensive as it was, this may well have been the norm for that stage of the slave trade.

To comprehend how this treatment affected those who were subjected to it, let us look at a particular aspect of African sensibility. In much of the research that has been done into African culture a consistent finding is that music, specifically the master drum and master drummer, held a highly elevated station within a tribe or cultural group. Music was an integral and fundamental necessity for the social and political life of the people, particularly in West Africa. The role of the master drummer was so important that many daily activities and events could not take place without the master drum to introduce or initiate them. Every event, such as a birth, death, the celebration of rights of passage, must be accompanied by music: drumming, song and dance.

Once I was staying in the outskirts of Monrovia, Liberia. I have a vivid recollection of being awakened early one morning, sometime around sunrise, by the sound of drums and singing coming from somewhere nearby. I got up, still half asleep, and looked everywhere to see where it was coming from, as it seemed like it was coming from right outside the window. I could not locate the source and finally woke up enough to realize that it was coming from over the hill, beyond some woods I could see from my window. I listened for some time, fascinated by being where I was and having the experience of hearing this music coming from somewhere just beyond my field of vision but not out of range of my hearing. I finally gave up, as the music was obviously not going to stop any time soon nor was it going to come any closer to where I was. What a lovely way to be awakened. Later that day I told one of my friends in Monrovia about it. He inquired about the quality of the singing and I replied that it appeared to be rather joyful. He said that undoubtedly a child had been born in the village during the night and this was being celebrated at dawn with music – a new life and a new day –

in gratitude for God's bounty to the family and the village.

What I'm attempting to show is that music is so integrated into the African cultural milieu that not to have it in some form would cause the Africans to cease to exist as a people. The entrepreneurs of the slave trade learned this quite early on and, I imagine, found it to their advantage to permit the slaves as much music, singing and dancing as seemed prudent as a way of maintaining a healthy herd. This was pragmatic 'slave' husbandry. As long as they kept the real unifying focus and substantive leadership out of the picture, the rest of African culture worked to their advantage.

Now let's look at the situation from the African's point of view. You have been taken from your family, husband or wife, children, brothers and sisters, are forced into association with strangers whose language you probably cannot understand and are made to cohabit with them with the intimacy of a family. You may see others from your tribe or cultural group in similar situations with the same demands on them but you are not able to associate with them as you once had. The only thing you have in common with those you now live with is the need to express music in some form or another, to continue to breathe the breath of life. This common feature now becomes, through necessity, a bonding for survival.

Other cultures in this situation chose to die and ceased to exist. One such was the native Indians of South America, whose decimation required the introduction of African slaves into the coastal areas of Colombia, Ecuador, Venezuela, etc., under the Spanish. Slaves were needed to work the mines dug in the search for gold, other precious ore and gems, as the native Indian people would just lie down and die rather than work in those conditions. But the African willed himself to survive, one way or another.

Owing to the African's instinctual need to express himself through music, the process of acculturation and integration would have begun as early as the point at which the slaves were separated from each other in the slave pens and would have continued throughout the lives of the first few generations of Africans forced to endure such a dehumanizing experience.

As a result, the three predominant cultural scaler groupings – pentatonic, hexatonic and heptatonic with the resulting harmonic associations – came together in an environment that offered no other alternative but to find a way for each of these natural structures to accommodate the others. The need to do so far outweighed the obstacles to collaboration. Surely a way was found to adapt and adopt each structure within that of another so that each people could express themselves comfortably and this process was continued until each was a cultural part of the other. The end of all this, I believe, was that integration was achieved without any loss to the 'Africanness' of the music.

The premise I propose is that as a result of this integration of distinctive African tribal traits of culture, a composite music grew up within this slave population. As a result, Africans were easily able to adopt and adapt European expressions of music, particularly what we recognize as the basis of all European musical language and theory, triadic harmony.

Let me illustrate what I'm proposing and why I suggest it occurred in this manner. If, as I suggest, the fifths of the pentatonic cultures, the octaves of the hexatonic cultures and the thirds of the heptatonic cultures had been integrated, those expressing the resulting music would have been comfortable with all three characteristics. Because of this, the triadic harmony of European music would have been readily comprehensible. These musical characteristics are very pronounced in the church hymns of the time and the practice of lining out a hymn has a marked similarity to the call and response tradition that is so characteristic of tribal African vocal practices.

Of course, this is impossible to prove but there is evidence found in the music of the Gullah of the Sea Islands of South Carolina, in Georgia and in the musical expression of the African–Caribbeans, all of which retain some of the purity of the older African music, which bears out this premise reasonably well.

As this is not a scholarly paper, I merely set this premise before you to think about and ponder. It is just one possible explanation for the phenomenon that took place in these United States and provides a slightly different view of the history of jazz. Almost any jazz history textbook will supply you with relatively accurate information on the important personalities, periods of change, significant contributors, innovators and innovations in the evolution of this music. So take your pick from the myriad possibilities out there. My proposition is that this phenomenon prepared the African and the African–American community to become the womb within which this American music was conceived and had its embryonic development. My thesis also demonstrates the African roots of this music and explains how they were retained during its evolution and development.

To set out my premise clearly, I will use the analogy of parents and their child: jazz has as its parents an African mother and a European father.

Consider the process of acculturation and integration that I have described. These young men and women were captured, processed and transported to the east coast of the Americas as slaves to be sold by auction to various purchasers. The majority of these purchasers were landowners and producers of crops with a high market value. The predominant view of the slave owners, as history has shown us, was that the African was somewhat above an animal but not totally human either.

In this environment of slavery the African learned from the outset that the owners would not permit the use of any of the elements of musical expression that might be unifying. Thus the master drum or anything resembling it would not be allowed. So a music was developed that did not require the master drum and this was allowed because it aided both the health and the disposition of the slaves.

When the Africans began to imitate the hymns sung by the owners and their families, the possibility grew in the minds of the owners that perhaps the slaves could be taught and converted to Christianity. Efforts to Christianize the African became an acceptable part of plantation life. Interestingly enough, had the owners been able to understand the languages of the various Africans on the plantations, they would have known that many of the slaves already knew about Christ from their Islamic heritage. Of course, not all Africans were Muslims but many were and the celebration of God or Alláh, or any other name that had an equivalent meaning, as the creator was present even in pagan or shamanistic beliefs.

When the slaves became Christian the slave owners showed a little more toleration and the establishment of slave congregations was widely accepted. This afforded the slaves an opportunity to express their musical needs in a form other than work chants and field hollers – which also functioned as a communication network – and was readily accepted by them. Over the years their hymns became almost universally adopted as the African-style Christian religious observance.

In doing research on this subject I came across an evaluation of the singing of these early hymns by someone who had visited a plantation. The singing was described as ragged, badly out of tune and rhythmically frenetic and jerky. But because the slaves were singing Christian songs and therefore beginning to show signs of becoming civilized through their growing acceptance of Christian teachings, the reviewer felt that progress was being made. The reviewer's analysis of the singing was logical from the viewpoint of a person who had no understanding of the differences between African and European cultures or, for that matter, that there was such a thing as culture in Africa at all – a perfect Euro-centric orientation. The saddest thing about this is that after all these hundreds of years there are still many who do not have this understanding. The reason why it was thought that the slaves could not sing 'in tune' was because of the difference in the scale structure of the African heptatonic scale, which closely approximates the European diatonic scale structure with two major differences in pitch. The same goes for the perceived inability of the African to maintain the steady 1–and, 2–and, 3–and, 4–and beat characteristic of the western European meter. The African meter is just different.

Back to the African mother who has embraced, adapted and adopted the European mode of expression to her own unique musical sensibility and is now pregnant with these hymns. In addition, she has even adopted as her own some of the secular reels, jigs and other dance tunes used by the owner in social situations. Like all pregnant mothers, she nurtured this embryo growing inside her body – which is the African slave community – with all the resources available yet she retained the uniqueness of her expression.

So the African mother nurtured this embryo, taking in what she could use and discarding the rest. Every mother will understand this. Years passed before this child, having been nurtured by its mother – who adapted and adopted whatever would feed it while still retaining its African understanding of the significance of its existence – was born. This birth was the appearance of a music, emerging from the obscurity and protection of its black environment into the larger, white European population where it became known for its vitality and creative energy and uniqueness of expression.

Many jazz historians have equated this coming out or birth with the emergence of jazz in New Orleans, Louisiana. I disagree with this idea and propose that wherever there was a substantial population of African descendants, which was certainly the case in urban areas, music was created and expressed that could have been called jazz.

Like any newborn child, jazz was, more or less, under the protection of its parents and, characteristically, the mother was the most dominant and responsible parent. The child, jazz, then began to investigate what was around it and to explore what was outside its immediate environs, again taking whatever it could adapt or adopt and discarding whatever did not fit or nurture it. All children grow little by little and each step of the way the child learns more about the larger world around it. The child will continue to take whatever is usable and add it to the growing process. If something burns, the child will let it go and stay away from it. On the other hand, if something makes the music more clear or meaningful, then it is adapted as a natural way of expressing oneself and the child evolves further.

If you follow the history of jazz you will see how and when this music reached its various stages of development and how it acquired its sophistication. It has now reached maturity and is entering the stage of being an internationally-recognized art music, greatly admired and loved throughout the world as American music, or as some of us now identify it, 'American indigenous classical music'. I like to keep 'indigenous' in the title because the environment in which it evolved is unique to this country, as was the process of acculturation that led to its development and evolution. This evolution could have taken place under no other circumstances except through the introduction of the odious practice of slavery into America with the slaves having come from the continent of Africa.

Whenever a creative energy as commanding as this makes an appearance it will be imitated, philandered, misused and prostituted in the hopes of capitalizing on its vitality. This does not detract from its value to humanity. In the greater scheme of things, all of humanity should and will begin to cherish this incredible gift that has been brought to us as a result of this phenomenon of history. What began as an abomination of human dignity and in the oppression of a highly sophisticated and culturally elevated people ended in the creation of a world-embracing cultural prodigy.

15

Academia

Oakland hired me to conduct a wind ensemble, teach some courses in theory and begin a jazz program. I accepted their conditions but by the time I was in my second year it became obvious that my knowledge and expertise in jazz was going to take precedence over all other activities. During the first semester at Oakland I decided to demonstrate to the students and the community the concept and focus that I would be pursuing in the jazz program. To emphasize this, I brought Sam Rivers, Warren Smith and Richard Davis to the school for a week of workshops and clinics. These workshops then culminated in a performance of the fledgling jazz ensemble and the trio of these guest artists. This blew the minds of some within the university community as they had never before heard jazz at that level of proficiency and creative ingenuity.

It suddenly became clear to the university and my colleagues that what they thought they were going to get and what they got were two different things. In addition to this shock, I brought into the campus, from Detroit, a staff of the leading exponents of the jazz idiom. The precedent had already been set by the music department to use professionals from the Detroit Symphony as instructors at Oakland so I used that to justify using professional jazz musicians as instructors for the students who wanted to study jazz. There was no way, without serious contention, they could deny me the right to do this.

What was the most difficult for many of the music department faculty was facing the reality that all these instructors, with the exception of one, were black. It wasn't long before I heard rumblings within the department about these men.

This finally came to a head at one of our faculty meetings when one of my colleagues expressed serious concern and obvious fear by asking, 'But how are we going to control THEM?' To which I replied, 'That is my responsibility and as long as you feel you need the DSO musicians to teach here for the quality instruction our students have come to expect, then my jazz students deserve a comparable quality of instruction. Symphony musicians are not qualified to teach jazz at the same level of expertise that my instructors are and therefore I will continue to use the very best jazz musicians I can find to teach our jazz students.'

That began a 17–year drive, under duress, to maintain the integrity of what I knew were the essential components of a real, viable and meaningful program of jazz studies. Out of the entire department one man, David Daniels, who was the conductor of the Oakland Symphony Orchestra and professor of most of the courses that related to that sphere of musical knowledge, was consistently in support of what I was doing for my students. He was also the only member of the faculty who would come to the concerts in which we presented our student ensembles. He was also probably the most respected musician in the entire department for his erudition. During the final years of my tenure a composer with solid credentials, Stanley Hollingsworth, was hired to teach theory and composition. After some of the jazz students studied with him, he investigated the program and became another source of moral support and validation.

I sacrificed a lot to keep the program alive, as did the men who made up my staff. They participated in the rehearsals for all the ensembles (we eventually had three) just through their interest and without compensation for their time. As the program grew, one would be chosen to lead one of the ensembles for remuneration but that did not alter the participation of the others. Their commitment to what we were trying to accomplish was magnanimous and it came through in the excitement and effort on the part of the students to learn and excel. The staff knew that this was an opportunity to foster an understanding of what this music really is and of the true foundation of its origins, so they felt their commitment almost as a mission.

To be involved in an activity that was pure and unblemished by unspoken racial bias was too good an opportunity to pass up. I was convinced that if I could establish a quality product, eventually even the most arrogant professorial attitude would have to accept its validity and give the program the recognition it deserved. The rest of the state sure did, though more out of a desire to keep up rather than from a belief in the concept we employed. By the end of the second year of the program at Oakland almost every college and university in Michigan had begun some kind of jazz studies program. Before we began our jazz program all that existed in the state was a couple of extracurricular jazz ensembles that were largely student run and operated. This was very reminiscent of my days at Phillips University so many years before. By this time the collegiate jazz organization NAJE was in place and beginning to make strides in establishing jazz programs around the country but it had not at that time had any effect on Michigan. Oh, yes! The Oakland University jazz program was very successful in the eyes of other institutions because students were transferring from their schools so that they could participate in it.

We created a degree program in jazz studies and within a few years had expanded it to offer a Master's degree in jazz performance – quite unique among schools except Berkeley and North Texas State. I'm not sure that even North Texas offered a Master's degree in jazz at that time. I should imagine that there are quite a few by now.

The Michigan state government recognized the validity of our program and provided financial support for it for one year. The administrator in charge of such things at Oakland assured me this was absolutely not going to be granted. The poor man had egg all over his face when the grant came down with all the money we had asked for.

Then the review of my appointment came up and the possibility of promotion to associate professor with tenure. The department voted against my appointment and I realized

that the only support for me had probably come from Dr
Daniels, who had always been there for me, though I don't
know for sure as he was too honorable a man to divulge what
took place. However, it didn't matter in the final analysis
because the president of the university and the provost came
to me and asked if I would stay at the university, with job
security, as a special instructor. My only question was what
this would do to my salary. They assured me that I would
continue on the same salary scale and on the same track for
increases that I would have had had I been an assistant
professor. Since I had nothing to lose and I wasn't going to
be an accepted member of the department's faculty anyhow,
I figured, 'So what else is new?' and agreed. Here's that
proverbial fence again.

During the first years of the program we attended collegiate jazz festivals. I found that they were really competitions,
with which I conceptually disagree. We would come away with
glowing accolades for the ensemble and our soloists but the
standards were predicated on qualities that were the antithe-
sis of what I had learned from my years as a jazz musician
and the adjudicators were held to those standards. Despite
their knowledge of the music they were asked to judge, by
those standards they could only go so far.

It was very interesting to me to observe my students'
reactions to the results of one festival in which we participated.
We had been chosen as one of the outstanding ensembles,
yet almost every person in the group was upset because
everyone knew that a band from Southern University at New
Orleans had been head and shoulders better than any other
band we had heard. Yes, you heard right. We stayed to hear
all the bands we could, which was in marked contrast with the
usual behavior of the good bands, who would come, play and
then leave. Usually their instructors/professors had the attitude
that they had shown everybody how it should be done and to
listen to others was pointless.

When this band from Southern went unrecognized – except
for one soloist, who was given an honorable mention – we were
all appalled. 'Kid', if you happen to read this, let me share

with you the overwhelming reaction of our students. They all knew that your musicians played jazz well beyond the rest of us. The only distinction between our two bands was that you were an all-African–American group and we were predominantly white. The very qualities that caused us to be recognized were, we were sure, the same qualities that were held as undesirable in your group. Your band was able to express more clearly and effectively the essence of the music and my students all recognized it. This is a clear example of the reason why we quit going to those festivals, even though we were often recognized.

It was like being on the Kenton band again and finding nobody willing to even consider the value of the criteria and the contribution of the African–American musical heritage to this idiom. We have now come to the point where the truth has become the lie and the lie has become the truth. Consequently, the attributes of the music so cherished by Kenton and his like became the standard which 90 per cent of the institutions and their respective instructors advocated for their students. I could not, and still cannot, accept this standard as the definition of jazz. We can see clearly the result of the error of this thinking. Unfortunately, this music has been popularized and marketed, erroneously, as jazz. Thank God, there is music being created and shared by those who adhere to the reality and pursue its continuing evolution. (Thank you Faddis and all your associates.)

To bring this subject to a close, at least for now, let me share with you the attitude that at least one person had about my work at Oakland. These are the words of a fellow educator in the Detroit area who was overheard to make this comment about my program as he spoke informally with a group of jazz teachers: 'That program Holladay has out at Oakland isn't a jazz program; it's a nigger club music program.' Need I say more?

By this time, circa 1976, my marriage had got to the point where it was virtually in shreds. My wife, even though totally sober and working professionally in the field of alcohol abuse counseling, could not resolve her basic difficulties with the male gender. I believe that this was a direct result of the relationship she had with her father who was of an old western baronial landowner mentality which didn't place much value on the females of the family. Without going into her less than desirable childhood, let me simply suggest that her inability to accept the situation that brought about her life's burdens did not change with our attempts at nurturing each other into a positive familial relationship. This eventually resulted in our entering into a year of waiting as required by the Bahá'í teachings.

The year of waiting is a wonderful practice. It requires that instead of running out to a lawyer and instituting the proceedings for a divorce, you are required to spend a year living apart, fulfilling all your parental and spousal responsibilities. This offers each member of the relationship, during that year, time for meditation and reflection on what has brought about the need for the separation. Following that period and after efforts to resolve the difficulties that perpetrated the year of waiting, a Bahá'í divorce may be granted. Even then you are required to sit down together and consult with each other to determine whether the source of the demise of affection can be overcome, remedied, compromised or circumvented so that the union can continue. If that is not possible, or the reconciliation proves unsuccessful, it is then permissible to file for a legal divorce.

In the year prior to applying for the year of waiting I had borrowed the money to cover the expense of going on pilgrimage to the holy ground at the World Centre of the Bahá'í Faith at Haifa, Israel. I had applied for this pilgrimage some years before and when the time came for me to go, I either had to decline the opportunity or go to the bank – which, of course, I did.

The remains of Bahá'u'lláh are buried in Bahjí, which is across the bay from Haifa and just a few kilometers outside the old prison city of 'Akká where He had been imprisoned upon His arrival there. The Herald of Bahá'u'lláh's coming and an independent Revelator Himself, the Báb, is buried in a shrine on the side of Mount Carmel overlooking the bay in Haifa. Also buried in that same shrine is 'Abdu'l-Bahá, Bahá'u'lláh's son. Identified in Bahá'u'lláh's Will and Testament as the Center of His Covenant with humankind, 'Abdu'l-Bahá is the perfect exemplar of His father's Revelation.

The most compelling request of my prayers at the shrines was to resolve the failure of my marriage and to seek guidance on how to address the disunity that had become so intolerable and which was beginning to affect our children, though I later found that they were, at that time, unaware of it.

Upon my return from pilgrimage and after the passing of a few months, I felt it necessary to embark on the year of waiting. I subsequently moved into faculty housing at the university and from there I was able to effectively co-parent the children with Jo and we actually became better friends. An example of this was Jo's automatic response when she was involved in a car accident and was taken to hospital: she had the hospital call me at the university to come and be with her, for both her sake and the children's. It is really funny how we became better friends – Jo was more supportive of me in separation than she had ever been while married. I've never really understood what that was all about and got to the point where I really didn't care if I did know, since the relationship we were having apart was so much better than it ever was when we were together. God knows! I'll have to ask her in the next world.

We followed all of the stipulations of the year of waiting without any resolution to our difficulties. I did not immediately pursue the civil divorce, as much for the cost as for anything else. We co-parented the children throughout this entire ordeal and were able to remain rather good friends, under the circumstances, but were unable to get beyond our dislike of each other as marriage partners.

I had moved out twice before while we were in New York and once when we were living together in Denver. Why I thought it was going to be different each time I went back into the relationship is beyond me, as I look back on it. Of course, then there is the other side of the coin which says that had I not gone back our children, Bud and Helen, would not be here on the planet. I can't wish for that, for they and our grandchildren, Joseph and Leslie, are all very precious. So you can see that there is always a greater reality to perceive in all things great and small.

Sometime later our marriage counselor, who had attempted to assist us, though to no avail, suggested that what I needed now was a friend. He offered his friendship on a weekly basis to help me get through the year. This was definitely of value to me as Jo, for whatever reason, was not open to counseling – or at least to that particular counselor – as a way of resolving our marriage difficulties, leaving it up to me to find a resolution.

Many years later our daughter helped me realize that Jo felt she could not have done anything different with her life. Jo had decided that she would not make any effort to have a marital relationship with another man because she was afraid that she would only pursue the same course of action and she was reluctant to inflict that on another man. She did, however, have a very deep, close and personal, though detached, relationship with a priest she met while acting as a counselor at a treatment facility – sponsored by the Catholic diocese – for priests with substance abuse difficulties. Their relationship was long and true and we all comforted her in the days leading to her passing in 1995.

16

Diane and the Fortress for Well-Being

Upon my return from pilgrimage I was asked to join a group of people who had been appointed by the National Teaching Committee of the National Spiritual Assembly of the Bahá'ís of the United States to function as the Mainland Michigan District Teaching Committee. We had the responsibility to oversee and assist all the Bahá'í communities in mainland Michigan, which is one big area covering the complete hand, as it is often described, of the lower peninsula of Michigan. Every month we would meet for a weekend and sometimes we met every other weekend. This gathering would be held at various locations throughout our designated area of the state so that we could consult with one spiritual assembly or another to assist in their teaching efforts.

The relationship we developed within the committee was extraordinary and I looked forward to our meetings, which as I have said, were rather frequent. This service also gave me an opportunity to become acquainted with many of the Bahá'ís throughout the lower peninsula and to interact with them in a very positive way. It's a good thing I was relatively young, as we were on the go a lot and I was still able to maintain my responsibilities at the university as well as a relationship with the family. Often the children would spend their weekends with me and during the summer they would move in and live with me. I was able to spend many evenings with them during the school year and I would often share in their activities at school and in their community. All this was made possible by our close proximity to each other.

About two months after the end of the year of waiting I met, quite by accident – or, one might say, by intervention of providence – a young lady who, in her capacity as secretary of the local assembly, requested the District Teaching Committee to consult with the Ann Arbor Spiritual Assembly's Teaching Committee on a project that they were contemplating. Since the members of the District Teaching Committee took turns to respond to such requests, I was informed that this was my turn. So I dutifully made a call to the contact person in Ann Arbor and set up a meeting with the teaching committee. The lady with whom I made the initial contact was Diane Wood, who had made the original inquiry.

Well, I went to the meeting and met and talked with the members about how this project might best be realized. Following this consultation the group moved to a more informal social environment and we made small talk on a variety of topics, one of which was my particular interest in the music cultures of the world. Apparently I piqued the interest of my host, Ms Wood, by the comments I made; she had been a student of social anthropology and found my comments intriguing.

She approached me during the social part of the evening in such a way as to cause me concern: the look in her eyes was all too familiar to me from my years on the road as a musician. I was afraid that she was a frustrated, most likely married, woman who was overly attracted to an imagined source of compassion. Not wishing to embarrass her or myself, I backed away a bit. I saw in her eyes that she recognized what was happening and she backed away as well. We continued the conversation on social anthropology and world music, setting up a defined comfort zone between us. She was as cute as she could be and nicely put together, which was always appreciated by yours truly, and I left that evening with great relief that the entire incident hadn't compromised either of us.

The next day I called a dear friend who lived in Ann Arbor, a member of that Bahá'í community, and asked if she knew Diane Wood. She replied, 'Oh, yes! She's a very nice girl.' So then I asked, 'Is she married?' She first giggled and then said, 'No!' That, naturally, prompted the next question, 'How old is she?' I thought she was probably in her late twenties at best and I was then almost 50, so it was very important to me. Her answer was 'Oh! I think she must be at least 30.' All the time she was giggling, as it was obvious why I was asking all these questions. She continued by suggesting that I give Diane a call and get better acquainted, which I did. It was September of '78.

We visited Diane's parents in Bay City, Michigan, at Thanksgiving. By Christmas we had flown to Kansas to visit my mother and she and Diane immediately fell in love with each other. This was a monumental contrast to meetings with other women, as my mother hadn't cared much for any of the girls or women I had brought home, though she would not have said so in so many words. (She wasn't at all happy with my marriage to Jo, though she didn't oppose it at the time.) However, I would hear about it and then some after the relationship was over. Diane and I were married in March of '79.

After all this stress, before the marriage I began to have physical symptoms of all kinds of maladies, particularly an attack of arrhythmia that wouldn't go away. Part of it was brought on, no doubt, by my recognition of the need to bring the old marriage to a legal end through the court. Also, I was embarking on a new marital relationship and I had no idea of its potential, other than that we had approached it from the direction presented to us through Bahá'u'lláh's writings on the subject.

Having put off legal proceedings because of monetary concerns, I had avoided the reality of what one must go through to effect a legal divorce. It was much more stressful than I thought it would be even though the advantages of a new marital relationship were becoming evident. Oddly enough, the day of my court appearance for the divorce, 22 December, was the same day that the marriage had begun 20 years earlier. So you can see the potential for high stress levels.

Diane and I had set the date for our marriage to coincide with our winter breaks at our respective universities and as the time came nearer I truly started to get cold feet. This wasn't because I didn't know whether I loved Diane or not but was due to the years of travail in my first marriage and the insecurity I felt in fulfilling the role I should in a Bahá'í marriage. As I got shaky I suggested to Diane that maybe we should postpone the marriage to a slightly later date. She responded in a most mature and loving way by suggesting that we would always be friends and that she would love me as a friend whether we were married or not but she would not accept a postponement of the wedding. It was the calm assurance of her love and her willingness to forgo the marriage if that is what I truly wanted, without that changing her feelings for me, that allowed me to exorcise, to some degree, my fear of entering into another marital relationship.

We were married on 3 March 1979, which happens to be right at the beginning of the Bahá'í month of fasting. We had set the date without taking into consideration that fact. Fortunately for us, we attended a Bahá'í meeting at which the speaker was an old friend of ours, Peter Khan, whom we had known while he and his wife Janet were at Michigan University and Eastern Michigan respectively. Peter and Janet now reside in Israel at the World Centre of the Bahá'í Faith, where he is serving on the Universal House of Justice. However, when this event occurred they were living in Australia, their original home.

Peter and Janet were very happy about our coming marriage and advised us, since we had chosen the date of 3 March, to be sure to travel at least nine hours away from Ann Arbor before we stopped for our honeymoon. The reason they recommended this was that by doing so we would be exempt from the fast until we returned to our home. They shared this bit of advice with us because they too had married in March during the fast but had not traveled for a honeymoon and had attempted to fast as a newly-married couple. This, they explained, was a horrible mistake and extremely difficult on both of them and on their marriage. All of this was offered in a most humorous and good-natured manner, while they shared with us the reason for their recommendation.

We dutifully projected the driving distance of nine hours

from Ann Arbor and chose Berea, Kentucky, as our honeymoon location, which turned out to be a great choice in every respect. We met some wonderful Bahá'ís there who made us feel like Berea was our home. We returned the next year, at their invitation, to present a program for their community at Berea College.

I was still having some difficulty with the arrhythmia and was on medication that had a side effect that was not particularly conducive to a satisfying new marital relationship. Diane never brought the issue up in any conversation we had but I sure could feel the angst. I decided to get off the medicine and prayed that the arrhythmia would not reappear. It didn't. In a subsequent conversation with a friend who was a doctor, I found that the whole business had been blown out of proportion and that the medication was probably unnecessary. My attending physician had, apparently, found a great opportunity to make a large payment on his Mercedes.

The spring brought the Duke Ellington Orchestra to Detroit for a gig. Diane and I had, for our first date, attended a concert by the Ellington Orchestra at the university in Ann Arbor a few months before. This time Mercer had sent a message to me requesting that I come to this gig in Detroit. We responded positively to the request and I was, therefore, able to introduce my new wife to everybody I knew on the band.

That evening Mercer offered me the baritone chair, starting in July, which was, I think, the next month. Since I had played with the Ellington Alumni Orchestra in New York, this was an opportunity to associate myself once again with the most legendary of all orchestras in jazz history. It was also an opportunity to get away from the stress of trying to remain detached and stay focused and creative at Oakland during some very trying times there for me. Diane and I talked about what it would entail and the pros and cons of the life of a road musician with respect to one's family, particularly as we were just starting out on this new relationship. She concurred that the change would be good for me, both professionally and psychologically.

By 1 July 1979 I was on the road traveling all over the country. This situation challenged our new marriage to survive extended separations with, of course, very dynamic reunions from time to time. Diane went on the road with me for a two-week period and realized, emphatically, that the road was not her cup of tea in any way, shape or form.

Diane and I have shared with each other at various times our recollection of those early years of our marriage and have become extremely aware of the wisdom and value of the teachings of Bahá'u'lláh about marriage. He refers to it as a 'fortress for well-being and salvation', which has far-reaching implications and ramifications. These have been explored extensively by Bahá'u'lláh, 'Abdu'l-Bahá and Shoghi Effendi in various writings which give great emphasis to the responsibility and importance of this association. You may have noticed that I have not used the term 'institution' when I refer to marriage. The reason for this is that I believe that for the majority of people the relationship that is implied by this word is a unit which is realized by the wedding vows to 'love, honor, cherish and obey'.

In contrast, the wedding vows for a Bahá'í marriage are 'We will all, verily, abide by the Will of God', spoken in turn by each marriage partner. As you can see, this is a pledge each makes to God and, by association, to each other. It offers no specific definition of the respective roles to be played by the man and the woman; it merely rehearses their willingness to be obedient to the Will of God.

Dr Hossain Danesh, a psychologist and currently director of Landegg Academy in Switzerland, presented a talk on this subject many years ago at the Louhelen Bahá'í School in Davison, Michigan, which Diane and I attended. The imagery he used to explain his understanding of what Bahá'u'lláh intended was, we found, both fascinating and illuminating. Dr Danesh drew two circles close to each other but not overlapping. These he identified as the husband and wife – distinct, separate yet close in association. He then drew a third circle that intersected both of the other two. This he identified as the 'marriage'. By this we came to understand that we are individually accountable to God only but we each also have a second relationship, which is with the marriage, which truly embraces us both. Since this is a spiritual union as well as a physical one, our responsibility to each other is to assist the other in his or her spiritual growth by being a source of strength and support when the other is in need – as anyone would do for his best friend. This is my simple way of describing my understanding of this unique relationship. Bahá'u'lláh also has said that marriage is for eternity, not just until we leave this plane of existence, or, as the standard vows suggest, 'until death us do part'.

'Abdu'l-Bahá, the son of Bahá'u'lláh, the Center of His Covenant and the sole interpreter of His words states:

> Marriage, among the mass of the people, is a physical bond, and this union can only be temporary, since it is foredoomed to a physical separation at the close.
>
> Among the people of Bahá, however, marriage must be a union of the body and of the spirit as well, for here both husband and wife are aglow with the same wine, both are enamored of the same matchless Face, both live and move through the same spirit, both are illumined by the same glory. This connection between them is a spiritual one, hence it is a bond that will abide forever. Likewise do they enjoy strong and lasting ties in the physical world as well, for if the marriage is based both on the spirit and the body, that union is a true one, hence it will endure.*

I guess you've got the idea by now that I kind of like this woman and that the thought of spending eternity with her is very appealing. In our early days together we were so anxious to follow the guidance of the Revelation regarding marriage that we sat down together and read the whole compilation *A Fortress for Well-Being*, which had been put together for the Bahá'í Comprehensive Deepening Program. We purposely set aside our natural inclinations and kept a space between us that would allow us to become acquainted

---

* 'Abdu'l-Bahá, *Selections from the Writings of 'Abdu'l-Bahá*, p. 117.

with each other's character, with the goal of seeing if we could, in fact, become each other's best friend.

Not only did Diane become my best friend but she has also made it possible for me to realize that the person I thought I could be was, in fact, who I was. She has said to me on many occasions during our 21-going-on-22 years of marriage that I have made it possible for her to be who she really is without fear of repercussions.

To keep this chapter from becoming toooooooo verbose, let me say that Diane is the personification of the title of my CD and is the person for whom the title track was written, 'Sweetness and Light'. I always talk about her when I perform this composition and I usually close all my concerts with it, to her embarrassment, though she is beginning to get used to it a little. I tell audiences that I originally wrote it for her and then discovered, after the birth of our first grandchild, Joey, that the same qualities of light and sweetness flowed from the eyes and the inner soul of this child, qualities I had found in the inner eyes of my beloved Diane. To take this adulation just one step further, you can ask anybody if they know Diane Holladay and they will identify her with those same qualities. All the Persian Bahá'í women who know her dearly love her and she doesn't understand why. Men are drawn to her and they don't know why; they usually assume it's chemistry, although the Bahá'í men admire the qualities they perceive in her. In a former life I would probably have been extremely jealous of the attention she receives. This is not a factor now – or maybe I growed up just a little bit since meeting her, as Diane is very clear about how she feels about moi. It ain't goin' to git any better than that.

17

Duke Ellington Orchestra

My association with the Duke Ellington Orchestra lasted for a year and two months before I returned to Oakland to begin teaching again. During that time all my physical maladies went away and I was reinvigorated both spiritually and physically by getting back in touch with my real self and putting my instruments under my fingers again, where they should have been all along. As a result I resolved never to let that happen again – playing is an essential ingredient of my life.

The tour itself was quite an experience as we went not only all over the United States but to many countries in Europe and South America and to Japan and Canada. Fortunately from my perspective, Cootie Williams had agreed to come out with the band for this tour, in response to a great deal of pleading and negotiating by Mercer, I'm sure. Having the opportunity to get to know Cootie and hang out with him during that year was one of this life's cherished events.

The only members of the band under Mercer's direction who had experienced the essence of what the Duke Ellington Orchestra was about were Cootie, Chuck Conners, Malcolm Taylor, Barrie Lee Hall and Rocky White. Then there was 'Geezle', Harold Minerve. Geezle had worked with Duke but mostly as a sub, I think. However, he did have a grasp of what it took to make the band sound like an Ellington organization and had often worked with Mercer both before and after Mercer took over the band. I believe that he was a part of the Ellington Alumni Orchestra that I had worked with some years before in New York.

It was always interesting to me, and somewhat disconcerting, that the men who really knew how to make the band sound as it should didn't try to bring that about either directly or through off-stage consultation with the men who hadn't experienced it for themselves. It doesn't matter, they didn't – but it was always a bit frustrating to me. I did, one time, in a private conversation, suggest to Mercer that he might take advantage of the presence of these men who were on the band to help convey the process by which the sound of the band could be reconstructed. I was met with resistance, not in an aggressive manner, but with the resolve that he would get the band in shape without anybody's help.

That proved not to be forthcoming. I then realized why none of the old members were taking responsibility for helping to shape the sound of the band. Rehearsals were a great disappointment for me and a frustration for everyone else that I observed. Still, we were playing the music of the master of orchestral composition and arranging in conjunction with his musical alter ego, Billy Strayhorn. The greatest fortune for the band was to have, besides Cootie, Mulgrew Miller on piano. He played so beautifully and in keeping with the tradition associated with the master himself. Not a clone, by any means, but clearly in the style.

As before with the Alumni Orchestra, I was having a ball playing all of Harry Carney's notes and expressing them in his fashion. You may remember my earlier reference to playing baritone as if in duet with the lead alto. That eventually turned out to be the means by which Geezle was willing to accept me into the band as an integral member.

Geezle was always challenging my ability to phrase with him and play with a conception of time that was reminiscent of the old band. This was most noticeable when we played 'Jeep's Blues', which was a VERY slow blues – slow blues might just be the most difficult time concept to gain command of, when done right. There was a phrase of descending 16th notes on the end of the fourth bar that Geezle would really lay back into. Fortunately, my earlier days with Ron Washington in Denver had prepared me for this eventuality very well, as Ron loved to play slow blues. Anyhow, Geezle was sure that he was going to lose me in that concept and got so far back one night that he about lost it for himself and for the band but to his chagrin I was right up his b***. From that moment on we were buddies musically and he would often lean over to me, after we had played a phrase of a similar nature, and say, 'Man, I wish these other cats would play with me like you do.' Thanks Ron!

The bookings for the band often left us with time off after three or four weeks of one-nighters. The time off was long enough (four days to two or three weeks) to permit me to return to Ann Arbor to be with Diane. She was handling this itinerant life of mine pretty well, I thought, for a newly married woman whose husband was not around a whole lot. Then there was the occasional long weekend when Diane would drive to wherever we were going to be in the midwest to spend time with me. Those were wonderful occasions, like a honeymoon all over again. She tried to travel with the band for a couple of weeks during a vacation from her gig at the University of Michigan but found that one-nighters were not for her, to say the least. She found the constant travel with new hotels or motels each night – and sometimes only every other night – to be too unsettling for her constitution, which wasn't the strongest to start with. Life on the road is not for everyone.

During that year (1979–80), whenever the band was to go out of the country I would share with the Bahá'í National Center a copy of our itinerary. They would then communicate with the various national assemblies of those countries who would inform their local assemblies of the arrival of the Ellington Orchestra in their cities and of the Bahá'í saxophone player who would be a part of the band. This led to some very interesting encounters.

The tours that stand out most in my memory are ones of Australia, Argentina and Japan. The aspect of the tours that made them most notable was this connection between myself and the Bahá'í communities in which we performed. More often than not, when the band arrived and the plane had taxied to the terminal, a large group of Ellington fans would be waiting, complete with a musical group of some sort. Most often, particularly in Australia, the band would be a traditional New Orleans style group. Whenever we got off the plane there was also a small group of people holding a sign saying something like 'Welcome to Buenos Aires' or Adelaide or wherever, often with Alláh-u-Abhá inscribed on the banner along with my name.

This happened so often that Mercer took me aside after one such arrival somewhere – I can't remember whether it was in Australia or Argentina; it seems to me that it was in Argentina, in a place rather remote and not a major city. Mercer was a bit perturbed that a crowd, small as it was, greeted me every time that the band was being met. 'What's the deal here, Marv?' he asked – he knew me from the days when I was Marv Holladay, before the Doc was added. 'Who are these people who keep meeting you at the airport whenever we arrive? It ain't cool for you to be seen as special in the band.' I replied, 'This is my family who have come to greet me. They're not identifying me with the Ellington Orchestra at all, are they?' Realizing that this was true, his response was that there was no way I could have family at every place we had been. In turn, I told him that, indeed, I do have a Bahá'í family in every place on the globe, wherever we might appear, and that they would continue to come to greet me. However, I said, if ever they should publicly associate me with the band I would ask them to cease and desist. That never happened. I don't seem to recall any such incident occurring in Japan or in Europe.

In January we had the pleasure of touring Japan. Japan was a great trip for me. The Japanese jazz fans were really something to behold. They knew more about each one of us than we did. They knew who we had played with, what our strengths were and what we had been doing for the past 20 years or so. I couldn't believe that anyone knew what I had been doing for the past year, let alone the past 20. But that is the total immersion so characteristic of the Japanese when they become interested in something.

Most of our time was spent in Tokyo but we did get to Osaka, Niigata and Hiroshima (pronounced He-do-she-ma.

I've been bothered by the mispronunciation of this city's name ever since the second world war. The r is a soft d sound, as in prodigy). I remember the train trip from Niigata back to Tokyo because Niigata is in the northwest end of the island and is extremely cold, traditionally having heavy snow falls each winter. Since we were there in January, you know that the snow was deep. It was fascinating to watch the people up on their roofs with big plows, like you would expect to see on the front of a small truck or something, which were pushed by hand to shove the snow off the roofs. The snow would be as much as four to five feet deep and the weight could have been too much for the roofs and thus very dangerous.

The high speed trains were really a gas and the accommo- dation was excellent. We used these trains for all of the band's travel throughout the main island of Japan with the exception of one flight to Osaka for the first concert of the tour with a return to Tokyo the next day.

During our sojourn in Japan I discovered that a former student of mine was residing in the Suginami-ku area of Tokyo. Bob and Maki Rann had been good friends from the early days of their relationship and when they decided to get married Maki's father held me responsible for the success of their union. This, I found, was the tradition in Japanese culture. So when I decided to stay in Tokyo for a week after the band returned to the States, the first act I had to perform was to go to Maki's father's house to pay my respects to both him and his wife. They are wonderful parents and very hospitable hosts. They even insisted that Maki arrange for me to experience the tea ceremony, which she did of course, and it was truly an honor to be so feted. The tea ceremony is not an activity that one can experience as a tourist but only at the request of someone who is respected. This was therefore a gift to me from Maki's parents.

Also during the week I spent in Tokyo I had the opportu- nity to perform with a terrific cellist/bass player who was widely respected in the more avant-garde musical circles of Tokyo. We played concerts at two different venues, one in a large department store and another in a smaller coffee shop kind of place. At the larger venue we were booked to play both as a duo and as a back-up to Kazuko Shiraishi's reading of her own poetry. At the smaller venue, it was just Keiko Midorikawa (me-do-di-kah-wah, remember Hiroshima), which I found out means Green River, and myself. Keiko was on cello and I was playing bass clarinet on both these occasions.

Playing with Keiko was like playing with somebody inside your head. It was a special kind of musical experience where we would begin as two independent units but would immediately become, rather mysteriously, a part of each other, so much so that I would be aware that I was leading the flow of the music and then, without any warning or preparation, I would find myself following. This would go back and forth until we would suddenly realize that we were coming to the end of the piece we were constructing. We would then begin to find our way to the end. We would know that it was over and would stop playing after the final notes were allowed to blend into each other long enough to bring closure to the experience.

I've only had that kind of musical experience with two other musicians, both bass players, Richard Davis and my current bass man Eliot Wadopian. Yes, that is the premiere bassist Richard Davis who is currently a professor of music at the University of Wisconsin and one of the most widely sought after bass men in the business. Eliot does not have Richard's fame but is one of the finest bass players I've ever played with and that does include Richard.

During the time we were playing our concerts with the Ellington Orchestra I was able to meet with the Bahá'ís of Tokyo at their Center in an area called Shinjuku-ku. I was invited on one of our days off to make a presentation at the home of a Japanese Bahá'í who was married to an American. They were responsible for the establishment of a number of English-language schools throughout the area. They had a very substantial home by Japanese standards. Kimiko acted as my interpreter. John and Kimiko Schwerin are now serving at the Bahá'í World Center at Haifa, Israel.

Bob and Maki made it possible for me to attend a

performance of kabuki at the National Theatre in Tokyo with a friend of theirs as my host and interpreter. I had heard recordings of kabuki but they didn't come anywhere close to the experience of being there. So nearly 28 years after I had been at Camp Drake outside Tokyo and had turned down an opportunity to see it, I finally saw a live performance of kabuki.

There was one other high mark of my stay in Japan. My visit coincided with the sumo grand national championships. Bob and I watched the matches every night on TV and I became fascinated with the sport. Bob promised that the next time I was in Japan he would find a way to get me to some of the matches. Maki sent me a cup with all the grand national champions' names engraved on it in Conji. I still have it on my desk with pens and pencils in it. I'm afraid to use it as a cup.

I could have spent another week with the Ranns in Tokyo but both Bob and I were coming down with something that was reminiscent of the flu so I felt it would be better for me to get back home to recover. I didn't want to be bedridden in Tokyo in the Ranns' apartment, which was about the size of a small efficiency in New York City. Three definitely made a crowd.

I got a flight out the next day and was very happy to get back to Diane and Ann Arbor, Michigan. As it turned out, it wasn't the flu so it didn't get much worse.

Then came the tour of Australia. I must share with you our rather dramatic preparation for that trip. Before we left for Australia we had a most interesting experience in Portland, Oregon. We were billeted in Seattle but flew down to Portland to play a concert with Ella Fitzgerald. Our return flight was to be that same night so we could prepare for our flight to Australia. We flew down from Seattle early that day for a rehearsal with Ella that afternoon. The rehearsal went very well – work with Ella always did. That evening we had a sold-out crowd for the concert and Ella was, as usual, in fine form and the band was pretty good as well. We finished the concert and were on our way out the stage door when we found ourselves in a kind of snow storm, only it wasn't cold and the flakes looked and felt more like ash. It was then that we found that Mount St Helens had erupted that night while we were performing. We couldn't take our return flight to Seattle as all air traffic in the area was grounded. The dude in charge of the concert was able to find us accommodation at a local motel but we had to double up to get everybody in a room. There were many stranded air travelers in Portland that night. The next day we flew back to Seattle and on the way were able to see the result of the eruption the night before. The day after that we were on our way to Australia.

One story about the Australian tour took place at the Opera House in Sydney. I think I have made clear my aversion to electronics, particularly when they are used in concerts of what are essentially acoustical orchestras. (Let me qualify that: this is not applicable to outside arenas or parks or, for that matter, huge barns or hangers, where some kind of sound reinforcement is necessary.) Here we were playing in one of the world's most acoustically faultless venues and to my shock there were banks of huge speakers on both sides of the stage. You would have thought they were expecting at least a heavy metal rock group to be appearing. Nothing was said about using this gross sound reinforcement, which had obviously been planned and arranged for us. When we began to play you could hear that the sound coming from the speakers was way beyond what the band was producing and the resulting sound was a grotesque perversion of what we actually sounded like.

It came my turn to do my thing, which was always the same tune, 'Sophisticated Lady'. This was a feature that Harry Carney had traditionally done throughout the years. I went to the microphone and began to play the first note that leads into the melody. When I heard the God-awful sound of my first two notes emitting from the speakers I immediately walked away from the mike and continued to play the first bar of the tune. The sound engineer, assuming that I had no idea of how to play on microphone, began to run gain on the mike to pick up my sound so that by the second bar he began to get feedback from his speakers. My response to this was immediately to walk to the lip of the stage of this grand, acoustically beautiful, opera house, and continue to play the third bar of the tune. I continued to offer the beauty of one of Duke's most enduring compositions from that location. The band, understanding what I was doing and why, really backed off its volume so as to defeat the sound system that I might be heard in what I had, obviously, declared as an acoustical offering of 'Sophisticated Lady'. This allowed me to end the piece, as was my habit, with a cadenza that ended with a sub-toned dominant to tonic conclusion. The audience loved it and I allowed them to hear my sound as it truly existed and not through the predetermined mind set of a pair of rock-and-roll ears.

The importance of this story is demonstrated by what took place two or three tunes after my solo. Cootie was introduced to play 'The Shepherd of the Night Flock'. He came out of the wings playing the opening bar of the tune and walked straight to the lip of the stage where I had stood and proceeded to offer his entire performance from that position, again with the very enthusiastic appreciation of the audience.

My first realization of this current use of electronics was during a jazz festival the Ellington band was playing in Munich, Germany. We had arrived early, which allowed us to hear some of the other groups who were scheduled to play before us. There was a big band on stage beginning its performance – I think it was a European big band but I'm not sure. I decided that I would walk out front and hear the band from the audience's perspective – we usually listened to the bands from the side of the stage or from the back. When I got out front I was clearly in the back of the arena that we were to play in. The sound was loud even there and the sound board, complete with the engineers, was in that same area. I decided that I would walk forward to try to hear the band from the stage. All I could hear was the banks of speakers on both sides of the stage and they were very loud. I continued to approach the stage, assuming that if I got close enough I would be able to hear the band. Finally I was standing at the edge of the stage, not more than 20 feet away from the saxophone section, and still could not hear the band on the stage at all. Only the sound emanating from the speakers was audible and from my perspective it was a distortion of what the band actually sounded like. It was at that moment that I realized that this was a phenomenon of the contemporary music industry with its orientation to what it believes constitutes an appropriate concert ambience.

When I was in my first years as an undergraduate at Phillips University the recording industry came out with a new improvement to recording reproduction technology. Of course, everything was acoustical then. It was called FFRR, a way of fine tuning frequency to create a clearer image than had been previously possible. A few years later the industry came out with stereo, which really began to reproduce sound that was close to the natural acoustical properties of sound. The objective had always been to come as close to the acoustical sound as was scientifically possible. We were amazed that you could almost hear the bow as it was pulled across the strings of a violin or cello and the occasional gurgle of saliva from a jazz saxophone player in the heat of a profound improvisational rendering. We were constantly amazed at the realness of the sound.

Now let's step forward a few decades. Here I am, standing in front of a big band. They are playing with intensity and obviously shouting out the chorus. Yet I am hearing a concert whose aesthetic philosophy is to create for the audience a sound that comes as close as possible to that of a recording. The purpose of the entire recording industry has made a complete 180 degree turn. At that moment I knew what I must do when the opportunity arose – and the concert in the Sydney Opera House was the first of many opportunities. The fascinating thing is that when audiences are afforded the opportunity to listen to jazz performed in an acoustical setting, most show a marked appreciation of the end result. The European classical milieu still demands such an acoustical setting, as it should.

I was captivated by the quality of life and the cleanliness of the environment that seemed to prevail in the cities of

Australia. It was a shock to realize that Sydney was like an American city would have been 50 or 75 years ago. There were no signs of X-rated theatres, girls were not working the downtown streets and you were not constantly being lured to get this or that for your enjoyment. Our hosts, however, believed that as we were from New York City, we would prefer to be billeted where the action was, so they booked our lodgings in the area of Sydney called King's Cross. You Aussies may appreciate this. What happened in Australia was similar to what would have been the norm in most major American cities 90 years ago. In those days in the US, if you didn't know anybody in town, you would ask a cabbie where the action was. Nowadays it's in your face and you can't get away from it. I saw Sydney, Melbourne and even Adelaide as being like those old American cities. Brisbane was a little bit more open but not so that you would know it. Darwin and Townsville were very provincial, although beer halls were abundant. A couple of years later I had the privilege of returning to Townsville to participate in a festival and had a grand time with the many friends I met while there on tour with the Ellington band.

We left Adelaide to fly to our next engagement in Darwin, on the northern-most edge of Australia. When we arrived in Alice Springs for refueling a few hours later, we were informed that the members of the band would be going on to Darwin by a two-engine puddle jumper instead of by the jet we had been on. The exception, of course, was Mercer and his family, who continued on by jet. We were all a bit miffed but accepted our fate, as it were, rather calmly. Two things occurred as a result of this change of flight plans. First, when I left the plane I was met by an individual of typical Aussie-outback appearance. He approached me as I got off the plane with the greeting of 'Alláh-u-Abhá'. I was not only surprised but shocked, since there was no way for him to know which of the musicians with the Ellington Orchestra was Doc Holladay. His answer was that the people in Adelaide had sent him a picture of me by fax and had described me, which isn't too hard to do, so he knew who he was looking for. I also realized, of course, that I'm white – I think there were only two of us on the band who were somewhat light in skin pigment. So while everybody on the band was grousing about the delay, I was having a great time talking with another family member about everything from what it was like living in the outback of Australia to what activities were on going in the Bahá'í community of Alice Springs. It turned out that there was a sizable community there but he was the only one who had the flexibility to come to the airport in the middle of the afternoon. The joy of having such a great extended family is beyond words.

The other gift that was given us, in place of being allowed to continue on to Darwin in the jet, was very eventful. The pilot told us as we were arriving in Darwin that since most of the passengers were members of the orchestra, he was going to take us on a side trip through the Australian version of the Grand Canyon. He hung a right and flew into a canyon where we could all see the expanse and beauty of the terrain. When he reached the end of the canyon he made a u-turn and came back down through it so that we could all view the canyon from the other side. What a bounty! When we arrived in Darwin none of the previous complaints were heard.

While in Darwin I got my first opportunity to make contact with Aboriginal Australian lore and artifacts; this was through an Australian lady who was married to an Aboriginal gentleman. She owned and operated an art store that sold Aboriginal artifacts for the artists themselves. It was through her that I was able to purchase a bark painting and a medium-sized didjeridoo or yidaki.

On this tour of Australia I was playing a piece featuring the baritone sax which was from a suite that Duke had written and recorded as a part of the album *Afro–Eurasian Eclipse*. The title of the tune I played each night just happened to be 'Didjeridoo'. Ellington was famous for composing impressions of the music he heard while touring around the world and recording his compositions when he returned to the States. 'Didjeridoo' was his impression of the Aboriginal instrument and its sound.

While in Townsville, Mercer and a small group of selected

members of the orchestra met with a group of educators from a college and a university there who wanted to know our views on how to educate young people in the art and history of jazz. They were specifically interested in the different approach one would use to teach jazz from that of teaching the European classical tradition that had been long established in Australia in colleges, universities and conservatories. This was right up my alley, as I had been doing that very thing at Oakland University for some 15 years by that time and so my input to the group was reasonably profound and current in practice. I guess it was because of my offering to that body of educators that they asked me to return at a later date to explore further my philosophy and approach to the subject.

The Ellington Orchestra appeared in most of the summer jazz festivals in Europe again that year and that allowed me another opportunity to meet and socialize with many of the great musicians with whom I had previously been associated during my years in New York and Los Angeles. That is probably the best thing about these festivals purely from the musician's standpoint. Everybody is so busy trying to make ends meet during the rest of the year that they usually don't have either the time or the opportunity just to socialize with each other. The need to travel, mostly out of the US for economic survival, keeps every musician on the move most of the time.

At these festivals upwards of a hundred musicians congregate in the same town for the same purpose. Consequently you keep running into other musicians as you get around to the various venues to hear this group and that, musicians you never get a chance to hear back home because you are most likely working at the same time somewhere else. The hotel bars and coffee shops during the day and after the festival has closed for the day are full of musicians you haven't seen in years. We would all hang until we couldn't hang any more.

Of all the festivals two stand out as my favorites, the North Sea Jazz Festival in the Hague, Netherlands, and the Les Jardin Festival in Nice, France. The North Sea Festival had more stages going on at the same time in one huge venue than any other festival on the tour and subsequently had the greatest number of musicians gathered at the same place. Nice had three stages going at the same time and appeared to make an effort to have as many big bands going at the same time as possible. All of the stages were outside in the gardens, which could have been a problem, but I never saw anything in southern France during that time of year but wonderful weather. I'm sure that there must have been exceptions to the constant good weather but I never saw it.

As you can see, my time with the Ellington Orchestra, though not the musical experience that I had enjoyed with the Alumni Orchestra, was a delightful one overall. When it came time to return to Oakland University the decision was very difficult to make. First of all, Mercer informed me that the band would be going on Broadway in New York with a show about the Ellington Orchestra entitled Sophisticated Lady and that he wanted me to be on the band for the run of the show.

Diane and I could have leased an apartment in New York City for the run of the show and been able to enjoy together the attributes of that incredible city while operating from a comfortable financial base. My university position could have been retained by extending my leave of absence but Diane would have had to resign from hers. However, her track record and expertise would most likely have qualified her for another position of equal stature at most any university in Michigan. You can see my dilemma. I also realized that the powers in place within my department had not made any effort to retain the vitality of my jazz education program, though I did not realize that it had been totally destroyed. I also wasn't really sure whether Diane would like living in Manhattan, as New York City is one of those places that you either love or hate. There is no middle ground about the Apple. I believe that the deciding factor was, in fact, just that. I wasn't sure whether Diane would even like New York, let alone love it like I did. She had already made a supreme sacrifice for me by agreeing that her newly-acquired husband could spend a year out wandering the earth in pursuit of his avocation, with just occasional reunions and weekend rendezvous on which to build a relationship. I owed her a major consideration.

My departure from the band was very satisfying. The men on the band, who hadn't before shown any appreciation for my being there, came to me and expressed their disappointment that I was leaving. One man even went so far as to say that he had finally got used to me being on the band and really wished that I would stay. That meant a lot more to me than he probably realized. Naturally, wouldn't you know, Sophisticated Lady seemed to run forever.

When I did return to my appointment at O.U. one of my colleagues, David Daniels, told me that he really didn't think I would come back to the university after being on the performance scene with such a prestigious orchestra. He was also very aware of what had been done to my jazz program in my absence.

18

Return to O.U.

When I got back to Oakland the next year I found that the then chairman of the department had totally destroyed the program I had worked so hard to build over so many years. He then had the audacity to ask me to rebuild the program to its previous standard. He suggested that I could do this without any help or assistance from the department, as I had done in the years before. This would allow him to put all his resources into the programs that he was interested in and wanted to keep supporting. It was bad enough to destroy what I had built up over those years but to turn around and tell me to do it all over again, with no help, was an insult to my intelligence.

I decided that my best course of action was to calculate the earliest date I could retire without losing any benefits. I then proceeded to put together as much of a program as I could with the energies and resources that were available. I wanted to give the students the best that we could offer them, while at the same time knowing that there was no hope of the program continuing once I was gone.

At the outset I had really thought that if I could create a great jazz program it would be appreciated and continued from then on. Through it I would have made a contribution to the future of the music and to the students who would come to Oakland, as well as to the stature of Oakland's music department. What I discovered was that no one cared, with the exception of David Daniels, the former president and the provost, who recognized the value of what had been accomplished. Realizing the futility of planning a future for jazz at Oakland, I retrieved as many of the old staff as I could and began to offer the students as much of a program as we could salvage, with the realization that when we were gone it would be gone as well.

The next few years were anticlimactic at best. However, as always, there were a few high spots to be remembered. One such occasion was my appointment as associate professor of music. If you recall, many years before at the request of the president and provost, I had accepted an appointment as a special instructor of music, with a job guarantee. I had not put any effort into bringing about a change of academic title and could see no real reason to do so under the circumstances. However, at this juncture the chairmanship of the department had been given to Dr David Daniels, my one source of support within the collegial structure. David decided that he would like to see my academic credentials reflect what he perceived as my contribution to the university over the 15 or so years that I had been there. He pursued that end and all I did was supply him with the information he requested. I held no expectation of any positive outcome for this venture and certainly did not harbor any hope in that direction, so when I received word that the change of academic classification had been approved, I was genuinely surprised. Not in my wildest dreams did I think that could happen. Thank you Dave!

The jazz program never again reached the level of participation or quality of product that had previously been taken for granted. There was, of course, an occasional participant who showed promise of reaching the level of accomplishment that had become the expectation of many of our former students. One such student was Regina Carter, a jazz violinist who was just as serious about her goal as any former student of the program had been. We treated her discipline with the same criteria that we would have had she been a saxophone player – no short cuts and the same attention to acquiring the craft as we gave any horn player. She sucked that discipline up like she was a sponge. I even used her with the big band in place of a lead alto saxophone. We amplified her instrument, set the speaker just behind the chair she sat in and set the volume of the speaker to establish a balance between her violin and the rest of the sax section. From there on the dynamics were under her control, just as they would have been as part of any ensemble. What came as a surprise to most everybody was that the band sounded very good with her in that role and the saxophone section responded to her lead immediately. She was also the best jazz soloist in the band and consequently was expected to fill that role in all of the band's performances.

During her years at Oakland, Regina joined a group of female jazz musicians, most of whom had been through the program. They put together a fine jazz ensemble which began to work quite a bit in the area and even recorded soon after that. The group still exists, from what I've heard, but Regina has gone on to New York where she has made a name for herself in the jazz world with her own group; she has a number of CDs out, to her credit. Give her a listen – she can play.

I did my job for the university and began to plan my retirement. The university started an early retirement incentive program for those of us who were getting to that age and I saw it as a good means for going on with the rest of my life. The jazz program as I had conceived it and built it no longer existed.

The jazz staff and I had created an educational environment for students of jazz that would, we had assumed, last as long as the university itself lasted. The program had been predicated on the concept of introducing the youngsters to the truth about this music, historically, aesthetically and philosophically, and offering them an environment that would essentially bring the jazz community into their institution so that the students could learn from these masters of the idiom in a manner most relevant to them. Now this was gone but it did make an impression. We were the first university in our area to offer both a bachelor's and a master's degree in jazz studies, concentrating on performance, composition and arranging, and history and education. We were even contemplating a doctoral program just prior to my year's leave of absence. As I have already mentioned, there were no jazz studies programs anywhere at that time in the state of

Michigan. By the time we were into our second year of the jazz program almost every university and many colleges had begun jazz programs as a part of their academic offering. So Oakland's program did make an impact. I'm sorry to say that most of the other programs did not, and still do not, embrace the historical, aesthetical and philosophical milieu of the African–American community which gave birth to jazz and where its greatest practitioners were spawned.

19

J.C.

I began to participate more in the musical activities around the Detroit area. J.C. Heard (J.C. lived in Detroit and was raised there after moving from St Louis as a child) asked me to participate in a tribute to Duke Ellington on Duke's birthday in April. He was putting together a combination that represented Ellington's band from the Cotton Club days. It was relatively small: three saxophones, three brass and three rhythm. He had found an arranger to transcribe the charts from recordings that J.C. had from that period. He needed a couple of musicians to fill out the ensemble and asked for my recommendations, which allowed me to introduce a couple of my best young musicians from the Oakland jazz program to him. The concert went so well that J.C. decided to try and get the band booked around the area, which he was able to do fairly easily since he was a known entity in jazz and enjoyed a substantial local following.

As the success of the band grew he gradually enlarged the band to four saxophones, five brass and three rhythm, using most of my students to fill the chairs of the ensemble. The original personnel of the band were unable to commit full time to it, thereby creating an opportunity for my former students. This band continued to function for the rest of J.C.'s life. I worked with the band for about six years and during that time we made a European tour with a sextet derived from the big band. The sextet did a number of the jazz festivals throughout Europe as part of the George Wein festival operation, sponsored by JVC. I had done those festivals in '79 and '80 with the Ellington Orchestra and it was great to be back in Europe at the festivals again.

J.C. was one of those unique individuals who we all have come to revere as icons of a bygone age. J.C., like Poppa Joe Jones, Gus Johnson, Osie Johnson, Denzil Best and many others, could swing a big band with a pair of brushes and kick the ! out of the shout chorus using just the brushes. In the years since, I've tried to instill in musicians the value of a drummer gaining expertise in the use of those beautiful implements but to no apparent avail as the industry has simply moved completely away from that kind of sensitivity. It may just be personal but I really miss it.

I believe that one of my former students and a stalwart member of J.C.'s band 'til the end, Walter Szymanski, has J.C.'s library. The original charts, as I said earlier, were for the early, nine-piece Duke Ellington instrumentation and J.C. later expanded this to 12 pieces by adding an additional trumpet and trombone and an additional tenor sax – which happens to have been the next version of the Ellington band's instrumentation as well. I don't know whether that was J.C.'s intention or not but it fits.

J.C. reflected the old values of the music so well that I can only hope that some of it rubbed off on the young cats he surrounded himself with. I do know that it rubbed off on a few of them, as they were former students of mine and had been prepared for that kind of experience from their early introduction into the O.U. jazz program. J.C. liked to sing and his rendering of some of the old Jimmy Rushing blues tunes was quite expressive. He did spice these up with rather racy undertones but I did say that he was a bit of a character, didn't I?

J.C. was also a great storyteller and had a wealth of stories to share from his experiences in the early days of the jazz scene on 52nd Street and uptown in Harlem. His stories of his association with Teddy Wilson, Charlie Parker and Dizzy, his duets with Buddy Rich while touring with Jazz at the Philharmonic and so on were legendary. Then he would share his experiences as a star on Japanese Radio (I don't remember whether this included television) and his professional work during the years he spent there.

When Dizzy came to Detroit, his usual domicile was the home of J.C.'s brother, David. There is a very long history there. Then, of course, there is David Usher, also of Detroit, whose years of association with Dizzy resulted in a recording label that eventually went under. In a sense, that label has been resurrected through Usher's association with Consolidated Artists Productions and Mike Longo, based in New York. I have the privilege of being one whose CD is presented by this label, a label which is of musicians, by musicians, for musicians. It's about time that we musicians took control of our own destinies instead of relying on business people who use our talents and efforts to make money, with the financial return to the artist being very negligible. I can say this, without any fear of contradiction: musicians are the worst business people in the world. This, of course, does not include those business- and marketing-savvy people who also claim to be musicians and whose record and CD sales demonstrate where their true talents lie.

J.C.'s passing brought out the entire jazz community of Detroit and those who associated with them – altogether a rather large contingent of the musical social fabric of Detroit.

J.C., it was a pleasure to have known you.

20

Wings for the Spirit

In the spring following our marriage and before I went out with Mercer and the Ellington band, Diane and I were invited by the National Teaching Committee to go to South Carolina to assist in consolidation work for the Faith. So in April of '79 we flew to Columbia where we rented a car and drove to Orangeburg. One of the people in Orangeburg who was involved in this work was a professor at South Carolina State University. She subsequently asked me to perform a concert for members of the South Carolina State University community. I agreed to do so if she could arrange for a local rhythm section to assist me.

One evening during our program of consolidation activities Diane and I met with one of the musicians who was going to back me at the concert. We had a very pleasant evening and discussed the material and established some parameters so that we could all be comfortable during the performance. The evening for the concert came but no musicians showed up, leaving both Dr Alberta Deas and myself wondering what to do. We had an audience but no musical support. She asked if there was something I could do by myself and I responded that I couldn't produce a reasonably effective concert without a rhythm section behind me.

Jazz is not an a cappella art form, generally speaking, though a cappella work has become a bit more commonplace in more recent years by a very few artists. Eric Dolphy is one who comes to mind who has utilized this format very effectively. While I was finding all the reasons why I couldn't satisfy Dr Deas's request, I remembered something that I had done, both in New York and at the Wesleyan University, with various poets from time to time. I then realized maybe I could get away with that type of performance without embarrassing either myself or Dr Deas too much.

Thus I began my first-ever solo concert with a rendition of 'Makin' Whoopee' and went on from there with a few melodies that I thought could stand alone without a clearly identified chordal underpinning. I then proceeded to engage the audience in a 'focus your thoughts on this subject and I'll attempt to create a musical impression of what I feel from your collective energy' format. It worked pretty well for a first-time effort, particularly since it had none of the poetic material from which to generate a lyrical and rhythmic orientation. This proved to be the first of numerous occasions on which I called upon this format in the following years. During my association with the Ellington Orchestra, particularly on our various tours outside the United States, I would often find that I was asked to perform in that solo mode for groups of Bahá'ís, having been invited into their homes after our concert or on nights when we didn't have performances.

My travel with the Ellington Orchestra outside the US enabled me to experience the extent of the Bahá'í family. We have subscribed to the notion that all humanity is but one family and that our differences are just 'vain imaginings'. But it wasn't until I was touring with the orchestra that I began to realize, in a very concrete way, the truth of this statement. Just as I told Mercer, I found I had a 'Bahá'í family' every-where – I've never been anyplace in the world where I didn't have a family to greet me. That is what the Bahá'í Faith is all about, in the final analysis: one God, one religion, one world, one humankind, all one family, all citizens of one country.

Going back to the concert at South Carolina State, what had started out as an emergency turned out to be an on-going means of expressing my musical creative self. After my stint with the Ellington Orchestra, I continued to find myself in situations in which I was called upon to play in this a cappella manner. One day it dawned on me that I should explore this format more seriously to see if it would result in a meaningful way for me to express a unique musical idiom. After extensive preparation, I went into a studio in the basement of the Bahá'í House of Worship in Wilmette, Illinois, and recorded an album of solo improvisations based on various images, or focuses, that were associated with the teachings and the major figures of the Bahá'í Faith.

Initially I put these out in a cassette format which has gone through two pressings and I am now exploring the prospect of releasing it as a CD for better air coverage, since radio stations won't play cassettes as a part of their normal programming. The title of the recording, 'Wings for the Spirit', was taken from the writings of 'Abdu'l-Bahá regarding music in this age:

> . . . although sounds are but vibrations in the air which affect the ear's auditory nerve, and these vibrations are but chance phenomena carried along through the air, even so, see how they move the heart. A wondrous melody is wings for the Spirit, and maketh the soul to tremble for joy.*

Let me tell you the story of that recording. When I decided to do the recording the only logical place to do it, from my perspective, was in the studio in Foundation Hall of the House of Worship. I contacted my friend Charles Nolley, who at that time was the chief engineer there and with whom I had worked on other projects. Charles agreed to the proposal and scheduled a time and date for the recording.

I spent the week before the recording in an apartment in St Joseph, Michigan, through the generosity of a long-time friend, Carol Handy – I was going to say 'old friend' but realized that might imply a degree of antiquity in both of us, since we are within three months of each other in age. I spent a week practicing, praying and generally getting ready for this event. I picked Diane up at the train station near St Joe and we drove over to the House of Worship, a couple of hours away.

Charles had set up the necessary microphones and related

---

* 'Abdu'l-Bahá, *Selections*, p. 147.

equipment in preparation for the recording, taking note that recording a single instrument such as a baritone saxophone and a bass clarinet requires very different and distinct characteristics of sound production. We spent a good bit of time getting the necessary placements and settings to eliminate as much key noise as possible. In this situation, with no other instruments playing, all the noises produced by the instrument itself and the sounds resulting from the manipulation of the instrument's mechanism are evident and unmasked, so to speak. When a number of instruments are being used, they each tend to mask the physical properties of the mechanism of the others. From this you can tell the difficulty I presented to Charles as he prepared for the recording itself.

When we finally got everything set up I returned to the sanctuary upstairs and said a few more prayers for my detachment from the outcome, thereby leaving it in God's hands. When I returned the only people in the studio were Diane and Charles's assistant, who was going to do the rest of the recording. All the hard stuff had been done by Charles and his assistant – now all I needed to do was play, with the assistant starting and stopping the tape between takes.

I began to play and after the first few notes I realized that I was into something extraordinary. In this technique of performance I arbitrarily choose the first two notes and the subsequent notes are a result of the intuitive direction of the creative process which forms a theme or melodic line that can then be developed. Towards the end of the creative development I recapitulate that theme, establishing a form that should express to the listener that I know where I'm going, where I've been and that I'm now bringing this exposition to a close in a logical and controlled way.

This was different. As I heard the theme flow out of the instrument I knew this was not like anything I had ever done before in my entire life as a performer. It was, in a word, beautiful. Never have I come close to that kind of beauty; and as I heard it come out the end of the baritone sax, I knew that I was not in control of this expression but that it was coming from some source beyond my understanding. As I listened to the music I began to say to myself, 'If I can just take that idea and develop it . . .' 'NO!' came another voice. 'Leave it alone. It's too good for you to mess with.' I continued to play, realizing all the time that this was extraordinarily beautiful. Amazed at what I was producing, I was in a state of wonder. Then I heard another idea that lent itself to further permutation and I thought, 'Hey! If I take this and . . .' 'NO!' Again that other voice shouted at me, 'Leave it alone. Don't mess with it. It's cool.'

Now this internal argument went on for a while. I haven't a clue as to how long or how many times I argued with myself but after a while I heard a third voice calling my name. 'Mr Holladay?' I then began to get a little freaked out as I was hearing voices from beyond. I continued to play, still in awe of what was coming out the end of my horn. Then I heard my name being called again, this time a little bit louder, which bothered me, as I couldn't understand who or why this was happening. I continued to play but I heard that voice much more loudly and somewhat authoritatively say, 'Mr Holladay!'

I continued to play, not wanting to let go of this incredible musical experience I was having, but I slowly opened my eyes – I always play with my eyes closed while improvising – and saw the engineer standing next to Diane shaking his head and cutting his throat with his finger, indicating that I should stop.

I slowly brought my playing to a stop, reluctant to let go of something I knew was special. I took my horn out of my mouth and looked at the engineer with, I'm sure, a degree of anguish. 'It's not recording!' he said. There was an extended period of silence. Then he told me that he had come out of the booth when he realized that the signal was not getting onto the tape and that he had asked Diane what he should do. He recognized the wonderful sound emanating from my saxophone and didn't want to stop me but he knew it was not being preserved. So he and Diane consulted about what they should do. They decided to let me know what had happened but not too abruptly so as not to upset the state that I appeared to be in.

Diane has told me, on more than one occasion, that in all

the years she has heard me play she has never heard anything as beautiful as what came through me at that moment. Needless to say, I was immediately distraught, knowing that I had never come that close before to such an expression of pure beauty when performing. With this knowledge and the extreme disappointment that enveloped me, I went back upstairs to the sanctuary and gave up my anxiety to Bahá'u-'lláh. I then had this clear realization that the music I had just played was, in fact, not for human consumption or to foster the musicianship of this individual but had been played for Bahá'u'lláh and the concourse on high and that it was still floating around in the ethers of both worlds.

I returned to the studio to continue the recording session. The first track on the recording entitled 'Bahjí' was actually the second track that was played that day.

Two years before I retired from Oakland University, Diane and I were in Chicago, as we were rather often since the Bahá'í House of Worship for the North American continent is located on the north shore of Lake Michigan on the outskirts of Chicago in Wilmette, Illinois. Next door to Wilmette is Evanston, where the Saxophone Shop is located. My mouth-piece man, Frank Wells, had his shop in the back of the Saxophone Shop and one of my former students, Mike Blanchard, was working there as an instrument repair man. He had apprenticed himself to Frank to learn the art and craft of making and customizing mouthpieces. Consequently Diane and I had many reasons to drive over to Evanston and Wilmette. This also afforded us the opportunity to enjoy the cultural life of Chicago and partake of the many epicurean delights the city has to offer.

On one of our trips to Chicago we were strolling around the art galleries on the near north side and encountered a showing of the water colorist Lee Weiss. At that showing Lee had a piece entitled 'Avenue of Light' and it seemed to me to be a visual rendering of how I perceived the musical essence of 'Wings for the Spirit'. Before Diane could figure out what to say to me, I had put a deposit on the painting and worked out the details of the purchase with the gallery owner. Diane thought I was nuts since she knew full well that we didn't have that kind of money. However, the gallery owner agreed that if after 90 days, when the note would come due, we could not pay for it he would take the painting back and even refund our deposit. As he said, he would have no difficulty finding a buyer for that particular painting.

I convinced Diane, somehow, that even if we couldn't pay for the painting, we would at least have it on our wall for 90 days with no worry as to whether we could afford it or not. There was no way to lose on that deal or so I thought. After the gallery showing was over, about two weeks later, the painting arrived in Ann Arbor, where we were living. We put it up on our wall and lived with it for nearly 90 days before we were faced with the prospect of having to crate it up and send it back to the art dealer. For some reason or other I didn't feel bad about having to send it back and felt that there might even be some way that we'd be allowed to keep it. How this might happen was not in my sphere of comprehension.

The weekend before we were to send the painting back to the gallery Dizzy came to Ann Arbor for a weekend gig at a local club and we were going to spend most of the weekend with him. When I saw him, the first thing he asked was whether I would be able to go out with his band on a tour of the jazz festivals in Europe. I said sure I'd go and the next day we called George Wein in New York to work out the details of money, etc. since the band was being put together through his organization. Well, the money we agreed on was enough to pay for the painting and then some – and that is how we acquired our Lee Weiss 'Avenue of Light'. It still hangs prominently over our fireplace, all thanks to Dizzy.

21

Dizzy

The tour with Dizzy was, undoubtedly, one of the highlights of my life. Also, coming at the time it did, it renewed my confidence in myself as a musician and brought me in touch with those values and principles that have become the standard by which I function, both as a human being and as a performer of American indigenous classical music – jazz.

Let me explain – and to do so we come back to the title of this book, *Life, On the Fence* and its relevance to my life. I'm not complaining, mind you, just using it as a setting for the display of certain truths that have come into focus for me in these later years, as one would hope, since learning and growing is what it is ultimately all about.

Compromise is the life-blood of human relationships and is needed for the peaceful resolution of interpersonal difficulties. Compromise, however, does not have the same connotation when applied to one's integrity or sense of values, either moral or aesthetic. I'll compromise with anyone, even quickly with a close friend or family member, to smooth the way for continued social harmony and to avoid causing pain or discomfort. On the other hand, to compromise one's integrity by agreeing to a half truth, or an out and out lie, about something that can and will affect others – no way man – it ain't worth it. And to justify such a compromise for the sake of being relevant or to gain some personal advantage can only end in a form of prostitution of the aesthetic that will affect one spiritually, if not materially as well. Again, it ain't worth it.

Maintaining my integrity is what kept me on the fence. When I was a young man I'd try to compromise that integrity in certain circumstances but when I did so I inevitably felt remorse for being a party to such injustice. To stand firm on issues that affected others and/or myself was the only way I could feel right about who and what I was. The significance of my position became clear to me after so many Afri-can–American men I knew shared with me their evaluation and preference for the stereotypical southern bias and prejudice simply because they always knew where they stood. Smoke screens don't work, particularly with those who have spent their lives having to recognize those screens for their survival. They could better maintain their integrity when they knew what they were dealing with – remember the Jerome Richardson story I told in chapter 10 about the insincere overtures of friendship he experienced.

Getting away for a year with the Ellington band, during those years at Oakland, preserved my emotional being. But when I returned to Oakland and the Detroit music scene, the pressure to compromise the high standard that I knew was appropriate for this music, to be one of the guys and to enter into a more lucrative association with my peers and colleagues became very compelling.

Philosophical isolation eventually brought many self-doubts. I was questioning my self regarding the validity of my stance on what this music was about and the criteria I had established and insisted upon, when I had the responsibility for engender-ing that quality. This was real and challenging and it was beginning to take its toll. I had been so far from experiences that resonated with the truth for so long that I would often think to myself, 'Maybe I'm wrong about all of this and everybody else is right' and/or 'Maybe I should give it up.' Very dangerous ground, particularly if you still feel the same truth strongly pulsating inside. As you can see, by this time, I was really being shaken and beaten up psychologically by much of what I had been confronted with, including the negative activity around me. As a consequence, I wasn't overloaded with self-confidence going into this gig with Dizzy. My desire to do the gig overrode my questioning, so I stuck my neck out and launched into the deep water again after all those years.

I got a flight into New York for a series of rehearsals with Dizzy's big band . When I arrived at the studio I found Jerry Dodgion, Garnett Brown and Virgil Jones there, as well as Sam Rivers. I knew Sam would be there, since he had been with Dizzy's small group for a few years by that time and was with him the night 'Birks' offered me the gig. (Birks was Dizzy's middle name and was used familiarly by many.) It had been years since I had seen the other guys or played with them, having been off the New York scene for so long. So it was a very heartwarming reunion, particularly since Jerry, Garnett and I had been on the Thad Jones–Mel Lewis Orchestra together.

Well, the rehearsal started and playing with that quality of musician helped my playing recover almost immediately from its atrophy and by the end of the first day I truly felt confident again in my ability to play my horn. During the second day of rehearsals we were working on 'Toccata', a selection from Lalo Shiffrin's *Gillespiana Suite*, which he had written years before. In one section of the piece there is a fairly long period of rest in the baritone part while the remainder of the band continues to play. I sat there listening to the band and was overcome with the realization that I was hearing all those criteria that I had been espousing over the years to deaf ears, or at least uncomprehending ears, and realized that I hadn't just been making a big deal out of my interpretation of this music and my concepts about it.

I sat there drinking in all this musical healing balm and was overwhelmed with the bounty that had been granted me to have my beliefs and knowledge confirmed and reinforced in such a dynamic way – and I wept. I wept tears of joy and relief and gratitude to Dizzy for having given me this opportunity to experience again what I had known to be the truth about this music and the history and heritage and strength of the people through whom it had come.

This belief has not left me since, nor do I have any doubt about it or question my ability to stand firm with the integrity and dignity it deserves. Good things can come with age and I know I have nothing to fear or to gain by what may happen as a result of telling you how it is and how it was. You must go for yourself!

The tour was a gigantic success for the band and for Dizzy, although he didn't need any help.

I am fascinated to see today, as we did then, some of the young Turks of the popular jazz scene walking around with outsized attitudes. This brings to mind a story about the first outing for the band in Philadelphia.

We did three concerts in the US before we left for Europe: Philadelphia, at the Academy; Pittsburgh, at some concert hall; and New York City at Carnegie Hall. At the Academy the opening act was a young saxophonist who had achieved a great deal of recognition from the public. It turned out he believed his marketing success was an indication of his musical stature. Some of the guys on Dizzy's band were walking around backstage, although most of us were in the dressing room, since we weren't to go on until this warm-up act had finished. The guys came back to the dressing room to tell us that this young saxophonist was raising hell backstage because he had to warm up for Dizzy Gillespie. He apparently felt that Dizzy should have been opening for him and he was very upset by this affront to his station in the music world.

Many young musicians have bought into the idea that being able to manipulate the material of music, on which the tunes they play are structured, is the epitome of jazz improvisation. This belief is not, totally, one of arrogant ignorance but can be laid at the feet of their university instructors. This belief became so prevalent while I was teaching that my staff and I began to refer to improvisation as 'extemporaneous composition' which, in the final analysis, more accurately describes what it actually is. We also identified chord manipulation, which was being promoted, as the craft of improvisation.

The institutions have been masterful at introducing a huge cadre of 'chord manipulators' into the business. There are exceptions to this, of course, and there are some absolutely dynamic young purveyors of this music out there. They have committed themselves to the truth and have sacrificed their material comforts to explore the ramifications of the music set out by those giants who came before them – Dizzy and legions of his kindred.

Oh, yes. By the way, when the band hit, following this young, internationally famous saxophonist's offering, you could feel the audience come alive and Dizzy kept them there for the rest of the night. Dizzy was his usual entertaining self and the band was smokin'. The reviews in the papers the next day, which we read on the plane heading for Pittsburgh, bore out what we suspected: the critics were unanimous in their appreciation and praise of Dizzy's band and in their castigation of the arrogant young Turk who was so full of himself.

After a great concert at Carnegie Hall in New York we left for Europe to begin our JVC Jazz Festival tour. Actually, the festival had started with the other concerts in the States, since they were all a part of the Wein festival operation.

Our first destination was the Tivoli Gardens in Copenhagen, Denmark, so it was a fairly long trip, particularly after a nearly three-hour long layover in London. When we arrived at the hotel all the young cats on the band were saying how tired they were and how they just wanted to take a nap. It was in the middle of the afternoon in Copenhagen but it corresponded to the middle of morning back in New York and we had been up all night. We warned them not to go to bed until later that night so that they would be on a Copenhagen schedule. They were sure that they would feel better after a short nap. Needless to say, they went to sleep and woke up in the middle of the night and were stuck in that mode for days until they adjusted to the new time zone.

This is one of the first things I learned about international travel: you either decide to continue to live on your stateside clock, no matter where you are, or you force yourself to adopt the new time as the real time as soon as you arrive. It is kind of hard for the first day because that it is anything from 30 to 36 hours long but the end result puts you in sync with the new time from then on. Jet lag can really be a drag if you don't find a way to adjust. On tour, like we were, you don't have three or four days to make the adjustment since you have to be on the bandstand that night, or at least the next night, and you have to be in shape to produce. Of course the next day after the concert we were up early in the morning to get to the airport in Copenhagen to catch our next flight to – wouldn't you know? – London, where our next gig was to be.

The organizers of the tour couldn't possibly have done it the other way around. No, that's not the way to book a tour. Many of us believe that the organizers of these tours have a secret method for ordering the tours and the first rule is 'never use a direct route'. It is imperative that you must run from one end of the continent to the other and back again following, blindfolded, the schedule apparently determined by some form of dart game.

We played 18 concerts in 16 cities in eight different countries in 21 days. That included a day off in each of Copenhagen, London and Istanbul. If I sound like I'm complaining, I'm not. I had a ball. I love the travel and for some reason or other I don't find too taxing the inconvenience of very little sleep, delays at airports, bus rides from airports in one town to another on the other side of the country with a return bus trip to the other city for a couple of hours of sleep before having to get up and go to another airport, for another flight, to another city, most likely in another country. Just a normal day in the life of a jazz musician on tour. I suppose that if it continued month after month after month, like Dizzy's schedule usually was, I might get tired of it but at this point in my life I didn't find it to be too much. Besides we were giving our lives to an avocation that we loved. Actually, sleeping on the plane or bus is much easier if you are exhausted. All of your energies go into the performance and the concentration you can muster is spent on stage doing what you came there to do.

One of the many benefits of this kind of travel is the food. I love being able to have a meal at a different restaurant each night and eating a different ethnic cuisine almost every other day from the tables of their origin. One night Danish, the next English, the next French, the next Italian, the next Turkish, etc. And the different regions of those same countries – wow! For one who really likes that kind of diversity, it is a dream trip.

The premiere experience of the entire tour – probably as much for the way it happened and the result of the experience as for the quality of the cuisine – took place on the island of Sardinia off the boot of Italy. Let me set the stage for this occasion because the emotional and psychological state of many of the men involved played a role in the dynamic of this particular event.

We arrived in the middle of the afternoon at Caliglari, Sardinia, by way of a change of plane in both Paris and Rome and after a very long flight from Bordeaux which had started very early that morning. We checked into our hotel in Caliglari and immediately got into vans to go to the concert venue at St Anna Arezzi. St Anna Arezzi turned out to be on the other side of the southern end of the island. Dizzy was taken separately by car, the Sardinian version of a limo.

The trip was very long over desolate terrain, somewhat reminiscent of the coastal areas around Bath, Maine, and as the trip seemed to run on and on some of the guys began to grumble. After all, they had been up since very early that morning traveling and waiting and traveling some more. We finally came to a town after hours of travel and the time was drawing near to when we were supposed to start playing. But instead of stopping in this town, which we understood to be St Anna Arezzi, we kept going through the town and on into more desolate country. Out-and-out complaints began in rather graphic tones and language, complete with unsubtle anger showing in the voices. The van I was riding in was blessed with the presence of Jerry Dodgion, who doesn't get ruffled over much of anything, and he kept saying, 'Relax, you're in Italy. They will see that you get where you have to be in time. Not to worry. The Italians do not have the same concept of time that we are accustomed to.' That only appeased the fellows for a short while, as it appeared that we were going to continue over the craggy roads forever.

Fortunately I had a great deal of faith in Jerry's experience and understanding, and from my own association with other cultures I didn't find this delay was anything to worry about, at least not as much as many of the others did. Finally we turned off the main road onto a path of two tracks obviously made by and for cars. We approached, over a small crest, a relatively small structure set out by itself with a sign hand-painted on it reading 'Pescatore', which translated into English is 'Fish House'. The vans stopped and we were escorted into the Fish House. Inside were a few tables at which a few people were eating. There was also a very long arrangement of tables set up for us, all in a line. They were obviously waiting for us.

At this point it was already 30 minutes past the time we were supposed to have started playing the concert and some of the guys were very testy and unruly. Jerry kept saying, 'Relax fellows, you're in Italy. They will get you where you're supposed to be when they want you there. They know what they are doing.' Well, between the exhaustion and the hunger they didn't hear him very well, so things got rather uncomfortable.

The first things that came out to the table, of course – this was, after all, still Italy, even though it was an island off the coast – were bottles of wine. These began to moderate the negative energy a wee bit but some were still somewhat testy. Then the waitresses brought out three huge platters heaped with shrimp. The attack was frenzied, like sharks feeding. Less grumbling but still some concern that we were so late for the concert. Jerry continued to reply, 'Relax, fellows, you're in Italy. They will get you where you are supposed to be when the time is right.' Somewhere between the bowls of sea snails, the mussels and the razor clams, Dizzy and his companion showed up and, of course, by this time the guys didn't care if we played at all that night.

As the waitresses were trying to catch Dizzy up with the rest of us, they came out with platters of small mounds of what I later found out was roe, either shrimp or lobster, in olive oil – absolutely delicious. Now the girls asked if we preferred spaghetti with garlic and butter or tomato sauce. Since no decision could be arrived at, they brought platters of both.

I've feasted before and gorged myself from time to time but I must confess I have never had a meal that was so expertly prepared and amply served in my life. Every dish seemed to be better than the one before it. While we were finishing up the spaghetti they brought Dizzy a huge stuffed crab. We did not get any crab but by that time who cared? Everybody was now very pleased and so satisfied with the culinary excellence that we insisted that the waitress, Donnatella, bring out the chef so that we could show him our appreciation.

She went into the kitchen and later came out with the most beautiful young woman I had so far seen on this tour. We thought that Donnatella had somehow misunderstood what we had said and had brought the owner's daughter or something. Not that everyone in that group didn't appreciate her choice but we said that we really did want to give the chef our personal appreciation for such a wonderful meal. Then to everyone's surprise Donnatella said, 'This is the chef.' You could feel every man's mind going into action formulating the same question but, as usual, Dizzy got it out first. 'Will you marry me?'

This incredible creature who was so lovely was also the cook who had prepared this exquisitely memorable meal for us. That took care of any concern for the gig or for anything else for that matter. We could have made the ride back to Caliglari right then and felt the whole trip worthwhile. Come to find out the owner of Pescatore was also the promoter of the concert that night in St Anna Arezzi and he had been in the car with Dizzy all along.

After the feasting was finished we all got into our vans and drove to an amphitheater in the middle of the town. By this time it was at least 12:30 or 1:00 a.m. and the concert was supposed to have begun at 10:00. We were three hours late and the place was still packed with people awaiting our arrival. There was no sign of concern or discontent with the delay at all, just a warm, friendly welcome. We even took time to do a sound check before we played and the audience enjoyed that as well. Dizzy did not shorten the program one iota. All the tunes were played and the soloists, which included everybody on the band in some slot, were allowed, even encouraged, to stretch out as they normally would. Two hours later we finished the concert.

Well after 3:00 a.m. we began our return to Caliglari over all those miles of desolate terrain. Most of us were asleep. Back we went to our hotel, in time for us to check out and go to the airport so we could fly out to the next engagement.

I can't recall how many times I've got back to my room only to look at a beautiful, invitingly soft bed and contemplate how wonderful it would be to lie down there and catch some sleep, knowing full well that I didn't dare do so because I most certainly would not wake up in time to catch the bus to the airport for the next flight. I'd get my bags and take them downstairs to join the rest of the band having a cappucino or something. The lack of sleep really didn't matter because we were doing something that we had prepared all our lives to do. And with this group of musicians, nothing could have been more satisfying than working with Dizzy.

The experience of checking into first-class accommodation (we had four- or five-star hotels in every city we stayed in) which we could not use except possibly to take a shower and change clothes happened more times than you need to hear about. Just imagine: a room big enough to hold a small convention with a balcony overlooking a gorgeous courtyard, a bed big enough for a family and even the bathroom big enough for a committee meeting. This kind of accommodation was the norm for us on this tour and all because we were the Dizzy Gillespie Orchestra.

The last concert of the tour was in San Sebastian, Spain, and we were to return to the States the next morning. We flew into Bilbao and took a bus to San Sebastian. To return to the airport in Bilbao for the first leg of our journey back to the States would require a similar bus trip. The return flight was to take us through Paris to London and then on to New York. After our arrival in New York, I was scheduled to take another flight out of JFK to New London, Connecticut, to meet Diane. We were going to spend a few days with some of her family and then take a leisurely drive back to Ann Arbor by way of Montreal and Toronto. With all that facing me I felt that I really had to get as much rest as possible. So after the concert in San Sebastian I decided to use the bed in my room for a little sleep before we caught the bus for Bilbao, even if it was for only a couple of hours.

The next thing I heard was a phone ringing off in the distance somewhere and I finally figured out that it was in my room. After finding the phone, I answered to hear Jerry saying, 'Hey man, the bus is ready to leave and all the guys are here but you.' 'Oh my God!' I said. 'I didn't hear the wake up call at all. I'll be right there.' Jerry said that he would be right up to my room to help me. As I was throwing things together Jerry came in, collected my stuff and began to take it downstairs while I finished dressing. I rushed down to the lobby, stopped at the desk to settle accounts, which meant that I signed off the register since everything was covered, and got on the bus apologizing profusely as I entered. Nobody seemed in the least concerned or had even noticed my tardiness as the majority of them were asleep, including Dizzy. I still felt like a fool because I had so carefully avoided this very situation throughout the entire tour, knowing what would be the result of such an indulgence. So here on the last day, and the most important trip of them all, the one home, I messed up. *C'est la vie*.

I must tell you more about Dizzy as a man, musician, leader and teacher. During this tour, including the rehearsals, I never heard him say anything critical to anyone in front of others. I do know that during the rehearsals we had a musician or two who was not there at the next rehearsal or who was not on the plane when we left. Dizzy never addressed anyone during the rehearsal but when he didn't feel confident that a particular musician was right for the job, he would privately inform that person of his decision – or he might delegate the responsibility – so as not to embarrass him in any way.

I remember one occasion when Dizzy had to defend his time and obligation to others from a well-meaning but thoughtless attempt to impose on his time and attention. This inadvertently involved a commitment I had made to a family in France. Dizzy had to do an interview with a member of the French press and was trying to get free from a number of people who were trying to pay homage to him in the lobby of our hotel. The family I had agreed to have dinner with before the concert came to pick me up. Seeing Dizzy there, they were certain that he would come with us, as they had suggested when we had first talked. I replied that I had not arranged anything for Dizzy and that my commitment to them could not in any way include him. That did not deter them from insisting that Dizzy come with us. They were putting Dizzy through this when I arrived in the lobby. Seeing what was happening I stepped in and explained to them that I had not committed Dizzy to anything. I was ready to honor my agreement but they should not presume to include Dizzy.

Dizzy was, as usual, gracious to all but very firm in his commitment to the journalist who had been waiting so long to speak with him. The friends and I then left the hotel and I spent a delightful afternoon and dinner at their home on a mountain overlooking the Mediterranean Sea and from where you could see, at a very great distance, the island of Elba. They returned me to the hotel in time for me to change and pick up my horn and then delivered me to the gardens where we were to perform that evening.

It was also in France that I learned a very important lesson about laundry services. I assumed that the hotel laundry service would be similar to the one we enjoy in the US, only to discover that it ain't necessarily so. There are many places that do laundry but if you use the hotel service, be prepared to have it cost you an arm and two legs. It was ridiculous, so be advised. The cost of the laundry far exceeded the cost of the room, if you can imagine it. Of course, most of the responsibility falls on me since I didn't pay much attention to what the prices were on the laundry slip and I failed to compute francs into dollars.

One assumes that a musician of Dizzy's stature will naturally be a great leader, which of course he was, but you can see from references I have made to other band leaders that this is not universally true. I could expound at great length on the exceptions.

Dizzy, very much like Duke Ellington, was not only a masterful musician himself but was also very perceptive about the latent musical potential of his fellow musicians. He would therefore create opportunities that would bring out those latent abilities and put each of us at our best advantage. He did more by example than by instruction. I remember many a night that the four trumpet players on the band – John Faddis, Virgil Jones, Byron Stripling and John Mitchell – all with exemplary reputations and recognized musical stature, would stand with their mouths hanging open listening to Dizzy turn a phrase. At those moments they became even more aware of who the master was. That is not to say that Dizzy had that spellbinding quality in his playing all the time, as he had had when in his prime, but he sure could when he felt like it. Considering that he was at that time 72 years old, the dominance he could express was remarkable and memorable. There were occasions when he would actually mesmerize the entire orchestra with a melodic line of such profound beauty and inspired genius that it went beyond creativity and into the realm of the sublime.

As I have already said, Dizzy taught more by example than by overt instruction. But there was one occasion when he spoke to us directly regarding this music and how understanding it would improve our ability to produce it with integrity. We were traveling by bus from somewhere to somewhere else and, as usual, John Lee was holding forth on the bus microphone, expounding at great length about everything imaginable and being very entertaining as well, since he had a very well-developed sense of humor – not in the same league as Redd Foxx but very expressive nonetheless. For some reason or another John had enlisted everybody on the bus to comment on his feelings about the trip and about anything that came to mind regarding this experience. We all participated, including those who were normally rather quiet and somewhat reclusive. That, in itself, was a revelation. Then Dizzy decided he wanted to say something to the group.

He began with a question. 'Do you know what the difference is between a bebop musician and all other musicians?' No one would venture a response to that question from the innovator himself. That would been sort of like having God ask you if you knew the answer to what life was all about. After a brief moment's hesitation he began to express the essence of what this music was about. He spoke not in technical or analytical terms but about spiritual values and about concern for the enhancement of those with whom one is playing and about the intrinsic value and station of each musician with whom one is enmeshed in the expression of a greater entity, which is defined by this music. These are my words, not his. What I remember him saying is this: 'The difference between bebop musicians and all other musicians is that bebop musicians play so that everybody else sounds good.'

From this I understood the essential importance of letting the expression of another musician be paramount to one's own – when that is a priority, the result is more expressive and communicative to the people who are receiving the music. As a result of placing another musician's expression above your own, you enhance the quality and content of what is collectively being expressed.

Too often an individual or a group of individuals realizes the errors that another player makes and shows up that mistake by playing to draw attention to it. Boy, does that sound familiar! I still experience that with entirely too many people who claim to be jazz musicians. This doesn't have anything to do with doing your best or being professional or performing with technical proficiency. We are all striving to do just that. The difference is in the attitude that prevails within the group when it is performing. Drawing attention to the mistakes of others was characteristic of the bands I was on in high school and college and, unfortunately, was all too prevalent in many of the professional bands I played with, particularly those that had not achieved a level of musicianship that could be compared with the Dizzy Gillespies and the Duke Ellingtons. It's sad for me to have to say but the most grievous examples of this attitude I found mostly in white bands and much less so in black bands, although I acknowledge that it does happen in them as well on occasion.

In his talk on the bus Dizzy went on to cite an example from the performance we had played the night before. He was in

Dizzy at Oakland University

Dizzy at Oakland University

Dizzy with Diane in Ann Arbor

Dizzy before his gig at the Bird of Paradise Club, Ann Arbor

Peace Fest Orchestra at Louis Gregory Bahá'í Institute, Hemingway, South Carolina

the middle of his solo when he started to run out of gas and his chops were beginning to give out on him. We could all hear it and were alert to it when all of a sudden his sound got strong and the line that was beginning to diminish became clear and defined and flowed on as if being regenerated by some mystical musical energy. To our surprise Dizzy put his horn down and walked away to the side of the stage. Recognizing the difficulty Diz' was getting into, John Faddis stepped up to the microphone in the trumpet section, picked up the line that Dizzy was playing and took over for him as if it were Diz' himself playing.

For those who don't know, Faddis learned to play by listening to all of Dizzy's records and imitating him and in fact he could play every solo Diz' ever recorded. In Dizzy's own words to me years before, 'Wait til you hear this young cat who just got in town from 'Frisco, John Faddis. This cat can play all my sh** an octave higher.'

Dizzy stood at the side of the stage working on his chops and listening to Faddis play. After a couple of choruses, Diz' walked back to the microphone, put his horn to his mouth and took over the phrase that John was playing and continued the solo as John stepped away from his microphone. This allowed Dizzy to take the solo on to the end of the chorus. It was so perfectly rendered that everybody assumed that Dizzy and John had worked this little exchange out as a trick, not realizing that what they had seen was an example of the greatness of both of these magnificent trumpet players. The men in the band were the only ones who knew what transpired that night on that stage.

The frequency of the opposite proposition – drawing attention to oneself – is much more the norm than not and always occurs at the expense of someone else. This is not a matter of applying the golden rule. No, there is now a new golden rule, brought to us by Bahá'u'lláh, which says that we must prefer others to ourselves. This new perception of our relationship with one another was emphatically described and demonstrated to all of us on that bus, that day, somewhere in Europe, in a manner that we will never forget.

Translate this idea into your daily life and into your relationships on a personal as well as collective level and you begin to get a hint of what could happen in this world.

22

Peace Fest

Prior to this European tour in September of 1986 I was asked to join Dizzy and Mike Longo to perform at a festival at the Louis G. Gregory Bahá'í Institute just outside Hemingway, South Carolina. It was the first of what was to become an ongoing annual event held on the third weekend of each September. After the success of our performance the first year, I offered to try to put together a big band of professional musicians from around the country who also happened to be members of the Bahá'í Faith to play Dizzy's big band library. This whole idea came up while Dizzy and I were walking in the area around the Institute during our stay at the Peace Fest, as they called it.

Dizzy, who had grown up in Cheraw, South Carolina, not too far from LGI, suggested that we take the walk. The first thing he did was to take off his shoes, get his feet into the soil and remark how good it felt, like it had when he was a kid growing up in Cheraw. After we had walked and talked for a while I broached the subject and asked him what he thought of the idea of putting together a big band to play behind him the next year. His response was very positive and he said he liked it.

I began to find musicians who I knew to be of a profess-ional caliber and from each I found other musicians who met the criteria for the project. It wasn't long before I realized just how many professional jazz musicians had found their way to the Faith and who were very much interested in a project like this one.

The next year we brought together the musicians for rehearsals about three days before the Peace Fest was to take place. It turned out that Dizzy had a previous engagement that he couldn't get out of scheduled on the same night that we had intended to perform at the Peace Fest. Since the festival ran for the weekend plus Thursday, it was decided that we would do Dizzy's concert on Thursday and have the band do another concert on the Friday. So members of the orchestra brought music from their own libraries for us to prepare as well as Dizzy's library. This opened up the opportunity for the members of the orchestra to share different musical concepts. Dizzy's concert went over great, as one would expect, but the concert of the orchestra without Dizzy went over just as well and gave us an opportunity to show off more of the talents of the members of the orchestra.

From that moment on the big band concert became the pivotal event around which the Peace Fest was structured. I took responsibility for organizing the orchestra and the music for Peace Fest for the next six years until I felt it was time for others to take on that role. My decision to take on the Peace Fest also had a lot to do with Diane and me deciding to move to South Carolina.

In 1992 all of these musicians, and many more, participated in various capacities and in many different combinations at the Second Bahá'í World Congress in New York City during 23 to 26 November at the Jacob Javits Center. Musical organizations and artists from all over the world participated, as well as a 400–voice choir and a 70–piece symphony orchestra of Bahá'í musicians. Approximately 27,000 people attended this World Congress, which was a phenomenal experience for all involved, whether on stage or out front.

23

The Power of Music

Music and the other arts are expressions of things to come. Consequently we have in these times a dichotomy between negative and positive expression in the arts. Which do you want to foster and support? How would you prefer the world to be? How will that condition be realized? Artists are playing a very important role in bringing about a new condition in the world and in determining how it will come about and when it will be achieved. You may say that's ridiculous, that art can't change or affect anything, except maybe some dude up in a tower who doesn't have to worry about the real deal out here on the street. Yet the harmony of life and the unifying principle that underlies all existence is expressed in the arts and most emphatically in music. Music enters the auditory canal immediately and affects the auditory nerve and consequently the nerves in the brain, which respond instantaneously throughout the body and influence all of its functions. The way musicians express themselves musically has a whole lot to do with the way the world and all those who are in it react and respond. No, this is not mumbo-jumbo. It's real and affects how we relate to each other as a result. Yes, it does have an effect on that too. Sound can produce a physical phenomenon and has been known to upset the world's physical equilibrium. It can just as easily bring equilibrium back into the world and ease human suffering as a result because it can bring about a change in the way the human psyche reacts.

The idea that music has powers that are mystical or at least mysterious is not new. Every culture in the world, certainly all those that I have had some opportunity to explore, have within their milieu some reference to this power. A brief look at a few representative cultures will demonstrate how widespread this idea is. What follows is not intended to be a treatise on the characteristics of all the world's musical expressions in the context of their power. For that you should explore any of the good ethnomusicological studies that are readily available. But do understand that this phenomenon of the belief in the power of music is universal and not just an occasional superstition found here and there in the world.

The music of Java and Bali, though differing in structure and organization, share, as an emotional, psychological and philosophical root, a similar reverence and respect for the power of music. For example, the colotomic (rhythmical order) of the music is delineated by the striking of a succession of gongs and at its cadential closing one particular gong is struck. In the case of the Javanese colotomic structure it is the gong Agung. The belief is that if the Agung is struck inappropriately or, God forbid, at the wrong time, it will drive the people performing and listening insane. I know your response, so go ahead and throw this away as superstitious nonsense. But could there be a kernel of truth there? I can state from experience that you most certainly will feel the vibration of the Agung pass through your body when it is struck.

In Bali there is a tradition of dance that represents the spiritual ability to transcend physical reality and counteract physical laws. A trance-like state is derived from the music that accompanies this particular dance, allowing the dancers to impale themselves upon their daggers with no resulting bloodshed or damage to their bodies. I can't explain it, nor can I explain how it is that some cultures create conditions which allow one to walk through a bed of burning stones or lie on a bed of nails or cut glass without experiencing bodily damage, yet these things do occur and are practiced. In every such situation, you might note, music is an integral part of these activities and without it the activity could not have taken place.

We are, perhaps, more familiar with the practice of voodoo. I dare say that any Haitian, Jamaican or, for that matter, New

Orleans resident will confirm that what happens when voodoo is practiced is not imaginary and, again, that it is the music which creates the environment for this to occur. Voodoo has its origins in traditional African cultures, which have similar experiences that relate to certain expressions of music, many of which are secret.

Native American traditions identify music as a voice of the Great Spirit and consequently 'drum' is revered in light of that awareness. Drum is not just an instrument but rather refers to those who participate as singers and who collectively sing and produce the rhythmical pattern on the drum. At the end of a pow-wow awards are given to the most successful dancers in various categories of dance and another award is given to the most successful 'Drum of the Pow-Wow'. This is considered to be a great honor.

The association of spiritual realities in the music of the Karnatic and Hindustani traditions of India are so integral to the lives of Indian peoples that they have identified the various musical structures, called Ragas, as expressing those spiritual qualities. They also distinguish the season and the time of day during which these expressions may be offered without disturbing the spiritual balance of their world. The resulting discipline that is demanded to fulfill this expression is, by western standards, unimaginable. The meticulousness of the tuning of the instruments, including the pitch of the drums, must be so exact as to allow an audible pitch to be heard that is not being played. While at Wesleyan I was associated with Laxmi Tewari, a very accomplished traditional Hindustani singer. He shared with me the necessity for the tamboura, a drone string instrument, to be so perfectly in tune that he could hear the third even though the tuning on the tamboura used only the root and the fifth in the tuning of the four strings of the instrument.

The Aborigine of Australia associate music with their sense of the Earth Mother, not unlike the relationship expressed by American Indians. Corroboree is an expression of the love, respect and physical association that they share with all living things, as was taught to them by those they refer to as the Mimis – almost mythological ancestral people of their history. Transcending one's physical reality goes readily with the use of the didjeridoo and rhythm sticks. Deep meditation is achieved through the rhythmical drone of the didjeridoo and subsequent connection with the Mimi.

China has a long history of understanding the power of music and has utilized that power for reflection, as well as for warring with the enemy. Korea and Japan have similar associations with this power and do not treat its expression lightly. Each instrument has its sphere of influence and the performance of that instrument must be in accord with that awareness.

'Abdu'l-Bahá also explained the power of music:

Music is one of the important arts. It has a great effect upon human spirit. Musical melodies are a certain something which prove to be accidental upon etheric vibrations, for voice is nothing but the expression of vibrations, which, reaching the tympanum, affect the nerves of hearing. Musical melodies are, therefore, those peculiar effects produced by, or from, vibration. However, they have the keenest effect upon the spirit. In sooth, although music is a material affair, yet its tremendous effect is spiritual, and its greatest attachment is to the realm of the spirit. If a person desires to deliver a discourse, it will prove more effectual after musical melodies. The ancient Greeks, as well as Persian philosophers, were in the habit of delivering their discourses in the following manner: first, playing a few musical melodies, and when their audience attained a certain receptivity thereby they would leave their instruments at once and begin their discourse. Among the most renowned musicians of Persia was one named Barbod, who, whenever a great question had been pleaded for at the court of the King, and the Ministry had failed to persuade the King, they would at once refer the matter to Barbod, whereupon he would go with his instrument to the court and play the most appropriate and touching music, the end being at once attained, because the King was immediately affected by the touching musical melodies, certain feelings of generosity would swell up in his heart, and he would give way.*

I do know from my own experience as a musician how these effects are realized. The effect through the medium of jazz, because of its extemporaneous and improvisational nature, is as immediate as any musical expression I have encountered. The one other musical expression that might equal the immediacy of jazz is traditional African drum ensemble patterns which tend to elicit that same immediate response.

I know this immediacy is also prevalent in all the different expressions of rock-and-roll and in much of the current pop music such as hip-hop, rap, etc., though they differ dramatically in the type of impact and effect that result. My objective here is not to critique or evaluate the quality of an expression but rather to reinforce the premise that music has this power.

I was asked by some young rock musicians with whom I had a very positive and mutually respectful relationship to attend one of their concerts so I could hear and assess their efforts. At the concert, after my ears adjusted to the volume, I attempted to hear the musical content of their expression. When the group took a break we all stepped outside for a breath of fresh air and I explained to them what I understood to be the effect and success of their musical offering. I shared my observation that the structure was comparatively basic and not too complex or sophisticated from a harmonic analysis. They concurred. Then I asked about the purpose for the extreme volume and they explained that the volume and the structure of their music was designed to maintain a peak balance of emotional energy at such a level as to keep the audience just shy of reaching a state of violence. Their term was 'controlled violence'.

When I left their gig I had time to reflect upon this. I realized that the excitement created by the expression and the accompanying volume did, in fact, cause a rush of adrenaline to the brain, which in turn triggered a release

---

* 'Abdu'l-Bahá, quoted in *Bahá'í Writings on Music*, p. 6.

of endorphins into the bloodstream thereby causing a sensation that, in many ways, was essentially like being high or stoned. I therefore concluded that the format was an extremely effective way to elicit support for the experience from the audience.

In contrast, let me share with you the spiritual purpose of music as proposed in the writings of Bahá'u'lláh:

> We have made it lawful for you to listen to music and singing. Take heed, however, lest listening thereto should cause you to overstep the bounds of propriety and dignity. Let your joy be the joy born of My Most Great Name, a Name that bringeth rapture to the heart, and filleth with ecstasy the minds of all who have drawn nigh unto God. We, verily, have made music as a ladder for your souls, a means whereby they may be lifted up unto the realm on high; make it not, therefore, as wings to self and passion. Truly, We are loath to see you numbered with the foolish.[*]

* Bahá'u'lláh, *Kitáb-i-Aqdas*, para. 51.

24

South Carolina

Diane and I are now living in Mount Pleasant, South Carolina, a suburb of Charleston, east of the Cooper River. We moved here after living for two years near Myrtle Beach, South Carolina, to be near the Bahá'í Institute. Our stay in Myrtle Beach was a time for self-reflection and activity on behalf of the Faith. We found that we frequently went to Charleston for cultural life and to dine. Our taste in food was not particularly satisfied by the proliferation of deep-fried everything, identified as calabash-style cooking. The few really good restaurants on the Strand were too expensive for us other than on special occasions. Consequently when Diane was offered a position with a college in Charleston we decided that we should take it and move to the Charleston area. We were spending much of our social time in Charleston anyway and it also seemed likely that there would be greater opportunities for my skills to be used there.

We moved into a winter rental on the Isle of Palms while we looked for housing. We had found a place in an apartment complex but upon moving in discovered that the apartment was uninhabitable. When we presented a four-page damage report to the management they declared that our relationship would not work and allowed us out of our contract. We spent the next three months looking for someplace to live. Fortunately, Dr Alberta Deas was now working in Charleston as a real estate agent and she assisted us in our search for housing. It became obvious early on that rentals were either way out of our financial range or not habitable, particularly for Diane and her allergies. Alberta showed us a way to purchase a house for about the same monthly expenditure that we would have incurred for an apartment or town house. We finally decided on a lovely home in Mount Pleasant that was perfect for Diane and only about seven minutes away from the ocean.

Diane dearly loves the ocean. She was born and spent her earliest years on a cove off Long Island Sound in New London, Connecticut. Being so close to the ocean and appreciating it as she does, this has been the ideal environment for us. Our friends in Michigan thought we were nuts moving into South Carolina since Hurricane Hugo had just destroyed much of the area where we planned to live. However, we had already gone to South Carolina for the Peace Fest and had stayed over for few days to look for housing in preparation for the move when Hugo appeared. We knew 48 hours before Hugo hit where it would make landfall, when it would hit the mainland, how severe the damage would be and how long the clean-up would probably take. We were then told to pack up and leave since there was nothing we could do to help. So we did just that and drove to Asheville, North Carolina, where we checked into a hotel and watched the storm on TV.

I grew up in Tornado Alley in southeastern Kansas. I know, firsthand, how much warning you can expect from a tornado. And I have also spent two years in Los Angeles over the fault line that has produced many earthquakes and is expected to produce the Big One some day in the future and I have experienced some rather minor quakes. In both of these places the warning given is almost non-existent, particularly for a tornado. Contrast that with the 48 hours' notice we had on every aspect of the hurricane that hit South Carolina. Such notice would allow us ample time to board up the house, pack those few things that could not be replaced like my wife, my baritone, our dogs and a few important papers, and leave for a location far enough inland to avoid the brunt of the storm. Whatever would be left upon our return we could replace and/or rebuild with the insurance we were obliged to have.

Since our daughter, her husband and our grandchildren are now living in the Knoxville, Tennessee area, we don't even have to decide where to go, should a hurricane occur. We've already gone there once and on that occasion the storm decided, at the last minute, to turn north and make landfall much further north in North Carolina, which hardly ever gets missed particularly on the outer banks. Obviously I find hurricanes much less of a difficulty than other situations I have lived in.

Diane is very happy with the work that she is doing. She is associated with an Educational Opportunity Program designed to assist those who are the first of their family to go to college, those who are disabled and students from low income families to access the academic world.

I have tried for a number of years to establish a jazz repertory orchestra here to offer a greater variety of quality musical experience for an under-served population but have found no financial support for such a project. Unfortunately, I do not have the personal resources to underwrite this undertaking, so I am forced to rely on a consortium of interested people and businesses to bring this project into reality and they have not been forthcoming. *C'est la vie*!

We have a wonderful two-week festival of music each summer, the Spoleto Festival. During Spoleto there are many venues that present a variety of media but for the rest of the year the Charleston community only has a concert series presented by the Charleston Symphony. Occasionally the Coliseum will offer a concert which is always a high-priced, multimedia theatre production by one, big-ticket, rock, country or mainstream pop group. There is very little quality, moderately-priced meaningful musical experience provided and none on an ongoing, regular monthly basis. Just recently an organization has begun to provide a short series of quality opera offerings that serves one segment of the population at least. However, there is still a large under-served population here in Charleston that should have an ongoing concert series of the masterworks of American indigenous classical music.

I've pretty well given up on that idea as I don't have the energy or the expertise for the kind of fund raising that is necessary, so I will have to leave it to a younger, better equipped person to bring new cultural life into the community.

I do continue to tour occasionally, primarily for the Faith, with concerts and presentations on 'The Evolution of American Indigenous Classical Music: Jazz'. From time to time a college or university will offer a residency for a few days or a week at their institution where I can work with their students. I've begun to explore the possibility of offering a two- or three-day survey of world music, exploring the traditional music of peoples from many world cultures. Since I do have those academic credentials it seems logical to do so while I still can. I do enjoy the interchange with young people. I'm glad I retired from the university but I do miss the process of teaching and communicating with students.

One of the draws of South Carolina for both Diane and myself is the aura of spirituality that we have sensed ever since our first trip here in '79. It isn't an overt, in your face, kind of thing but very prevalent throughout the state. We have attributed that spiritual energy to the vitality and depth of the African–American experience here in the low-country and that community's relationship with the Creator which pervades it and is readily expressed in its culture.

I knew an elderly gentleman on Pawley's Island, on the Grand Strand, and during the time that I worked with him building a small cement block shed around the water pump in his yard – a pump I had inadvertently backed into on one of my visits – I became aware of his and his friends' consistent attention to creating a loving relationship with God. I have associated with many people from a large number of social and political groups who have had many spheres of interest but this gentleman's concentration and focus on a relationship with God as the paramount interest in his life stands out in my experience as unique. It is this overriding impression of a spiritual aura that we continue to receive, particularly in the rural areas of the state, which has only confirmed our first impressions.

25

The Bard

While in South Carolina I began to develop, in collaboration with and initiated by Michael Fitzgerald, a poet from Winchester, Virginia, a performance format using poetry and jazz. Winchester is located in the Shenandoah Valley up in the northwest corner of the state, tucked in between the borders of West Virginia and Maryland. We had met for the first time at a week-long symposium on poetry in honor of Robert Hayden at the University of Michigan at Ann Arbor. I was participating in a dramatization of some of Robert's poetry by students from the university and other actors, dancers and musicians from the area, under the direction of John Schak. The performance was to be the culmination of the symposium. My responsibility was to give a musical impression of the theatrical rendering of the poetry and to provide a thematic transition between the different dramatizations using the extemporaneous improvisational techniques I had developed over the years.

Michael was at the performance and spoke to me afterwards. He suggested that we collaborate sometime in the future, using his poetry and my music. I gave him my card and more or less forgot the matter until he called many months later. After a couple of attempts at putting his poetry together with my improvisations, we found that the collaboration was working quite well, so we continued to develop the format by performing at Bahá'í functions around the country and in Canada. Each time our work seemed to get better and our performance more effective so we decided to record it. We have now done five or six recordings with various combinations of musicians, two with just Mike and myself. The most recent of these recordings, *Report from the Edge*, is, I believe, the best offering thus far.

Michael's newest collection of poetry is *The Holy Passions*, which I have found to be his best compilation yet. We recently had a conversation in which we discussed the emergence of maturity in one's creative work and recognized that after the publication of *The Holy Passions* Michael's work reached what appeared to be a new level of maturity. It is interesting to contemplate the creative process and to realize that it does not necessarily flow in a logical, sequential fashion. Yet in Michael's case it appears that everything he has written before this book has been a prelude to it and to what is yet to come.

The humanity of his family, particularly his parents John and Bessa, and their love for each other exemplifies what we could all achieve were we to approach our familial relationships with selfless and compassionate empathy for one another, placing, as Bahá'u'lláh has directed, the welfare of others before our own. I don't know of a better example of that teaching than the family of John and Bessa Fitzgerald of Winchester, Virginia.

Michael is, within the limits of his resources, a supporter of many causes – artists, schools and institutions that represent his ideal of what this life is truly about. I personally have Michael to thank for supporting my efforts to produce my CD *Sweetness and Light*, which had been sitting on the shelf for a few years for want of the necessary funds to manufacture the product. His sole purpose in providing the funds was his desire to see it available to the general public, as an expression of my particular voice in the world of creative jazz. Now he wants me to do a CD reproduction of the much earlier cassette recording *Wings for the Spirit*. He has had a personal copy of both these recordings for years, so his interest in seeing them made available to the public is purely philanthropic. He has nothing to gain from such a project except the sense of having made something of value available to everybody in the world of creative arts. It's just his way!

For years we have had a standing engagement in Winchester at the end of February: a performance of Michael's poetry and my jazz improvisations in support of his readings at a venue of his choosing, followed the next evening with our participation in an Ayyám-i-Há celebration with the Winchester Bahá'í community. These past few years the venue for the performance has been a unique bookstore and coffee house called The Satisfied Mind, owned and operated by Lorne Bair, who has become both a friend and a great fan of Michael's poetic talent.

Michael is another individual whose history has been a life on the fence – never compromising, accommodating or modifying his standards and belief in what is most important. He has received more than his share of difficulties but he continues on undaunted with that which he knows to be the truth. Part of his strength has come, as has mine, from the recognition, along with millions of others around this planet, of the advent of Bahá'u'lláh's Revelation to human-kind, which has been the source of our ability to 'hold to the course'. Values change but truth is ONE.

Admiration, respect, love, appreciation, esteem, honor, veneration, deference – I'm sure there must be more. Those are the words that come closest to expressing my feelings for Michael Fitzgerald.

26

Epilogue

This is both the most important chapter for me to have written and the most important for you to read. It is, essentially, a reflection on my life's experiences and may bring into focus many ideas for you to see, contemplate and digest.

Life, On the Fence is not intended to be a 'poh me' book. It is, rather, an expression and to some degree an analysis of what I have discovered and explored in my life. The findings of my research are stark, real and, I hope, helpful to the present generation of Americans, particularly to those of African–American and European–American ancestry. What I have discovered affects the lives of those who share these ancestries, ancestries which encompass all the populations of the world and whose fortunes are inextricably bound together in this American nation, under God, who live in allegiance with that universal home we call planet Earth.

In these latter years I've come to realize just what it was that so embraced my being, that drew me – unknowingly but not reluctantly – into such intimacy with the African–American community that it confused and confounded my family and friends: it was the spiritual integrity prevalent in that community, 'what you see is what you get'. Certainly this was not universally true, just as with any community, but this overriding quality was ever present. It was a welcome relief from what I had come to see as hypocritical, two-faced and downright devious actions justified by those in power and authority as the way one gets ahead in the world and accomplishes the goals one sets for oneself.

What brought this to light for me were my many attempts to be a part of the mainstream and to work with the system as it was. But every time I began to achieve some gains, the whole thing would fall apart or crumble at my feet. As the expression goes, I was constantly shooting myself in the foot. Again I would find acceptance and nurturing in the African–American community to which I have been continually linked. When I returned to the fold, so to speak, my good fortune would begin to reappear. Then came my discovery of the Revelation from God for this age, once again giving guidance and direction through the Glory of God, Bahá'u'lláh.

My way was made clear and my commitment to the cultural and community environment which exemplified these values was clearly established. This was where I would choose to reside, even when the circumstances of my residency demanded a separation from the immediate surroundings of that desirable community. Living in South Carolina has made embracing that community life a bit more difficult for Diane and me since we are not native to this soil. Our hearts, souls and minds are there, as they have always been. Our dedication to the growth of the Bahá'í communities in this area is the way we retain the spiritual closeness of our lives with these beautiful souls, who continue to nurture our beings, even though they have reservations as to our true motives.

What I'm about to share with you may be, initially, difficult to swallow. This is understandable, particularly as it comes from one who has never had to endure the oppressiveness of racism himself. I have chosen to associate with this culture because of my awareness of its beauty, integrity and innovative creativity, which satisfied my cultural sensibility and which I could only find in these surroundings. In my discussions with the numerous friends I have acquired over the years who truly constitute my family, I have discovered that my observations and analysis of where we have been and where we appear to be going are synchronous with their views.

While I was yet a relatively young man I knew that the racial divide between black and white could, from the black viewpoint, have easily been overcome. All that was needed was a level playing field: opportunity based on one's ability; access to the ideal of American life – being able to own a home wherever one chose, based only on one's ability to purchase it; a job that would allow one's efforts and talents to determine one's advancement; respect as a member of the community that one chose to live in based on, again, one's contribution to the betterment of that community; the freedom to access all educational levels for one's children and the same admission requirements for all children. Though it seemed simple to acquire these and easy to achieve a logical and comprehensive resolution to such inequities, yet there remained a fierce resistance to providing such a solution and powerful reasons for ignoring the need for it by the majority population of the community.

How many times during the years of my youth and young adulthood did I hear such views expressed by my friends in the African–American community? More than I can possibly count. At the same time, I have heard opposing views and resolutions from the other associates. The solution offered by the blacks was so logical and simple it boggled my mind and the minds of those with whom these ideas were shared.

Smitty and I had shared these questions back in our high school days in 1945–6. Remember our discussions about the beauty of the human race when people interracially married and our perceptions of what the children of those unions would look like? The most physically beautiful person I have ever seen, apart from the lady at the Charles Hotel in DC, was an Afro–Eurasian woman I came across in Europe. She epitomized the essence of what Smitty and I had proposed those many years before. Stunning didn't even come close.

The integrity I have referred to so many times in my descriptions of the black community has its roots in the spiritual essence that pervades the core reality of that community. I don't attribute that exclusively to the churches, though they are an extremely dominant part of the culture. God was, and is, at the center of African–American life, as I understand it. Even if one is not a church-going person, God is still at the center. Probably 90 to 95 per cent of all the musicians I've known have come through the church in one way or another and they have never lost awareness of the soul connection within the music. Many books have described this characteristic quality of African–American life far better than I can hope to express, so let me refer you to them. What I'm getting to is this: that my life's experience acknowledges the outstanding quality and ensign of the African–American community's reality, what I refer to as its spiritual ascendancy. That spiritual ascendancy has always been there and has sustained that community through its darkest years. It has helped them to persevere under extreme duress in a way that I honestly can't hope to really comprehend. And all this has continued through many generations and on to today.

We have a unique opportunity to embrace the truth of our oneness with all our fellow human beings, an opportunity which is a bounty and a blessing conferred on us by the concourse on high. We have each been given the privilege of acknowledging and supporting this awareness in our everyday lives. It is my belief that we must each be ready and willing to be counted as stalwart ensigns of this truth and to stand uncompromisingly for this reality.

An outstanding example of what I mean is the life of Richard Price of Walterboro, South Carolina, who tragically died when his beloved ultra-light airplane crashed. Richard had been a pilot since his early years and was highly respected by all who knew him. As a teenager he would spend as much time as he could hanging around, running errands and generally being helpful to the Tuskegee airmen who were training at the airport at Walterboro. They took him in and, recognizing his sincerity, gave him the respect and assistance he needed to gain greater knowledge of flying.

In turn, Richard's willingness to assist those who were learning the intricacies of flight was legendary. He was also a drummer and, next to flying, loved nothing more than to sit down behind a set of drums and play with anybody in any style. His forte was the traditional New Orleans style of playing but he would do his best to kick a big swing band just as readily. He wasn't a bebopper by any means but his love for that medium and respect for all those who excelled there was voluminous.

As the cultural director of the city of Walterboro for many years, Richard was able, despite some local political opposition, to bring Dizzy Gillespie to play for and speak to the public school students, which the children loved. Unfortunately, owing to the opposition, only a few hundred turned out for the concert that evening. This was just one of many examples of Richard doing what he knew was right and the best thing to do for the community despite the disapproval of others.

Here was a white southern gentleman whose historical association with Walterboro was many generations long, who knew the truth of things and who began to demonstrate those beliefs well before it became acceptable to do so in his home town. I believe, and this is strictly my conjecture, that he was relieved when the civil rights movement of the '60s became successful, as it gave him a justification for relating openly to the black population as he had always wanted to do and which he had done surreptitiously. Richard Price was one unique son-of-a-gun and a prime example of the new southern gentleman who will arise from the dross of the old.

The long fight to gain some modicum of justice for the African–American community has been fraught with peril and disappointment. Thanks to those who have been committed to this goal, some modest accomplishments have been realized even though many of them are still only on paper. We all know that the only true justice comes about when hearts are changed. However, there are some indications that there are new opportunities and progress in the area of political and social life, which have resulted from successes in business, entrepreneurial activity, education and politics. These accomplishments are greatly overdue.

However, I must share with you a phenomenon which my friends and I have viewed with growing concern. I'm sticking my neck out, so to speak, to share this observation with you.

The spiritual ascendancy which has been the hallmark of this community from its beginnings and roots in Africa, through all the various periods of travail, is now, it seems, being sacrificed at the altar of material accomplishment. Yet we know that true material accomplishment will be realized only as the value and integrity of spiritual attributes begin to take precedence in the world. Those who epitomize these qualities will be brought forward to fill responsibilities in all our national and international activities.

Who will best be prepared to step into that arena? Those whose lives have reflected these attributes and there are, in my opinion, no people more prepared for these responsibilities than those who have held on to their spiritual ascendancy and have continued to nurture and model it for the world to see. Was this not shown dramatically in the '60s by the peaceful sit-ins and demonstrations advocated by Martin Luther King Jr? These followed in the wake of the race amity activities fostered by Hand of the Cause of God Louis G. Gregory in the early years of the 20th century that took place primarily in the south.

The people of African ancestry, who have contributed an enormous amount of invention, innovation and ingenuity to the quality of American life, are at the forefront of those who exude spiritual qualities. They have been identified by Bahá'u-'lláh as the pupil of the eye through whom the world will be able to see the spiritual reality of humankind's existence and its guiding influence. It is these people, we are assured, who will lead the world into the age of fulfillment and to the establishment of God's kingdom on earth.

Please let us not sacrifice this spiritual ascendancy that has been our birthright for what, temporarily, may appear to be an ascendancy of stature in a crumbling world of material wealth, comfort and pleasure, a world that may well disappear in a twinkling of the eye.

We can do both. We can and will ascend to positions of great importance in the world of humanity without sacrificing the spiritual ascendancy which has been the hallmark of all our accomplishments, be we black, red, brown, yellow, white or all the possible combinations thereof. Personally, I've declared myself 'other', since my bloodline is so diverse. And to those who continue to ask, I can only respond with, 'Which do I deny?' I know where my heart is and that may well be the most important thing to know for this life.

One closing observation. Have you noticed how wide this fence is becoming? It used to be very narrow and scary at times but lately it is getting to be wide and full of so many people, throughout the world, that I'm beginning to feel like 'the fence' may be the 'in' place to be.

Glossary

A and B♭ clarinet B♭ is the standard clarinet and therefore the most familiar one. The A clarinet looks exactly like the standard B♭ but is a few inches longer, lowering the overall pitch by a half step from B♭ to A.

bad, baddest Excellent, the best, superlative in accomplishment, beyond comparison.

bad rap An undeserved reputation.

bebop A style of jazz identified with Dizzy Gillespie and Charlie Parker and characterized by virtuosic solo improvisations based on complex harmonic progressions.

began to run gain Increased the volume.

bill Program order of a concert. The word was taken from Vaudeville.

bird colonel A US military designation rank of colonel, identified by the insignia of a silver eagle.

blasted Inebriated to the extreme.

the book The library of a band or the collection of parts from arrangements for individual instruments in a band or orchestra.

brother Usually refers to an African–American but is also used to signify soul brother or one who understands.

bulldog Strong, commanding.

to burn Intensity of feeling and/or sound.

cadenza An elaborate improvised passage by a soloist at the end of an arrangement.

cats Jazz musicians.

changes Chords that support and harmonically identify a tune or composition.

charts Musical arrangements or orchestrations of compositions.

chops Refers to one's technical readiness to perform. Can be used in reference to either instrumental or vocal performers. Also used to refer to an instrumentalist's embouchure.

copped Imitated.

cornet A trumpet with a tubing of a larger bore, creating thereby a softer edge to the sound.

draft Not feeling welcome, a cold shoulder, sensing you were in a place where you didn't belong.

drum pad A small piece of wood, square or circular, with a rubber patch glued to the center which is used to practice drum techniques and to gain control and coordination of the sticks.

dude A person, usually male, who is something of a character or is unique in personality.

efficiency A one-room apartment.

embouchure The method of applying the lips and tongue to the mouthpiece of a wind instrument.

fattest notes Those notes of a chord or voicing of the chord, that have the greatest effect on the subsequent sound of that chord or voicing.

FFRR An electronic innovation by the recording industry that preceded stereo.

gig A job or engagement.

glockenspiel A percussion instrument with chromatically tuned, flat metal bars set in a frame, that produce bell-like tones when struck with small hammers.

goose eggs Whole notes.

groove The flow of the time resulting from the quality of the pocket.

hip Aware, knowledgeable, in tune with the times.

IRS United States Internal Revenue Service.

jam session An occasion when musicians improvise individually on a pre-selected tune whose melody is initially rendered collectively.

jazz heads Familiar tunes from the lexicon of jazz tunes used as a vehicle for further improvisation.

jive Phony, incompetent, pretentious, etc., depending on the context.

knocked him out Liked a lot.

kvetching (Yiddish) Complaining.

line Melodic statement, singly or in concert with others.

lining out a hymn Group singing in which one person sings a line and the rest respond with the same line.

the local The local chapter of the Musicians' Union.

Mickey Mouse A reference to the characteristics of commercial music commonly used in hotel ballrooms from the '30s to the '60s.

MOMA Museum of Modern Art.

Monkey Wards A term for Montgomery Wards, a department store.

MOS Military Occupational Specialty

NAJE National Association of Jazz Educators

ofay A white person; could be interpreted as pig-latin for foe.

Penny's An abbreviation of J.C. Penny's, a department store.

phrasing Manner of expressing musically a line collectively or singly, unifying the overall impression.

pocket, poquette Quality and character of the pulse of the time with which one is playing.

pull my coat tail Let me know.

R and B Rhythm and Blues.

reach to the bottom of your book Pull out your very best chart so as to demonstrate your prowess.

run gain Increase the volume level from a sound board.

scene The music industry or local musical activity.

skate To glide or float over without much musical substance, creating the appearance of competence.

smoker A chart that creates the qualities of smokin'.

smokin' Exhilarating, impressive, dynamic, awesome.

SNCC Student Non-violent Coordinating Committee

soli A segment of an arrangement written to emphasize the musical qualities of a specific section of an orchestra or the entire orchestra with a harmonization of the primary melodic line in a unified exposition.

sub-toned (very soft) A technique of altering the airflow and vibration of the reed to create a subdued sound, similar in some ways to *sotto voce* in classical singing.

take A recording effort, i.e. take 1, take 2, etc.

TDY Temporary Duty, US Army designation

tight Close, best of friends, an intimate friendship.

turned left Turned against you, turned away, ignored you.

turn in the barrel Exposed, down front, on the spot, in the spotlight.

up tempo Fast, bright, etc.

voicing The ordering or placement of the notes of a chord to affect the overall sound and/or the movement of the voices from one chord to another.

woodshedding Practicing.

Bibliography

'Abdu'l-Bahá, *Selections from the Writings of 'Abdu'l-Bahá*. Haifa: Bahá'í World Centre, 1978.

Bahá'í Writings on Music, comp. by The Universal House of Justice. Oakham: Bahá'í Publishing Trust, no date.

Bahá'u'lláh, *The Kitáb-i-Aqdas*. Haifa: Bahá'í World Centre, 1992.